WHY MUSLIMS REBEL

WHY MUSLIMS REBEL

Repression and Resistance in the Islamic World

Mohammed M. Hafez

LYNNE
RIENNER
PUBLISHERS

BOULDER
LONDON

Paperback edition published in the United States of America in 2004 by
Lynne Rienner Publishers, Inc.
1800 30th Street, Boulder, Colorado 80301
www.rienner.com

and in the United Kingdom by
Lynne Rienner Publishers, Inc.
3 Henrietta Street, Covent Garden, London WC2E 8LU

Published in hardcover in 2003.

ISBN 1-58826-302-9 (pbk. : alk. paper)

Printed and bound in the United States of America

∞ The paper used in this publication meets the requirements
of the American National Standard for Permanence of
Paper for Printed Library Materials Z39.48-1992.

5 4 3 2 1

In memory of Mahmoud
In honor of Inshirah
For my love Abeer

Contents

Tables and Figures

Tables

Figures

Foreword:
Rebellion in the Islamic World

Fred Halliday

Every rebel, like every nationalist, claims to be different. Those who oppose such rebellions may equally feel, and claim, that they are facing something distinctive, but here too impressions are misleading. Yet, the very first instinct of a social scientist, even before that of explanation, is to compare and to set that which appears as distinctive and unique, and which often thus presents itself, in the broader context of human and social behavior.

The question "Why do Muslims rebel?" invites, therefore, an initial, straightforward answer: "For the same reasons as everyone else." The study of revolt, and revolution, in modern history and sociology has produced a wealth of understanding as to why movements of collective protest develop, and as to the conditions under which they succeed or fail. Social and political factors may be at play, but often revolt is based on something equally widespread, the denial of national rights. If there is an argument to be made for the distinctiveness of the Muslim world, and of "Muslim" rebels, this is a case that has to be made, not assumed. Equally, claims made as to the uniqueness of particular acts of collective protest, be they the Iranian revolution, the activities of Hizb Allah in Lebanon, or the actions of Al-Qaida, need to pass, not be presumed already to have met, the criterion of distinctiveness.

The answer "for the same reasons as everyone else" is not, however, a sufficient answer, for any rebellion or group thereof. For even if the social scientist can determine what the reasons are, a greater incidence of rebellion (and of ideological definition) in one part of the world rather than in others invites the question as to why these factors are more prevalent. To answer this demands discussion of the factors that set the context for revolt, including forms of state, external control, ideological formation, mobilization capacity, and class structure, to name but some. A comparative, reasoned account of rebellion in the Muslim world, drawing on the political sociology of revolt and on social movement theory, inevitably involves a discussion of the kinds of state and society that shape these actions. The question is not therefore why Muslims revolt but why states in these countries have the authoritarian character they do.

For all that the social scientist compares, and is skeptical of, motives proclaimed and ideologies espoused, the very fact that such movements appear to espouse a radical particularism, derived from religion, merits attention. We do not have to accept that self-definition or imagined roles are the determinants of political behavior to see that ideology has its own salience and autonomy. Indeed, ideology needs to be rescued from the ideational.

Finally, of course, there is no one answer to the general question, no shared answer on what "the same reasons" are. The development and richness of social movement theory, as it has developed in Europe and in the United States in recent decades, has produced a variety of different analytic schools. Each case study engaged is also an engagement with theory and with a competition of approaches. The greatest test of any theory is not its conceptual precision or volume of data and cases but its ability to provide plausible explanations of social processes.

It is the great merit of this work by Mohammed Hafez that he engages with these and many other issues in the course of his analysis. This is a work that makes a major contribution to the comparative study of revolt in Muslim countries, by comparing different countries and situations in the Muslim world and also by setting these cases in the framework of social movement theory. Dr. Hafez uses the revolts of the Muslim world to address debates in the social sciences in general, drawing attention to what he sees as weaknesses in some established approaches, including those based on class, religious formation, or psychological disorientation. Instead, he develops a case for analysis in terms of political context and, in particular, the ability or failure of the state to provide openings to Islamist movements for participation in the political process and the manner in which it represses dissent. The espousal of antisystem worldviews by Islamists is, he argues, a result less of an inherent ideological proclivity, and more of political exclusion and repression.

This is, therefore, a work that is theoretically astute and innovative. It is, at the same time, based on thorough knowledge and research of unique Arabic sources. The dramatic irruption of radical Muslim movements onto the political scene has been a feature of the politics of the Middle East and of other countries for two decades past. It has become a major preoccupation of Western states since 11 September 2001, if not before. To understand such movements and to evolve a calibrated and informed response to them are a major challenge, intellectual and political, of modern times. In furtherance of that endeavor, Dr. Hafez has made a most original, and singular, contribution.

—Fred Halliday

Preface

This book puts forward a theoretically informed answer to the question: why do Muslims rebel? Since the 1970s, the Muslim world has given birth to a number of rebellious movements and violent insurgencies. Muslims in Iran rebelled to overthrow a dictatorship. In Afghanistan and the Palestinian territories, they mobilized to oust a foreign occupier. In Algeria and Egypt, they fought to establish an Islamic state. In the Philippines, Kashmir, and Chechnya, they struggled as separatist movements seeking independence as Muslim nations. In Central Asian states of the former Soviet Union, they have rebelled for a combination of those reasons. In all these societies, Islamic movements galvanized mass publics and won them over to the cause of violent insurgency. Explaining the underlying causes and dynamics—timing, duration, scale, and targets—of some of these rebellions is my objective in this book.

Despite the variation in the expressed aims and objectives of Muslim rebels, there is an elemental consistency among their rebellions that merits theoretical analysis. Muslims become violently militant when they encounter exclusionary states that deny them meaningful access to political institutions and employ indiscriminate repressive policies against their citizens during periods of mass mobilization. Political exclusion and state repression unleash a dynamic of radicalization characterized by exclusive rebel organizations that isolate Islamists from their broader society and foster antisystem ideologies that frame the potentially healthy competition between secularism and Islamism as a mortal struggle between faith and impiety. The cumulative effect of political repression, exclusive organizations, and antisystem ideologies is protracted conflicts against secular ruling regimes and ordinary civilians who are perceived as sustaining those regimes.

The title of this book intentionally echoes Ted Gurr's seminal work *Why Men Rebel*. My objective is not to ride brazenly on the success of a renowned piece of scholarship about the origins of political violence—although I do aspire to achieve comparable readership and accolades. My intention, rather, is to illustrate a point. Gurr's book put forward the theory of relative deprivation, which linked rebellious activity to feelings of economic deprivation. This theory has long been challenged—and one may say surpassed—in the field of political science. Yet, despite its limitations, Gurr's theory continues to prevail, explicitly or implicitly, as the leading explanation of Islamist violence and rebellion by area specialists, Islamic studies scholars, and journalists covering the Muslim world.

In this book I argue that contrary to prevailing academic and journalistic wisdom about why Muslims rebel, violent insurgencies in the Muslim world are not primarily an aggressive response to economic deprivation or psychological alienation produced by severe impoverishment or failed modernization. Muslim rebellions, generally speaking, are a defensive reaction to predatory state repression that threatens the organizational resources and lives of political Islamists. Hence the subtitle of the book: *Repression and Resistance in the Islamic World*.

My objective is to provide a convincing political process approach as an alternative to the relative deprivation theory of Islamist insurgency. In doing so, I engage in the comparative study of Islamist movements and rebellions. The two main cases I cover are Algeria and Egypt, but I also draw comparisons with the experiences of Jordan, Pakistan, Tunisia, Kashmir, the southern Philippines, Chechnya, Tajikistan, and Al-Qaida. In addition, I draw on recent innovations in social movement theory, especially the synthesis of three theoretical variables—political environment, mobilization structures, and ideological frames. To that end, I aim to contribute to the bridging of the gap between social movement studies and research on Islamic movements.

* * *

In the course of writing this book, I incurred the support of many mentors, colleagues, organizations, relatives, and friends to whom some recognition and appreciation are due. First and foremost, I am indebted to Fred Halliday at the London School of Economics and Political Science.

He was generous with his time, thorough in his reading of chapters, and constructive in his criticism.

I am also grateful to James Piscatori of Oxford University and Sami Zubaida at the University of London for their valuable feedback and suggestions for revisions during my doctoral examination.

I extend my appreciation to Laurie Brand, Michael Fry, and John Odell at the University of Southern California and Qunitan Wiktorowicz at Rhodes College for their support and guidance at various phases of this project. I am appreciative of Robert Gamer at the University of Missouri–Kansas City for encouraging me to pursue publication at Lynne Rienner Publishers.

A number of organizations have provided me with financial and research support, without which the following pages would not have been possible. I wish to express my sincerest gratitude to the Harry Frank Guggenheim Foundation for its generosity. I am also thankful to the U.S. Information Agency and the American Center for Oriental Research in Amman, Jordan, for financial and field-research support in 1998 and 1999.

A number of institutions were kind enough to allow me to "dig through" their archives and publications for indispensable documentation. In London, England, I am grateful to *al-Hayat* newspaper and its staff, especially Camille al-Tawil, for providing me with many communiqués and hard-to-get pamphlets of Islamists in Algeria and Egypt. Without their support the following pages would have been impoverished. In Cairo, Egypt, I am indebted to the Ibn Khaldun Center for Development, al-Ahram Center for Political and Strategic Studies, and al-Mahrousa publishing house. All three kindly provided me easy access to their reports, statistics, publications, and some of the primary documents of Egyptian Islamists. In Amman, Jordan, I am grateful to the French Cultural Center for assisting me in translating some of the French sources.

The following colleagues, relatives, and friends are recognized for their intellectual and moral encouragement: Adalah Hafez, Anja Graupe, Catherine Warrick, Chris Thiebes, Elizabeth Stephens, Guy Ziv, David Alpern, Kurt Zamora, Laura Hoegler, Mark Nierwetberg, Nick Bisley, Nisreen al-Shaikh, Ranjit Singh, and Osama and Salam Saifan.

Words alone cannot express the deep gratitude I feel toward my hardworking father, loving mother, and supportive wife, to whom this book is dedicated.

—*M.M.H.*

I

Introduction:
The Challenge of
Explaining Muslim Rebellions

The year 1992 witnessed the beginning of two Islamist rebellions, one in Algeria and the other in Egypt. Although Islamist violence was not a new phenomenon in either country, the 1992 insurgencies ushered in a distinct phase of political violence, characterized by sustained and bloody confrontations between Islamists and the state. Prior to 1992, Islamist movements in Algeria and Egypt chiefly relied on a mix of accommodative and reformist strategies to effect social change; violence was the domain of marginal Islamist groups that failed to garner mass support. Ideological radicals and proponents of insurgency did exist in the broader Islamist movement, but other representatives of Islamism, those who advocated working through state institutions, restrained them or undermined their revolutionary strategy. Things changed in 1992.

In Algeria, supporters of the Islamic Salvation Front took up arms after the cancellation of an election that held the promise of parliamentary victory for Islamists. Since that time, more than a hundred thousand people have been killed in an ongoing struggle between Islamists and the regime. In Egypt, the Islamic Group embarked on a campaign of violence in upper Egypt, with the proclaimed aim of toppling the secular regime and establishing an Islamic order in its stead. Although the violence was not as significant as in Algeria, thousands of people were killed and injured in the rebellion that took place between 1992 and 1997.

Islamist insurgents in Algeria and Egypt did not just wage war against the state and its officials; their violence was expansive, targeting secular intellectuals, journalists, foreigners, tourists, and ordinary civilians. In Algeria, entire families, towns, and villages became victims of massacres and wanton acts of violence. In Egypt, violence against tourists and Coptic Christians at times resembled massacres.

The conflict in Algeria and Egypt was a protracted one; violence persisted despite attempts by some of the combatants to bring the insurgency to a peaceful resolution and despite the apparent failure of rebels to spark revolution against the incumbent regime. In Egypt, violence effectively halted in 1997, almost five years after the beginning of the rebellion and ten years after the resurgence of Islamist violence in the mid-1980s. In Algeria, violence continues to this day.

The cases of Algeria and Egypt raise three sets of questions. First, why did Islamists rebel in 1992? What were the underlying factors that explain the timing, scale, and motivation of Islamist insurgency in those countries? Second, what explains the duration of the conflicts? Why did the rebellion in both countries turn into protracted conflicts, and why were the combatants unable to negotiate a peaceful resolution to the violence? Last, what explains the targets of Islamist rebels? Why did Islamist violence become expansive, striking at such a broad range of "enemies"? How can we explain the rise of anticivilian violence by rebels who claim to represent the people?

The Puzzle of Islamist Rebellions

The questions raised by the experiences of Algeria and Egypt extend well beyond those two countries. The 1980s and 1990s witnessed Islamist rebellions and violence in many countries and almost every region of the Muslim world, including Afghanistan, Chechnya, Indonesia, Iran, Iraq, Kashmir, the Israeli-occupied Palestinian territories, Philippines, Syria, Pakistan, Lebanon, Tajikistan, Uzbekistan, and Yemen. In many of these countries, Islamist insurgency garnered some, if not mass, support from the broader public; turned into protracted conflicts that produce "residual" attacks to this day; and witnessed expansive violence that went beyond the targeting of soldiers and government officials to victimize helpless civilians.

The focus on Islamist rebellions may at first glance give credence to Samuel Huntington's provocative thesis that Islam has "bloody borders." Such first impressions are misleading, however. Islamist opposition movements adopt a variety of strategies to effect social and political change. Some opt for militancy, violence, and revolution but many more eschew violence and seek accommodation with their secular states. Islamists in Turkey, Jordan, Indonesia, and Malaysia, to name a few, are generally committed to legality, gradualism, and constitutionalism. Many more avoid politics altogether and seek to effect change through education and social reforms at the grassroots level. A number of Islamists from Morocco to Bangladesh prefer to work peacefully toward the moral rejuvenation of their communities through informal social networks and neighborhood associations.

The focus on Islamist rebellion is intended to address dispassionately a recurring phenomenon that affects the lives of millions of people in the Muslim world and the governments that rule over them. Discovering the sources of rebellion in the Muslim world is a critically important but woefully neglected undertaking. Few studies of Islamist movements make the puzzle of Islamist rebellions their central concern and even fewer attempt to solve it by systematically applying theoretical propositions across a number of carefully selected case studies. Much of the literature on Islamist movements is concerned with the origins and resurgence of Islamic fundamentalism across the Muslim world since the 1970s (Arjomand 1984; Hunter 1988; Kepel 1994), its historical antecedents and intellectual sources (Esposito 1983; Choueiri 1997), the socioeconomic base of its leaders and activists (Ibrahim 1980; Ansari 1984a; Munson 1986; Hoffman 1995), and its impact on political processes (Piscatori 1983; Roy 1994; Guazzone 1995).

Those studies that address Islamist violence remain at the level of description. To the extent they provide an explanation, they do so in passing and only for the particular case under investigation. In other words, they are not concerned with the generalizability of their explanations or with formulating propositions that link cause and effect in a systematic and testable way.[1] Thus, what is missing is a sustained theoretical treatment of Islamist rebellion, and an attempt at an explanation of it, in a comparative perspective.

The resurgence of Islamism as a serious competitor in the political process has put many state regimes in the Muslim world on the defensive. Initially, many of these regimes sought to harness the political energy of Islamism to balance against internal opposition forces (mainly from the left), but they soon came to realize that Islamism has a momentum of its own that could bring its advocates to rule over the state, either through elections, as in Algeria and Turkey, or by force, as in Iran and Afghanistan.

Many state regimes have sought to discover through trial and error a formula with which to counter the "threat" posed to their rule by

Islamist opposition forces. Some have chosen a strategy of unmitigated repression (Tunisia since 1990, Algeria since 1992, and Syria in 1982). Others have opted for some form of inclusion (Jordan since the 1940s; the Sudan since 1977; and Indonesia, Malaysia, and Pakistan since independence). Still others have chosen a mixed strategy of toleration and repression (Egypt and Morocco since the 1970s).

It is safe to say that none of these state strategies have produced consistent results. In Tunisia and Syria, repression effectively eliminated the Islamist opposition; in Algeria, repression intensified its resolve. In Jordan, Indonesia, and Malaysia, political incorporation appears to have placated (or perhaps co-opted) the largest Islamist organizations; in the Sudan and Pakistan, inclusion gave the Islamists prominence without necessarily lessening their determination to Islamize society or eliminate acts of violence. In Morocco, a strategy of partial toleration and repression appears to have succeeded in keeping Islamist groups in line; in Egypt, this mixed strategy failed to prevent violence and insurgency during the 1990s.[2]

Thus, the puzzle of Islamist rebellion: why and when do Islamists rebel, and how can we account for the scale and duration of their rebellions and make sense of the people victimized by their violence? These questions deserve sustained theoretical attention. Recognizing the diverse strategies of Islamist movements is significantly easier than providing an explanation for them. Islamist rebellions do not lend themselves to easy generalizations.

This book attempts to go beyond this theoretical impasse. It seeks to address the puzzle of Islamist rebellions theoretically, by adopting theories and insights derived from social movement studies, and empirically, by applying these insights to explain the development of Islamist rebellions around the Muslim world. The aim is to provide a new way of looking at Islamist rebellions that departs from common wisdom about why Muslims rebel.

Concepts and Definitions

An analysis of Islamist rebellions must begin by defining the meaning of the terms *Islamist* and *rebellion*. By *Islamist* I mean individuals, groups, organizations, and parties that see in Islam a guiding political doctrine that justifies and motivates collective action on behalf of that doctrine. Many Muslims believe that their religion is a comprehensive one that regulates matters of worship (ibadat) and social relations (mu'amalat). Not all, however, translate this basic belief into a call for social and political action. Islamists are Muslims who feel compelled to act on the belief that Islam demands social and political activism, either to establish an Islamic state, to proselytize to reinvigorate the faithful, or to create a separate union for Muslim communities.

Rebellion refers to the efforts consciously undertaken by movement organizations to acquire and allocate resources for sustained violent opposition to an incumbent regime. Rebellion is different from riots, sporadic and spontaneous mass upheavals, or occasional terrorism. It refers to broader planning that involves organizational structuring, ideological formulations, and programmatic steps to acquire resources and allocate them to resist an established order through recurrent violence and mass mobilization.

Throughout this book I will use the terms *moderates* and *radicals* when referring to Islamists. By *moderates* I mean those individuals and groups that shun violence and insurgency as a strategy to effect social change and, instead, seek to work through state institutions, civic associations, or nonviolent organizations to Islamize society and politics. Conversely, *radicals* are those who reject accommodation with the state regime, refuse to participate in its institutions, and insist on the necessity of violent revolution or mass mobilization to Islamize society and politics.

My usage of the terms *moderates* and *radicals* focuses on the behavior and tactics of Islamists, not their ideological orientation. Conceivably, Islamists could be radical in their aims and objectives but insist on the gradual pursuit of those aims through nonviolent means. An example of such movements is the Jama'at-i Islami (JI) in Pakistan. It is generally recognized that Mawlana Mawdudi, the founder of the JI, was a forerunner of contemporary fundamentalism and influenced many radical ideologues, including Sayyid Qutb of Egypt (Nasr 1996). Yet despite his uncompromising views on the necessity of establishing an Islamic state and his enmity toward the West, the prevailing strategy of the JI under Mawdudi was to work through state institutions, courts, and party politics to achieve its goals (see Chapter 2). From my perspective, the JI is a "moderate" movement.

We could also find instances where Islamists might hold "legitimate" or uncontroversial goals but choose violent or confrontational means to achieve them. Indonesians in 1997–1998 mobilized en masse and rioted to oust Suharto from power and demand democratic change.

Thus, while their goals would be considered moderate, their tactics were radical.

One may object that my usage of *moderates* and *radicals* is too simplistic and ignores the fluid nature of Islamists. Rarely are Islamists clearly demarcated between radicals and moderates. Some may reject violence as a tactic in a given period in time but quietly acquire resources and organize groups to engage in violence at a later time. Similarly, a group that generally advances its aims through conventional or "legal" means may occasionally press its demands through extra-institutional mobilization or violence. How would we categorize these hybrids?

There is no easy answer for this objection, but my aim in this book is to explain prevailing movement strategies and tactics over time, not merely to label groups as moderates or radicals. In other words, I want to explain why we see upsurges in mass violence or mobilization in Islamist movements, rather than just episodes of extra-institutional mobilizations or sporadic terrorism. Thus, while categorization of Islamists is problematic, I attempt to mitigate the potential conceptual confusion by focusing on trends in Islamist conduct. Throughout this book, I will point out how "moderates" and "radicals" within a given organization or movement influence the debates over strategy or push the movement in one direction over another. Chapter 4 in particular highlights the schisms within movements and how those divisions contribute to protracted conflict.

In the following chapters these terms and concepts will become clearer as they are utilized within a theoretical framework that competes with existing socioeconomic and psychological approaches to Islamist rebellions. The next two sections outline the arguments of existing approaches to Islamist insurgency and offer a critique of these approaches.

Theorizing Islamist Rebellions

The prevailing explanation of why Muslims rebel focuses on the underlying conditions of poverty, deprivation, and alienation that exist in the Muslim world. Islamist rebellions and violence, it is commonly claimed, are the result of socioeconomic impoverishment and psychological alienation that stem from failed modernization and excessive Westernization (Ansari 1984a; Davis 1984; Arjomand 1988; Ayubi 1991a; Cassandra 1995; Dekmejian 1995; Faksh 1997). Rapid structural and demographic dislocations that have taken place in the Muslim world during the postcolonial era have contributed to this sense of relative deprivation and alienation. These social transformations entailed the expansion of secondary and university education, development of public-sector employment, implementation of land reforms and Western-style legal systems, nationalization of religious institutions, modification of personal status codes, and promotion of state-led industrialization. ⌡

A nationalist technocratic elite with an affinity toward Western models of development usually carried out these reforms. This technocratic elite often equated successful development with secularization and Westernization of society and saw institutions rooted in rural economies and religious traditions as impediments to modernization. The most notable examples of these transformations are Turkey under Kamal Ataturk, Iran under the Shah Muhammad Reza Pahlavi, and Tunisia under Habib Bourguiba.

These postcolonial transformations, despite improving the lot of many people, manifested serious contradictions. Industrialization, initially a source of national pride, quickly turned into a heavy burden on society that could only be sustained through national debt. The expansion of education significantly increased literacy rates and produced many engineers, doctors, and lawyers. However, prospects for meaningful employment for this "new middle class" diminished over time; many of the new professionals could not find employment or simply rotted away in state-sector jobs where their skills were underutilized.

Land reforms did not improve the lot of peasants either (indeed, that was often not the intent of those reforms). Instead, they forced many peasants to migrate to already overcrowded cities where they ended up in shantytowns. Nor did legal reforms ensure rule by law or put an end to corruption; instead, they became crude attempts at emulating Western states and the principal means by which to deprive civil society of independent expression.

More significantly, the rhetoric of "progress" that accompanied efforts at modernization produced high expectations among people. Many state regimes sought legitimacy by promoting grandiose national projects that promised to raise the living standards of ordinary people and combat poverty, inequality, and exploitation associated with pre-independence years. Thus, many people came to believe that hard work and education could result in a better life for themselves and their children.

Talk of progress resulted in a rapid increase in urbanization, as many peasants flocked to cities expecting to benefit from modern education and employment. As time passed, however, it became apparent

that the attempt at state-led development in Muslim societies dispro-
portionately benefited a well-positioned few while leaving many with
unfulfilled expectations and broken promises.

This failure to meet the rising expectations of ordinary people and
the crude emulation of Western lifestyles, it is commonly argued,
resulted in feelings of deprivation and "normative disorientation" (Arjomand 1988), which made many Muslims susceptible to Islamist radicalism and militancy. As Kepel (1984: 128) explains in relation to
Egypt, "in the ramshackle dwellings of the suburbs ringing the large
Egyptian cities, people by-passed by progress and development turned
towards other, more radical tendencies of the Islamicist movement."
This view is echoed by Cassandra (1995: 20), who claims that the
"youths most negatively affected by Egypt's faltering economy are the
ones most likely to be Islamist insurgents." Dekmejian (1995: 6) also
concludes that "the scope and intensity of the fundamentalist reaction,
ranging from spiritual reawakening to revolutionary violence, depends
on the depth and pervasiveness of the crisis environment."

If some place the emphasis on economic deprivation as the root
cause of militancy, others point to psychological alienation as an
equally important factor. Ansari (1984a: 140–141) asserts that Islamist
militancy is a product of the breakdown of traditional solidarity caused
by "rapid urbanization and rural migration." Ayubi (1991a: 176) talks of
"frustrated" and "shattered" expectations from development that drive
Muslims into militant Islamist organizations. Dekmejian (1995: 47)
describes ordinary Muslims who "tend to lose their psychosocial bear-
ings as they are bombarded with the values of an alien environment."
Whether the emphasis rests on economic deprivation or psychological
alienation, analysts tend to be in agreement that the developmental crisis of Muslim societies is the root cause of Islamist militancy today.

Sivan (1985: 188) articulates the policy implications of this type of
analysis as such: "A measurable success of the economic system and/or
the lowering of the level of expectations through deliberate acts of the
powers-that-be, would no doubt tend to diminish the appeal of the new
radicalism." Ayubi (1991b: 234) has a slightly different policy solution:
"Most analysts agree that the challenge of such groups cannot be
removed unless something radical is done to solve the socioeconomic
problems of the recently urbanized and formally educated youth, from
among whom the militant religious tend to draw their cadres."

Proponents of socioeconomic and psychosocial explanations of
Islamist militancy proffer the social background of Islamists engaged in

protest and violence as evidence for their contentions. This evidence, according to a number of studies, indicates that the familiar social base of militant Islamists is students and professionals in their twenties and thirties. These students tend to be educated in the technical fields (e.g., engineering and medicine) and exhibit high motivation and aspirations. Militant Islamists also attract members of the lower-middle class and recent migrants to cities (Ibrahim 1980; Ansari 1984a; Davis 1984; Munson 1986; Cassandra 1995; Hoffman 1995). Finally, many of these militants suffer from chronic unemployment or underemployment, or have not acquired the material status associated with their hard work and dedication (Ayubi 1991a: 162).

Although many of these conclusions are derived from the study of Egypt's militant Islamists, a survey of radical Islamist groups across the Muslim world indicates that many militants outside Egypt do share these characteristics. In Syria, some of the most militant elements in the Muslim Brotherhood movement between 1976 and 1981, a period of violent struggle against the Ba'athist state regime, were university students, engineers, physicians, teachers, and professionals (Batatu 1982). In Algeria, unemployed urban youths in their teens and twenties, as well as civil servants, professionals, and teachers, constituted the main social base of armed Islamists (Willis 1996: 297–298). In Pakistan, the Islam-i Jami'at-i Tulabah, a student organization with a tradition of militancy and a history of violence, drew its activists from small towns and rural areas, as well as urban lower-middle-class areas (Nasr 1994: 74). In Morocco, students constituted a large portion of the radical al-Shabiba group headed by Abdel Karim Mouti in the 1970s and early 1980s (Munson 1986). Thus, the socioeconomic and psychological approaches appear to be supported by empirical evidence.

A Critique of Socioeconomic and Psychological Approaches

Despite their plausibility and parsimony, the validity of socioeconomic and psychological explanations of Islamist rebellions must be challenged on both empirical and theoretical grounds. Although militant Islamist movements did emerge under conditions of social dislocation and economic stagnation, nonmilitant movements have also emerged under similar circumstances. Almost every Muslim society experienced major social, economic, and political changes and crises of poverty and excessive Westernization in the postcolonial era. Yet many of these societies have not had to contend with high levels of Islamist rebellion or violence.

A glance at some basic economic and demographic indicators of five Muslim countries—Algeria, Egypt, Jordan, Morocco, and Tunisia—prior to and during the early 1990s shows that there is little correlation between economic deprivation and insurgency. In all five countries, the Islamist current was thriving in the 1980s and could have potentially played a more militant role during the early 1990s, as evinced by the strong presence of Islamist organizing at the university and in civil society.

In Algeria and Egypt, Islamists rebelled in the early 1990s (although rebellion in Egypt was much more limited than in Algeria). In Jordan, Morocco, and Tunisia, Islamists either retreated from political confrontation (Morocco and Tunisia) or accommodated the state regime (Jordan) during the 1990s.[3] Given this variation in levels of Islamist violence, we would expect to see concomitant variation in the economic-demographic data of the five countries. The following indicators should serve as a basis for cross-national comparison:

- Average annual GNP per capita growth rates
- Population growth
- Urbanization growth rates
- Estimated contribution of rural-urban migration to total urban population growth[4]
- Unemployment rates
- Urban population under national poverty line
- Gini index (measure of inequality)

Table 1.1 indicates that there are no significant differences in the economic-demographic data of the five Muslim countries, or at least they are insufficiently significant to explain variation in patterns of violence. To the extent there are differences in economic and demographic realities, the relative deprivation theory would suggest that countries like Jordan and Morocco should have experienced higher levels of violence during the 1990s as did Algeria and Egypt, which was not the case. The following paired comparisons should help clarify this point.

When compared to Algeria, Jordan has experienced nearly similar worsening economic conditions during the 1980s and early 1990s (see Figure 1.1). Like Algeria, it witnessed negative average GNP per capita growth rates, high population and urban growth, high rural-to-urban

Table 1.1 Economic and Demographic Data for Five Muslim Countries

Country	Average Annual GNP per Capita Growth Rate (1980–1992)	Population Growth (1980–1992)	Urban Growth (1980–1992)	Estimated Contribution of Rural-Urban Population Growth (1980–1992)	Approximate Unemployment Rate in Early 1990s	Urban Population Below National Poverty Line	Gini Index
Algeria	−0.5%	2.8%	4.9%	43%	20%	7.3% (1988)	40.14 (1988)
Egypt	1.8	2.4	2.5	4	15	35.9 (1990–1991)	32 (1991)
Jordan	−5.4	4.9	6.0	38	20	15 (1992)	43.36 (1992)
Morocco	1.4	2.5	3.8	34	16	7.6 (1990–1991)	39.2 (1990–1991)
Tunisia	1.3	2.3	3.4	35	16	7.3 (1990)	40.24 (1990)

Source: Most of the data were collected from Richards and Waterbury (1998: 49, 79, 134, 252, 254). Gini index data was taken from "Global Poverty Monitoring" reports by the World Bank Group (www.worldbank.org/povmonitor).

Figure 1.1 Economic Indicators of Algeria and Jordan, 1980–1992

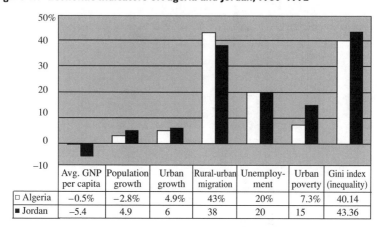

	Avg. GNP per capita	Population growth	Urban growth	Rural-urban migration	Unemployment	Urban poverty	Gini index (inequality)
□ Algeria	−0.5%	−2.8%	4.9%	43%	20%	7.3%	40.14
■ Jordan	−5.4	4.9	6	38	20	15	43.36

migration, a high percentage of urban population living under poverty, and a high percentage of people unemployed by the early 1990s. The level of inequality in Jordan is nearly the same as in Algeria. The latter witnessed urban riots in October 1988 as did Jordan in the spring of 1989. Yet despite having comparable economic-demographic data, Jordan had a relatively moderate Islamist movement during the 1980s and 1990s, one that eschewed violence and remained as a "loyal opposition" within the monarchy. In Algeria, Islamists rebelled.

A close look at Morocco's numbers in comparison to Egypt's raises similar conclusions (see Figure 1.2). Morocco's growth rate during the 1980s and early 1990s nearly matches Egypt's (the latter has a slightly better rate). Population and urban growth rates are also nearly the same (again, Egypt's is slightly better). During this time period, Morocco witnessed significantly higher rural-to-urban migration than did Egypt, and its unemployment rate was nearly the same as Egypt's. The only major difference is in the percentage of urban population under poverty. In Morocco it is significantly lower than in Egypt—but it was nearly the same as Algeria's.

What can we conclude from this simple comparison? One would expect levels of violence in Morocco to be nearly the same as in Egypt during the late 1980s and early 1990s. Yet this was not the case. Most groups and organizations that constituted the Islamist movement—the Moroccan Muslim Brotherhood, Al-Adl wal-Ihsan (Justice and Benevolence), and the Movement of Reform and Renewal in Morocco

Figure 1.2 Economic Indicators of Egypt and Morocco, 1980–1992

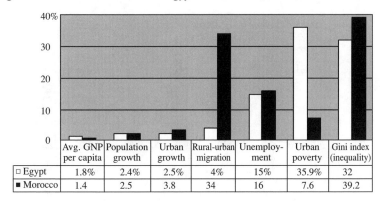

	Avg. GNP per capita	Population growth	Urban growth	Rural-urban migration	Unemploy-ment	Urban poverty	Gini index (inequality)
□ Egypt	1.8%	2.4%	2.5%	4%	15%	35.9%	32
■ Morocco	1.4	2.5	3.8	34	16	7.6	39.2

(HATM)—either sought to work through legal channels or avoided politics altogether. These organizations emphasized social reforms through education, preaching, and charity work (Entelis 1997).

Even the relatively small radical al-Shabiba group that existed during the 1970s and early 1980s suffered a split and effectively ceased to exist by the mid-1980s. HATM, which has its origins in the Shabiba group, adopted its present name in 1992 (removing all references to Islam) to avoid the charge that it seeks to monopolize religion (Shahin 1997). By the early 1990s the Moroccan Islamist movement was largely social reformist (Munson 1993).

Algeria's economic situation during the period from 1980 to 1992 was worse than Tunisia's, but not significantly so (see Figure 1.3). Algeria witnessed negative average GNP per capita growth, while Tunisia's growth was anemic. The population grew at a rate of 2.8 percent in Algeria, which is only slightly higher than Tunisia's 2.3 percent during the same period. The rate of urbanization in Algeria was not much higher than Tunisia's, and the same can be said for rural-to-urban migration during the period. Urban unemployment in Algeria was only slightly higher than in Tunisia, and inequality as measured by the Gini index was nearly the same in both countries. The percentage of urban population living below the national poverty line was the same in both countries. Like Algeria in 1988, Tunisia witnessed urban riots in 1978 and 1984.

Given this near carbon-copy data, one would expect to see levels of violence and rebellion in Tunisia nearly similar to Algeria, or at least

Why Muslims Rebel

Figure 1.3 Economic Indicators of Algeria and Tunisia, 1980–1992

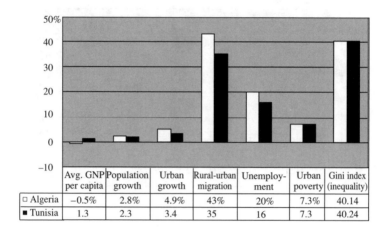

	Avg. GNP per capita	Population growth	Urban growth	Rural-urban migration	Unemploy- ment	Urban poverty	Gini index (inequality)
□ Algeria	−0.5%	2.8%	4.9%	43%	20%	7.3%	40.14
■ Tunisia	1.3	2.3	3.4	35	16	7.3	40.24

some sustained militancy. However, rebellion in Tunisia did not happen. In the early 1990s, there were few incidents of violence by Islamists, but since that time the movement retreated from the political arena under heavy state repression.

A comparison of Algeria's and Egypt's economic conditions between 1980 and 1992, the years preceding Islamist insurgencies in both countries, fails to suggest a clear correlation between economic deprivation and levels of violence (Figure 1.4). In Algeria, the violence was widespread and resulted in more than 100,000 people killed and injured. In Egypt, the violence was limited to the countryside and did not result in more than few thousand people killed and injured. Given this variation in the levels of violence, one would expect to see economic conditions in Algeria to be much more depressed than in Egypt.

However, economic conditions in Algeria are similar to Egypt's. A notable exception is in the area of rural-to-urban migration, which was much more significant in Algeria than in Egypt. Yet despite this difference, the rate of urban poverty—people living below the national poverty line—in Algeria was significantly lower than in Egypt in the late 1980s and early 1990s. While these numbers could possibly explain higher rates of violence in Algeria than in Egypt, they cannot possibly explain the huge gap in the rate of violence between the two countries.

The mere existence of poverty and deprivation is not sufficient to explain levels of Islamist rebellion. The case of the Iranian revolution shows that it is not even necessary. Between 1960 and 1977, the years

Figure 1.4 Economic Indicators of Algeria and Egypt, 1980–1992

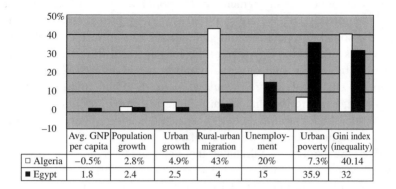

	Avg. GNP per capita	Population growth	Urban growth	Rural-urban migration	Unemploy-ment	Urban poverty	Gini index (inequality)
□ Algeria	−0.5%	2.8%	4.9%	43%	20%	7.3%	40.14
■ Egypt	1.8	2.4	2.5	4	15	35.9	32

preceding the Islamic revolution, Iran's annual real growth rate was nearly 9.6 percent, which was about double the average of developing countries. Moreover, absolute poverty was measurably reduced and unemployment was relatively small and localized (Amuzegar 1992: 414–415).

A number of writers point out that the initial participants in the demonstrations that eventually brought down the Shah of Iran were not the deprived or alienated. According to Denoeux (1993: 220), "Actors who mobilized first and asserted themselves most powerfully and effectively in the political arena were not individuals and groups that had been displaced and whose way of life had been disrupted, but those communities that had best preserved their sociocultural identities, cohesion, internal solidarity, and sense of unity and purpose despite rapid modernization." This claim has been confirmed by Kazemi (1980), Moaddel (1993), and Bayat (1997: 38), who emphatically adds, "Indeed the disenfranchised remained on the margins of the revolutionary campaign nearly until the end." The *bazaaris*—the merchants and traditional bourgeois sectors of the population—who were in the lead during the initial phase of revolutionary events, could hardly be considered marginal and alienated (Arjomand 1988: 107).

We should question the validity of socioeconomic and psychological explanations for another reason. Nearly all of the studies that investigate the social base of militant Islamists fail to analyze the social background of more moderate Islamists. In other words, while analysts do compare the socioeconomic base of militants across the Muslim world, they rarely conduct internal comparisons between moderate and

militant Islamist organizations within a given national context to show
that they attract different segments of the population. Indeed, as Krämer
(1995: 48) observed: "We are sadly lacking in empirical studies exam-
ining the social composition and generational set-up of major Islamist
movements such as the Egyptian or the Jordanian Muslim Brotherhoods
of the 1970s, 1980s, and more particularly the early 1990s. . . . More
systematic empirical research would allow us to either support or refute
the general assumption that by and large militancy coincides with a
modest social background and younger age . . . and pragmatic moderation with higher social status, income, education and age."

From the evidence we do have, there appears to be no such straightforward correlation. Hoffman's (1995) study shows that the social base
of Islamist organizations across the Muslim world is almost uniform—
students in the technical faculties, recent migrants to cities, and members of the urban lower-middle class. Yet not all of the movements she
studied could be considered militant. In Pakistan, the more moderate JI
is largely composed of a lower-middle-class membership that also
draws from university students and the intelligentsia. Its initial base of
support during the 1940s consisted of young religious scholars, but in
the 1950s and 1960s the JI increasingly appealed to those educated in
modern sciences and representing such professions as doctors, lawyers,
engineers, and government employees. After its election defeat in 1971,
the JI sought to expand its constituency by appealing to the uneducated
working class and peasants. However, its main base of support remains
to be the educated lower-middle class (Nasr 1994: 83–100).

In Egypt, the relatively moderate Muslim Brotherhood seems to
thrive in the professional associations of doctors, lawyers, pharmacists,
and engineers, all of which tend to attract younger professionals and
recent university graduates (Ibrahim 1996: 58–59). These sectors are the
ones most likely to suffer from relative deprivation due to the paucity of
rewards in their fields. Similarly, the Islamic Youth Movement of
Malaysia (ABIM), the most prominent Islamist organization in the 1970s
and 1980s, was mainly composed of young professionals and university
graduates. ABIM emphasized reform through education and has worked
through legal channels and official political parties to Islamize society.
These examples suggest that the social base of Islamist movements does
not determine their strategic orientation.

Another reason to question the validity of socioeconomic and psychosocial explanations has to do with the logic of the theories that
underpin them. The prevailing socioeconomic and psychological

approaches to Islamist militancy rely on a mechanistic understanding of political violence: individuals become aggrieved due to structural transformations, economic deprivation, and social alienation; they then develop particular worldviews and organizations; and, finally, they engage in political protest or violence.

This logic closely follows the "frustration-aggression" approach to collective action exemplified by Ted Gurr's seminal book *Why Men Rebel* (1970), which influenced earlier theorizing on social movements.[5] Gurr sought to link incidents of political violence and rebellion directly to feelings of deprivation that arose out of unfulfilled expectations.[6] These feelings of deprivation result in anger and anxiety that make ordinary people susceptible to aggression and rebellion. Although Gurr's model introduces a number of intervening variables, such as "dissident institutional support" and "regime institutional support" (Gurr and Duvall 1973), the defining feature of his approach remains the frustration-aggression nexus.

Gurr's frustration-aggression approach, however, has encountered a barrage of criticism both on theoretical and empirical grounds.[7] Three of these criticisms have specific relevance to the study of Islamist rebellions. First, it is not sufficient to show that individuals and groups engaging in collective struggles are aggrieved or deprived of something. After all, as Leon Trotsky (1961: 249) observed in 1932, "the mere existence of privations is not enough to cause an insurrection; if it were, the masses would be always in revolt." A satisfactory explanation of organized collective militancy must chart how grievances and deprivations are transformed into collective struggles.

To be able to wage a fight, individuals will have to mobilize resources, recruit committed activists, and establish organizational structures that can withstand repression. Many aggrieved groups cannot meet these requirements due to heavy state repression, lack of allies, lack of material and symbolic resources to motivate activists, and lack of experience in the underground. Socioeconomic and psychological approaches ignore these important considerations or, to be precise, assume that given enough discontent, determined activists will be able to overcome these obstacles. But this assumption is dubious. It suggests, as McAdam (1982: 12) points out, that "the absence of social insurgency is a simple product of low levels of strain or discontent in society [and] ignores the distinct possibility that movements may die aborning, or not arise at all, because of repression or rational calculations based on the imbalance of power between insurgents and their opponents."

This starting assumption, as we have seen, leaves socioeconomic and psychological explanations vulnerable to numerous counterexamples. A better way to proceed theoretically is by starting with the assumption that grievances are ubiquitous. What then demand an explanation are the special circumstances—political opportunities, nature of state repression, availability of allies, expanded capabilities—that enable groups to transform grievances into militant action.

Another criticism often leveled against the "frustration-aggression" approach is that even if aggrieved individuals are able to mobilize enough resources and activists, they do not necessarily have to turn to militancy and violence to alleviate their condition; it is just as logical to work through conventional channels to effect change. Organized individuals suffering from deprivation and alienation could seek reforms by lobbying, petitioning, and forming political parties.

To rebel, deprived groups must not only feel that they are denied fundamental needs, they must also feel that militant action is the *only* option available to them (White 1989). To the extent institutional channels for conflict resolution are perceived by aggrieved individuals to be blocked, these perceptions are a product of their political, not economic or psychological, environment. The key to explaining their militancy is not economic stagnation or excessive secularization, but the lack of meaningful access to state institutions.

Finally, even if aggrieved groups are able to mobilize resources and choose militant strategies to effect change, the nature of their grievances does not determine the purpose (revolutionary vs. reformist), scale (local vs. national), scope (limited vs. expansive), intensity (sustained vs. sporadic), and duration (brief vs. protracted) of their militancy. Economically deprived groups can demand major reforms through mass demonstrations (Tunisia in 1978) or they can attempt to launch a revolution through assassinations and bombings (Egypt in 1981). Why one strategy prevails over another cannot be explained by the socioeconomic and psychological approaches advanced above. Nor can they explain why some militant movements last for only few months (student movement in Indonesia in 1998), while others turn into protracted conflicts (Algeria since 1992 or Kashmir since 1989).

These criticisms are not intended to suggest that socioeconomic and psychological factors are not important for understanding the rise and appeal of Islamism. Socioeconomic deprivation and cultural alienation make up the structural conditions under which grievances are generated. Islamist discourse expresses the frustrations of ordinary Muslims who are surrounded by wealth they cannot partake in and are made to feel inferior to alien cultures in their own societies. Socioeconomic and psychosocial approaches highlight the contradictions that allow Islamism to thrive. However, these approaches point to relatively constant features of Muslim societies to explain variations in Islamist strategies. Economic deprivation and social alienation cannot be linked directly to Islamist rebellion, nor are they the most important factors for answering the question why Muslims rebel. An alternative explanation is necessary.

A Political Process Approach

This book puts forward a political process approach to Islamist rebellions. The political process approach developed largely in response to socioeconomic and psychological theories of social movements, which mechanistically link grievances to collective action. It begins with the premise that it is neither necessary for Islamists to be contented to become moderate nor sufficient for Islamists to be deprived to become rebellious. The political process approach to Islamist insurgencies analyzes the political environment in which Islamists operate, the mobilization structures through which Islamists acquire and allocate movement resources, and the ideological frames with which Islamists justify and motivate collective action.

To engage in collective action—be it peaceful or violent—Islamists must be empowered with resources that enable them to compete with, or "put up a fight" against, powerful opponents (Tilly et al. 1975; Tilly 1978; McCarthy and Zald 1973, 1977). There are at least three resources that Islamists could command to effect social and political change.

- *Material and organizational resources:* dedicated activists and experienced cadres; finances, property, facilities, and shelter; weapons, means of communication, and combat material.
- *Legitimacy and identity resources:* moral authority to command commitments and sacrifices from activists, sympathizers, and supporters based on perceived primordial ties; shared historic experiences; or possession of special knowledge, wisdom, or charisma.
- *Institutional resources:* access to public office and state ministries; support from influential state agencies and elites; and access to a political platform through parliaments and state media.

Each of these resources is a reservoir of power from which Islamists could draw to exert pressure against opponents, including an incumbent regime.

Material and organizational resources provide Islamists with the capacity to mobilize people for marches, demonstrations, and strikes, as well as for terrorism and guerrilla warfare. Legitimacy and identity resources, in turn, provide leaders and organizations with the ability to appeal to an audience beyond the core activists who make up the movement in its formative stages. The moral authority to command people is an indispensable resource for aggrieved groups seeking to effect cognitive and behavioral changes in society or mobilize the broader public for peaceful elections or violent disruption.

Institutional resources, in their turn, enable Islamists to publicize their goals and views through prominent channels, to exert pressure through elite ties, and to initiate change through legislation. Islamists who command some or all of these resources have many strategic options and are capable of collective action. Those who lack these resources will encounter difficulties and are likely to mobilize few people.

The types of resources movements accumulate, and how the movements allocate them, are partly determined by the political environment in which movements operate. The political environment structures the opportunities and constraints facing movements (McAdam 1982; DeNardo 1985). For example, in some repressive states the allocation of organizational resources to launch a demonstration might result in mass arrests, imprisonment, and the dissolution of the organization. Conversely, in a democratic political system that does not prohibit extra-institutional protest, participation in peaceful demonstrations is an option that opposition movements could exercise to exert influence. In both instances, the political environment delimits the possibilities for action and is likely to influence the choice of strategy, even if it does not entirely determine it.

The political process approach further contends that movement strategies involve more than decisions concerning how to exert influence and effect political change; movement strategies also involve decisions about what types of organizations to adopt and how to appeal to potential members. To respond to a repressive environment, for instance, social movement actors may choose to organize activists in clandestine cells dispersed across a national territory. They may also accentuate some grievances or perceived injustices to motivate high-risk activities.

Under pluralistic systems, on the other hand, social movements might form inclusive parties or public interest associations to take advantage of institutional resources and emphasize the possibility of "making a difference" through "proper" channels of conflict mediation. Therefore, an investigation of movement strategies must account for the spread of different mobilization structures and ideological frames in the movement in response to opportunities and constraints (McAdam et al. 1997).

Finally, the political process approach argues for the primacy of process over structure in collective action. Social and political movements do not respond mechanistically to existing conditions; rather, they "continually mobilize resources, apply them in various forms of collective action or 'tactics,' and experience the consequences of those strategies in a fully interrelated process that also affects subsequent 'rounds' of mobilization, action, and outcome" (Snyder and Kelly 1979: 219).

Rather than being an outcome of fixed circumstances, the political process approach treats social and political struggles as a dynamic of interaction, adaptation, and intended and unintended consequences that are likely to shape the strategies of movements over time. Thus, rather than ask *why* does a movement become rebellious, a more appropriate question becomes *what is the process* by which a movement becomes rebellious.

In sum, the precepts of the political process approach suggest at least three dimensions to the study of social movement strategies: political environment, mobilization structures, and ideological frames (McAdam 1982; McAdam et al. 1996). I argue that these are distinct aspects of a dynamic process that both channels movement strategies toward moderation or rebellion over time and determines the scope and duration of political violence.[8] The choice between moderation and rebellion entails cost-benefit calculations of different courses of action and the adoption of organizational forms and ideological symbols to best respond to the broader political context. The interplay among political environment, mobilization structures, and ideological frames is the key to understanding the strategic orientation of Islamist movements over time.

The Argument of the Book

The central claim of this book is that Muslims rebel because of an ill-fated combination of institutional exclusion, on the one hand, and on the other, reactive and indiscriminate repression that threatens the organizational resources and personal lives of Islamists. Exclusionary and repressive political environments force Islamists to undergo a near universal process of radicalization, which has been witnessed by so many rebellious movements, including ethnonationalist, socialist, and rightwing movements. This process involves the rise of exclusive mobilization structures to ensure against internal defections and external repression, and the diffusion of antisystem ideological frames to justify radical change and motivate collective violence.

Once movements disjoin into exclusive organizations that adopt antisystem ideologies, they witness intramovement competition that precludes a quick resolution to the conflict. Those who wish to continue fighting sabotage those that seek peace. Moreover, militants in exclusive, antisystem organizations undergo ideational transmutations that motivate expansive anticivilian violence. This violence becomes less and less rational and increasingly driven by emotive and group-maintenance goals. Over time, the convergence of a repressive environment, exclusive mobilization structures, and antisystem ideological frames determines the duration and targets of Islamist violence.

The Organization of the Book

The recent history of Islamist rebellions in Algeria and Egypt constitutes the central focus of this book. They are two countries that I have studied and written about since 1997. However, this book is concerned with the Muslim world at large and therefore draws upon evidence from many countries and regions, including Chechnya, Jordan, Kashmir, Pakistan, the southern Philippines, Tajikistan, and Tunisia.

In this chapter I have outlined the main precepts of the political process approach. In each of the following chapters, I begin with a brief theoretical proposition rooted in the political process approach and proceed to test the empirical validity of this proposition through case analysis. Thus, rather than present the theory all at once and proceed to case studies, I chose to divide the theory into themes to make the argument manageable and easily comprehensible for all readers.

The first half of the book deals with the political environment of Muslim rebellions, while the latter chapters investigate the mobilization structures and ideological frames of Muslim rebels. In Chapter 2, I analyze the impact of political exclusion on movement behavior and address the role of institutional closure in precipitating violent rebellion in Algeria and Egypt. I argue that political exclusion often contributes to the delegitimation of incumbent regimes and takes away incentives to seek redress through institutional channels.

I also examine how formal political access contributed to accommodative strategies in Jordan, while it contributed to both accommodation and militancy in Pakistan. I then show how political exclusion in Tunisia resulted in movement retreat, not rebellion. I conclude that the lack of institutional access is often a necessary, but rarely sufficient, condition for Islamist rebellions. Much like poverty, political exclusion abounds in the Muslim world, yet rebellion is not constant. This observation leads me to seek additional variables to answer the question of why Muslims rebel.

In Chapter 3, I introduce the variable of state repression into the analysis and show how varying patterns of state repression can affect the decisionmaking of potential Islamist rebels. Specifically, preemptive and selective state repression is likely to deter rebellious activity, even within a context of political exclusion, while reactive and indiscriminate repression promotes rebellion. In addition to Algeria and Egypt, I draw upon the recent histories of Kashmir, southern Philippines, Chechnya, and Tajikistan to show the deleterious effect of reactive and indiscriminate repression on Islamist movements. With few exceptions, the combination of political exclusion and reactive and indiscriminate repression is both necessary and sufficient to explain the timing and scale of Islamist rebellion.

In Chapter 4, I ask why do many Islamist rebellions turn into prolonged struggles? Under conditions of exclusion and repression, Islamists are more likely to adopt exclusive movement organizations, which in turn hinder conflict resolution. Exclusive organizations offer greater protection against counterinsurgency measures and solidify the internal cohesion of rebel organizations. However, these mobilization structures have consequences beyond the intent of the organizers. The chief outcome of such organizations is the intensification of intramovement competition, as well as the emergence of underground "careers" that institutionalizes rebellious activity within society. Hence, protracted conflict.

In Chapter 5, I address why many Islamist rebellions result in anticivilian violence. The diffusion of antisystem and polarizing ideologies that deny the possibility of neutrality in the conflict is the main reason why violence becomes an all-encompassing war against civilians. Antisystem frames, however, do not appear out of thin air, nor do they gain their virulent effect overnight. They emerge from the margins to gain resonance in the broader movement only under conditions of exclusion and indiscriminate repression, and within a context of exclusive mobilization structures. Once they solidify in the movement, these frames are difficult to uproot and serve to neutralize self-sanctioning moral codes against killing and maiming civilians. In addition to the ideological frames of Algerian and Egyptian Islamists, I explore the antisystem frames of Al-Qaida leaders to explain their anticivilian carnage.

I conclude the book by drawing out the theoretical and policy implications of my approach to Islamist rebellions. I propose five starting points for future systematic and comparative research on Islamist rebellions. The analysis presented in this book suggests tangible recommendations to those governments seeking to formulate a workable policy toward Islamist opposition, a policy that does not produce unrelenting suffering of people in the Muslim world.

Notes

1. See, for example, Luis Martinez's (2000) book on Islamist rebellion in Algeria. He offers a unique explanation that is specific to the Algerian context.

2. For an informative categorization of state policies toward Islamist movements, see Hudson (1995).

3. A perusal of the *Middle East Journal* chronology sections from 1980 to 2000 confirms that from the five countries under discussion, only Algeria and Egypt witnessed significant levels of Islamist violence and insurgency during the early 1990s. Studies by a number of authors also confirm that violence in Jordan, Morocco, and Tunisia during the 1980s and 1990s was relatively negligible when compared to the violence of Algeria and Egypt since 1992. For Jordan, see El-Said (1995), Robinson (1997), and Boulby (1999). For Morocco, see Munson (1986), Tessler (1997), and Shahin (1997). For Tunisia, see Waltz (1986), Hermassi (1995), Shahin (1997), and Hamdi (1998).

4. This variable is often cited as important for the rise of Islamist militancy because the harsh and "morally lax" realities of urban life result in frustration among traditional-minded migrants (Ibrahim 1980; Ansari 1984a).

5. Other works within the "frustration-aggression" approach include Davies (1962, 1969), Feierabend and Feierabend (1972), and Gurr (1968a, 1968b, 1968c, 1973).

6. Gurr distinguished between three types of deprivations that could eventually translate into political violence: (1) "decremental deprivation," where expectations are constant but individual capabilities to meet these expectations are declining; (2) "aspirational deprivation," where expectations are increasing

but individual capabilities to meet these expectations are static; and (3) "progressive deprivation," where expectations are increasing but individual capabilities to meet these expectations are declining (Gurr 1970: 46).

7. For some of the best-known criticisms of the frustration-aggression approach, see the works of Tilly (1978) and his colleagues (Snyder and Tilly 1972; Tilly et al. 1975), Oberschall (1973, 1978), Jenkins and Perrow (1977), Skocpol (1979), and McAdam (1982).

8. The idea of channeling-movement strategy comes from the works of Jenkins and Eckert (1986) and McCarthy et al. (1991).

2

Political Exclusion in the Muslim World

Social movements emerge in political environments that shape their opportunities and constraints for action. These opportunities and constraints enter into the calculations of movement actors and help frame debates over the efficacy and legitimacy of competing strategies (Eisinger 1973; McAdam 1982; Kitschelt 1986; Tarrow 1989; Kriesi et al. 1995; McAdam et al. 1996). One of the most important dimensions of any political environment is the degree to which social movements can participate in the political system. Movements can participate procedurally, through direct access to formal and informal policymaking channels, and substantively, by exercising real influence through those channels. System accessibility is important for investigating violent contention because it bears directly on whether a movement will advocate reform or revolution.

In this chapter, I draw on existing social movement theory to explain why institutional exclusion is a contributing condition for Islamist rebellions. The absence of institutional channels for conflict mediation and political contestation encourages rebellion by delegitimizing the ruling regime and disempowering moderate voices within the movement.

The cases of Algeria and Egypt show how shifts from political inclusion to exclusion contribute to the rise of rebellious Islamist movements. In Algeria, the shift was clearly marked by a bloodless coup that ended an electoral process favoring the Islamists. In Egypt, the shift from inclusion to exclusion was far more gradual and was characterized by legal restrictions and electoral manipulations that hindered the Islamists. I conclude by comparing the experiences of Algeria and

27

Egypt with other Muslim countries and discussing the extent to which the variable of institutional exclusion is necessary and sufficient to resolve the question of why Muslims rebel.

Exclusionary Systems and Mass Rebellions

The degree of political system accessibility often plays a critical role in shaping the strategic orientation and tactical repertoires of social movements. By the *political system* I mean the set of formal institutions of the state—parliaments, government ministries, policy-implementing agencies—and informal channels, procedures, and "policy styles" by which the state elite governs (Kitschelt 1986: 63). A political system is accessible to a movement when the state grants it the possibility to influence policymaking through governmental institutions; it is closed when the movement is prohibited from influencing public policy through institutional channels.[1]

Under completely accessible systems, movement actors encounter few restrictions on their ability to form parties, compete in elections, lobby state officials, hold public office, engage in policy formulation, appeal to judicial review, and challenge state policies through formal and informal channels of conflict mediation. Such systems include many Western democracies such as the United States and Germany. Conversely, completely inaccessible systems make illegal any attempt by movement organizations to engage in formal policymaking and instead opt to repress them. Iraq under Saddam Hussein, Chile under Augusto Pinochet, and many of the former single-party and communist states are examples of exclusionary political systems.

Between the two poles of open and closed access lies formal access to the political system. Formal access is circumscribed inclusion whereby legal restrictions to participation do not exist but substantive influence is denied. A state that only provides formal access to the system often expects to give the appearance of political openness without ever intending to cede consequential access to the levers of power. Indonesia under Suharto is a prime example of formal inclusionary systems.

The more accessible the system, the more likely Islamist movements will adopt accommodative strategies and shun violence over time. At the very least, a more inclusive polity will diminish the possibility of a united violent opposition with mass public support. Open access to the system means the movement has an option beyond disruption or revolutionary struggle to effect change. It creates the possibility for debate between moderates (advocates of nonviolent means to social change) and radicals (advocates of revolutionary insurgency) within the movement.

The possibility of pursuing "proper" channels of conflict resolution will entice many Islamists to choose the path of institutional bargaining and competition, resulting in a movement divided between two strategies. A divided movement, in turn, is likely to reduce the material and organizational resources of the militant wing. Closed or formal access, while it does not necessarily preclude debate over strategies and tactics between radicals and moderates, is likely to narrow the range of options from which moderates could draw.

To be sure, system accessibility is not a guarantee that those vying for power will not exploit political openness to dominate the system or engage in violence. Adolf Hitler's fascist party used its political access in Germany to exclude leftists and communists during the 1930s. Sudanese Islamists' access to the political system since the late-1980s resulted in a hegemonic alliance between the Islamists and the military, to the exclusion of other political forces. Secular regimes and parties in the Muslim world rightly express the concern that political inclusion of Islamists in a genuinely democratic process may result in "one person, one vote, one time." (Later on in this chapter, I will show how political inclusion of Islamists has not eliminated recurring sectarian violence in Pakistan.)

Generally speaking, however, studies of revolutionary movements have substantiated the claim that the more inclusive the state, even an inclusive authoritarian state, the less likely it is to unify opponents behind a revolutionary strategy or witness internal wars (Huntington 1968; Skocpol 1979; Zimmermann 1983; Dix 1984; Goodwin and Skocpol 1989; Goldstone 1991; Wickham-Crowley 1991; Cleary 2000; Gurr 2000; Parsa 2000; Sambanis 2001). The Iranian and Nicaraguan revolutions of 1979, for instance, were made by a broad-based movement against "personalist authoritarian" regimes characterized by "institutional detachment from the majority of the population" (Farhi 1990: 32).

Similarly, the Cuban revolutionary movement of 1959 engendered cross-national opposition to the state largely because Fulgencio Batista's regime was a personalist, rather than collective, form of dictatorship. In contrast, revolutionary movements in Colombia, Venezuela, Peru, and Bolivia were unable to forge unified movements partly because elected governments "contributed greatly to the weaknesses of the revolutionary opposition since the reformist option seemed to provide the opposition with an alternative path" (Wickham-Crowley 1992: 170).

Just as important, open access to the political system is likely to amplify the voices of moderate Islamists by giving credence to the idea that change could be achieved through extant state institutions. Open access allows moderates to argue that participating in conventional politics could offer a less costly path to social change. Closed or circumscribed access, by contrast, makes it easier for radicals to argue for disruption and violence by highlighting the inability of moderates to effect change through conventional politics. As Goodwin (1997: 18) explains, access to the institutionalized political process "discourages the sense that the state is unreformable or an instrument of a narrow class or clique and (accordingly) needs to be overhauled."

The perceived reformability of the state will lessen the sense of urgency for fundamental change in the institutionalized political process. Piven and Cloward (1977: 91), for example, attribute the demise of the unemployed workers' movement in the United States during the New Deal era to institutional channeling that "encouraged faith in the possibility of national electoral influence" and "destroyed the incentive of the leaders of the unemployed to exacerbate disorder." Conversely, Crenshaw's (1978: 7–8) study of revolutionary nationalism in Algeria points out that many of the leaders of the National Liberation Front at one point sought political office and were denied through fraud.

Furthermore, rebellious contention in a context of open institutional access might cause the Islamist movement to lose legitimacy resources (in this case, the moral authority to command its supporters). A movement that adopts militancy in the face of meaningful access to "normal" channels of conflict mediation can be portrayed as unnecessarily disruptive and perhaps illegitimate. This is what happened in the Venezuelan revolutionary movement during the 1960s. Democratization after the demise of the dictator Marcos Pérez Jiménez in 1958 resulted in the marginalization of the revolutionaries largely because, as one of the leaders of the movement put it, democracy "remained unbroken in the eyes of the masses" and the "electoral process became the most important phenomenon in the country, absorbing the interest and passion of the masses" (quoted in Ryan 1994: 33).

Che Guevara advised other revolutionaries to avoid insurgency under regimes that give the appearance of electoral legitimacy because "the populace will not turn in a revolutionary direction while electoral alternatives remain an option and retain appeal" (McClintock 1998: 5). If militant strategies are to acquire legitimacy in an Islamist movement, uncommitted supporters must come to believe that militancy is the only available form of contestation (Goodwin 2001a).

Finally, open access to the political system could potentially increase the institutional resources of Islamists—political recognition, free public platform in parliaments, elite patronage, and bureaucratic and ministerial positions. These resources, in turn, allow the movement to exert influence through elite ties, negotiate concessions with the authorities, put new issues on the political agenda, publicize the demands of the movement through the parliamentary platform, and solidify the role of the movement in society by working to undermine state repressive policies against the movement.

Access to the political system, as Oberschall (1993: 56) explains, "shifts some of the costs of obtaining resources onto institutionalized politics." The acquisition of institutional resources is important in the long run if the movement wishes to stabilize its resource base. Maintaining material and organizational resources through sustained mobilization is difficult due to declining commitments by movement supporters and the heavy toll of state repression (Tarrow 1989; Koopmans 1993).

Unless Islamists calculate that a brief series of demonstrations or incidents of violence could result in a quick victory for their movement, many will opt to take advantage of open institutional access to maintain a stable resource base. Consequently, militant activities will be rejected because they are likely to threaten these resources by inducing state repression. Thus, militancy will be viewed as entailing a dual cost, the cost of actual struggle against the state and the cost of losing institutional resources.

If the state provides Islamists substantive access to the institutionalized political system, Islamists are less likely to rebel. If, however, the state denies Islamists meaningful access to institutional participation, Islamists are more likely to rebel. The following examples from Algeria and Egypt will illustrate how system closures contributed to the outbreak of rebellion in the 1990s.

Overview of Islamist Activism in Algeria and Egypt

The contemporary Islamist movements in Algeria and Egypt were forged during the 1970s and 1980s as part of an Islamic revival that swept the Muslim world (Esposito 1983; Hunter 1988; Kepel 1994). Like all social movements, Islamist movements in Algeria and Egypt represented various tendencies, ranging from apolitical social reformers to violent ideologues and extremists. Overall, however, the Islamist movements in both countries did not emerge as radical projects bent on the revolutionary overthrow of secular states or violent destruction of secular societies. On the contrary, the prevailing tendency was oriented toward the gradual redirection of Muslims into a "more Islamic" path and competition with Marxist and nationalist thought, particularly on university campuses and through "free" or "private" mosques (Rouadjia 1993; Mubarak 1995).

The quiescence of Islamist movements in Algeria and Egypt during the 1970s and 1980s can be observed in their pattern of relative nonmilitancy, especially when compared to the 1990s. Islamists in Algeria and Egypt hardly engaged in any overt political opposition or extra-institutional mobilization such as demonstrations, marches, assassinations, or armed attacks against the state during the formative phase of their movements (Figure 2.1).

To be sure, armed Islamist groups did emerge during this time in both countries. In Algeria, the Mouvement Algérien Islamique Armée, better known as the Bouyali group, began to take form in 1982 after a merger of several smaller groups under the leadership of Mustapha Bouyali. Although this group did muster the support of approximately 600 activists (mainly south of Algiers), it never posed a serious challenge to the Algerian state and was largely shunned by other Islamists and preachers at the time (Khelladi 1992: 73–80; Ayyashi 1993: 192–207).[2]

In Egypt, the 1970s witnessed the rise of several radical groups, including Jama'it al-Muslimun (the Society of Muslims), commonly known as al-Takfir wal-Hijra (Excommunication and Emigration), and Shabab Muhammad (Muhammad's Youth), better known as the Military Technical (Faniya Askariya) group. Both of these organizations adopted a distinctively radical ideology and engaged in violent activities against the state. However, their violence was limited to a few noteworthy incidents and both quickly succumbed to state repression (Ibrahim 1980; Mustapha 1992).

During the 1980s and early 1990s, Islamist extra-institutional militancy and violent activities increased in both countries but remained well below the level of mass rebellion. In Algeria, the relative quiescence of the Islamist movement during the early 1980s was shattered by a series of demonstrations and rallies that brought together thousands of Islamists between 1989 and 1991. In those years alone, the number of overt Islamist activities (32) was double the number of activities in the years between 1975 and 1988 combined (16) (see Figure 2.1).

In Egypt, violence marked 1981–1982. The two most prominent incidents of antistate violence, of course, are the assassination of President

Figure 2.1 Islamist Militant Activism in Algeria and Egypt (number of violent incidents)

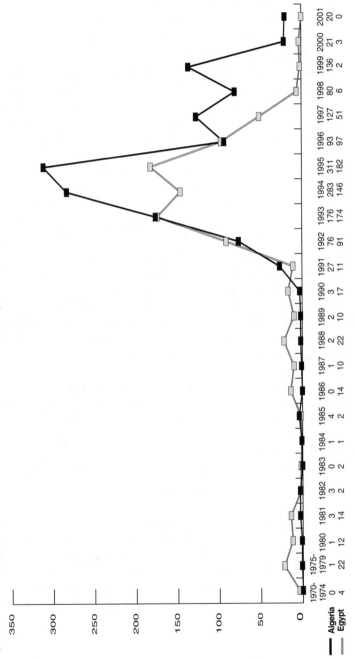

	1970-1974	1975-1979	1980	1981	1982	1983	1984	1985	1986	1987	1988	1989	1990	1991	1992	1993	1994	1995	1996	1997	1998	1999	2000	2001
Algeria	0	1	1	3	3	0	1	4	0	1	2	2	3	27	76	176	283	311	93	127	80	136	21	20
Egypt	4	22	12	14	2	2	1	2	14	10	22	10	17	11	91	174	146	182	97	51	6	2	3	0

Source: The data were collected from the *MEJ* quarterly chronologies, *MEI, ACR, and MECS* and episodes reported by Roberts (1988), Al-Ahnaf et al. (1991), Lamchichi (1992), Ayyashi (1993), Willis (1996), and Burgat and Dowell (1997).

Anwar Sadat in October 1981 and the aborted insurrection by radical Islamists in Asyut following the assassination. The expansion in violence coincided with the radicalization of some of the upper Egypt Islamist students organized around al-Jama'a al-Islamiyya (henceforth, the Jama'a), many of whom took up a revolutionary strategy by merging forces with an incipient radical organization called al-Jihad. This merger was the result of a split in 1978 when the Jama'a leaders in Cairo, Alexandria, and some al-Minya branches agreed to support the Muslim Brotherhood (MB) while the Asyut and other al-Minya leaders opted to formulate an independent position.[3]

Despite the noticeable increase in Islamist militancy during the first two years of the 1980s, the Egyptian Islamist movement did not turn to sustained insurgency, and violence was relatively limited and sporadic from 1982 to 1986. Islamist militancy reemerged between 1986 and 1991, when Egypt witnessed eighty-four incidents of violence. Much of the violence was carried out by the Jama'a and struck at "soft" targets such as musical festivals, weddings, cinemas, churches, and any individual perceived to be engaging in "sin" (munkar).

Patterns of violence significantly changed in 1992, the year that ushered in Islamist rebellions in both Algeria and Egypt (see Figure 2.1). In Algeria, the prevailing strategy of the movement from 1992 to 1997 was armed insurgency. Initially, this armed struggle took the form of dispersed and unorganized clashes with security forces. Over the course of time insurgents organized themselves into numerous armed groups, including the Armed Islamic Movement (MIA), Islamic State Movement (MEI), and Islamic Front for Armed Jihad (FIDA). However, the two most prominent armed groups to emerge in the post-coup era were the Groupe Islamique Armé (GIA) and Armée Islamique du Salut (AIS). The AIS officially gave up its insurgency in 1997 and disarmed its cadres in 1999. The GIA has split into numerous groups, many of which continue to fight to this day.

Egypt witnessed a total of 741 incidents of violence between 1992 and 1997. This is in stark contrast to the 143 incidents from 1970 to 1991. Whereas from 1970 to 1989, according to one estimate, Islamist violence resulted in the deaths of 120 people (Mubarak 1995: 374), between 1992 and 1997 violence resulted in 1,442 deaths and 1,779 injuries. Unofficial figures put the number of killed and injured much higher. The years between 1993 and 1995 were the bloodiest, witnessing almost daily incidents of violence. This violence was overwhelmingly the work of the Jama'a; al-Jihad played a minor role in the insurgency while the MB shunned violence altogether.[4]

The insurgency was largely limited to upper Egyptian towns—Asyut, Aswan, Souhaj, al-Minya, Qina, and Beni Swayf—even though the Jama'a tried to expand its recruitment and attacks into Cairo (Mubarak 1995: 370–371; al-Din 1998: 506). Just as significant, violence in upper Egypt did not come about simultaneously but appeared in some regions and spread to others over time, while it waned in the areas in which it originally developed.[5] This pattern is in stark contrast to Algeria, where violence arose in several regions and continued in full force until 1996 and 1997.

In sum, the Algerian and Egyptian Islamist movements that emerged in the 1970s and 1980s were not "naturally" radical movements bent on violent rebellion. Proponents of revolutionary violence were a small part of a broader social movement that sought nonconfrontational means to effect change. It took more than a decade before violence reached the level of rebellion. The political-institutional context prior to and during the years of Islamist rebellion in Algeria and Egypt demonstrates how Islamist rebellions were partly a response to political exclusion.

Exclusionary Politics and
Islamist Rebellion in Algeria

During the formative stages of its Islamist movement (1979–1989), the political system in Algeria was largely exclusionary, characterized by single-party rule and dominated by a military-led executive that did not brook any opposition to its rule (Entelis 1986; Hermassi 1987; Zartman 1987; Rakhila 1993; Roberts 1996). However, this institutional context changed in 1989, when President Chadli Benjedid embarked on major political and institutional reforms in the aftermath of the October 1988 riots. It was widely believed that institutional reforms were a way to absorb the anger of the public over economic crisis and mismanagement.

These reforms began with the announcement that the ruling National Liberation Front (FLN) would be "freed from participating in the direct management at all levels of the state apparatus."[6] Through a national referendum that was overwhelmingly approved in November 1988, the FLN was separated from the ruling government. Moreover, the FLN was no longer in a position to oversee elections and appoint FLN candidates. Other reforms were instituted in the 1989 constitution, the most significant of which was the right to form associations of a political nature (Article 40), thus officially abandoning one-party rule (Ali 1996; al-Amar 1996; Kharfallah 1996: 96–108; Rashid 1997).

There were additional developments in 1989 that signaled greater openness in Algeria. In March, the military withdrew from the FLN central committee; in April, the national assembly abolished state security courts; and in October, licenses to demonstrate and hold rallies were no longer necessary.[7] These reforms signaled a significant opening in the system and appeared to have ushered in a new era in Algeria. As Entelis (1992: 19) put it, "in only nine months, from October 1988 to July 1989, the Algerian political system was fundamentally transformed from a single-party authoritarian state to a multiparty, pluralistic nation of laws."

Islamists took advantage of nearly every aspect of institutional and political openness. In March 1989, Islamists came together to form the Front Islamique du Salut (FIS) as a political party. The formation of the FIS and its subsequent success inspired the formation of thirteen other Islamist political parties in the early 1990s. The most notable of the new parties were Harakat al-Mujtama al-Islami (HAMAS, Islamic Society Movement) and Mouvement de la Nahda Islamique (MNI, Islamic Renaissance Movement). Senior activists and preachers Mahfoud Nahnah and Abdullah Jaballah, respectively, led them.

Along with official Islamist organizations and parties emerged a number of small groups with a radical Islamist orientation. These groups carried titles such as Amr bil M'arouf wal Nahi 'an al-Munkar (Commanding the Good and Prohibiting the Forbidding), Takfir wal Hijra (Excommunication and Migration), Jama'at al-Sunna wa al-Shari'a (the Group of Islamic Tradition and Law), and Ansar al-Tawhid (Supporters of Unity). These groups were marginal in the movement, especially in relation to the FIS, which became the largest representative of the Islamist movement.

The Strategy and Discourse of the FIS

Although the FIS was a political party that sought to work within the system, it was also a populist movement that organized rallies, marches, and demonstrations to highlight its demands and exhibit its popularity to the larger public. Its rallies and demonstrations easily mobilized thousands of supporters and at times brought out hundreds of thousands. Most effective in terms of publicity, however, were the mass Friday prayers around key mosques in Kouba and Bab el-Oued. The mosques would regularly overflow onto adjacent streets, where worshipers would lay down their prayer rugs to pray.

The FIS combined moderation with radicalism in both its discourse and protest repertoire. Led by Abassi Madani and Ali Belhaj, two Islamist activists who gained notoriety in the 1980s, the FIS presented the public with two faces, one moderate and the other radical.[8] In its 1989 political program, the FIS described its method as that of "moderation, centerism, and comprehensiveness." According to the document, the FIS pursues its goals "without excess or negligence" because it believes in "persuasion not subjugation." It also seeks to "guarantee the interests of the nation, protection of its foundations and preservation of its gains."[9]

In addition to a moderately worded program, the statements of Abassi, the principal leader of the FIS, sought to reassure the public of FIS's good intentions and intrinsically moderate message, particularly when it came to issues of democracy and individual liberties. Although Abassi declared his preference for *al-shura* (Islamic tradition of consultation) over democracy, he defined the former as a system that permits freedom of expression, encourages self-criticism and accountability, and precludes political monopoly.

As for political opposition, Abassi declared that "al-shura permits multiple parties and opposition because the latter is necessary and existed during the time of the rightly guided caliphs." Moreover, in contrast to those who argue that "only God legislates," Abassi maintained that "it is the people that rule and no government should exist without the will of the people; Islamists are not enemies of democracy" (Ghanim 1992: 33–34).[10]

However, Ali Belhaj, Abassi's deputy, did not hesitate to give fiery speeches in which he denounced democracy, the state, and opponents in vitriolic terms. Belhaj views democracy as "an un-Islamic institution" and "a system that permits prostitution." Any victory for Islamists through the polls is "not a victory for democracy but a victory for Islam." He promised that the FIS "will not exchange al-shura with democracy" because the latter, according to Belhaj, is a "poison that leads to heresy" (al-Ahnaf et al. 1991: 97; al-Jasour 1995: 46; Ali 1996: 268).

Although Belhaj repeatedly declared his abhorrence for autocratic rule, he did not make it clear that his understanding of al-shura was as accommodating of opposition (especially secular opposition) as Abassi's aforementioned definition. On the contrary, he rejected the notion of majority rule by maintaining that "truth is not measured by counting the proponents or opposing voices, but with the authoritative proof that the creed presents. . . . Truth is not agreed upon by the majority even if the latter were Muslims . . . but is represented by adopting the divine truth, even if we alone do so."[11] This rejection of majority rule strongly implied that Belhaj did not believe in the alternation of rule if it entailed turning over power to those who did not represent the "truth."

Similar to its discourse, FIS's tactical repertoire from 1989 to 1991 combined militancy with accommodation. The FIS did not hesitate to rally people or challenge the regime, and it often thrived on confronting opponents, especially the ruling FLN. This populist militancy is best exemplified in three episodes: the April 1990 march, the demonstrations against the Gulf War in 1990, and the May–June 1991 general strike.

On 20 April 1990 the FIS held a landmark demonstration that brought together between 600,000 and 800,000 people to march in silence. The sheer size of participation and the discipline with which it was conducted were impressive enough, but what made the march significant was the fact that it was scheduled on the same day the FLN was scheduled to hold its own march against the political use of mosques by Islamists. This move by the FIS was clearly intended to confront and embarrass the FLN, who would have had difficulty matching the participation levels achieved by the FIS. The self-assurance of the FIS led Ahmed Sahnoun, the head of Rabitat al-Dawa (League of Islamic Preaching), to urge FIS leaders to cancel the march because it could result in violent clashes. Abassi refused, however. Instead, it was the FLN that called off its march (Ayyashi 1993: 71).

The boldness of the FIS was repeated during the Gulf War of 1990–1991. Although the FIS condemned the Iraqi invasion of Kuwait, it adopted a pro-Iraq stance as the United States–led international force began to prepare for war against Iraqi forces. The FIS along with other parties organized a mass demonstration of approximately 400,000 people on 18 January 1991.

However, while other parties participated, the FIS was the most vociferous in its calls against the West. More significantly, its principal leaders sought to embarrass the Algerian regime for its apparent passivity in the conflict by calling for jihad and demanding that the state open up training camps for volunteers to Iraq. Belhaj, in his usual truculent style, declared "we do not want power . . . we leave the thrones to you. We want jihad, only jihad and to meet Allah."

President Chadli Benjedid condemned the "demagogy" and "blackmail" of the FIS, but this did not stop the latter from organizing another demonstration that was equally belligerent in its tone. On 31 January 1991, the FIS mobilized about 60,000 supporters, some of whom carried signs that read "There is no God but Allah, Chadli is the enemy of Allah" (Mortimer 1991: 587; Roberts 1991: 141–142; Ayyashi 1993: 103–106).

The height of FIS's extra-institutional militancy came in May and June 1991 when the FIS called for a "general and unlimited" strike. The strike was in response to an electoral law that was blatantly intended to benefit the ruling FLN. It was widely denounced by the opposition, but the FIS in particular saw it as "high treason" (Mortimer 1991: 588).

The FIS called for a general strike on 25 May. Some parties voiced the opinion that the strike would be "dangerous" and undemocratic. The interior ministry issued a communiqué denouncing it as adventurism that could harm the democratic process and national security. The military deployed forces two days before the strike was to commence, signaling the potential for violence. Yet despite the bad publicity and threat of a clampdown, the FIS went ahead with the strike (al-Tahiri 1992: 94; Charef 1994: 148; al-Rasi 1997: 347).

The strike began with demonstrators calling for an Islamic state and presidential elections. Demonstrators carried signs that read "Down with Chadli" and chanted slogans denouncing democracy. When the strike failed to halt work, many Islamists took it on themselves, either by threat or by force, to prevent workers from entering factories, shopkeepers from opening their shops, and schoolteachers and university professors from teaching (al-Rasi 1997: 344–346). Some Islamists distributed a tract entitled "The Principles and Objectives of Civil Disobedience," in which the author, Said Makhloufi, a member of the FIS consultative council, argued that political work had reached an impasse and civil disobedience was necessary to bring about an Islamic government.[12]

The strike, which extended into June, turned into a series of rallies and occupations of public squares in the capital. The military finally decided to dislodge the demonstrators by force, producing a series of clashes and escalations that lasted throughout June and resulted in mass arrests and numerous deaths and injuries.[13] The confrontations also resulted in the dismissal of Prime Minister Mouloud Hamrouche and the declaration of a "state of siege." The state-movement confrontation culminated with the arrest of Abassi and Belhaj on charges of fomenting, organizing, and conspiring against the state.

Although these three examples highlight the populist militancy of the FIS, a closer examination of the period 1989–1991 indicates the extent to which the FIS was willing to accommodate the state and limit its militancy in order to remain a legitimate actor in the political process.

The April 1990 demonstration, while intended to confront and embarrass the FLN, was also aimed to counter charges of Islamist violence; hence the silent and disciplined march.[14] During the Gulf War, the FIS never went beyond vitriolic rhetoric, and its demonstrations were within the boundaries of legality and generally peaceful (Qawas 1998: 98).

Between the April 1990 demonstrations and the May 1991 strike, the FIS participated in local government elections as a political party. It appointed candidates and ran an election campaign that resulted in the FIS winning the majority of communal and departmental assemblies.[15] Its preelection rallies and marches were largely intended to give publicity to the Islamist party, not to denounce the system of party politics. After the June 1990 election, Abassi declared the willingness of the FIS to cooperate with other parties and guaranteed individual freedoms in FIS-controlled departments and communes.[16]

As for the general strike of May 1991, the FIS's militant action was counterbalanced by other measures that reflected the limited nature of its militancy. When they made the call for a general strike on 23 May, Abassi and Belhaj asked for a "peaceful" and "disciplined" strike "for democracy" (Charef 1994: 147). On the first day of the strike, organizers with loudspeakers urged supporters to avoid any violence, even in self-defense or in response to provocation (Ayyashi 1993: 248).

During the strike, the FIS maintained constant contact with government mediators and negotiated with Hamrouche an agreement to occupy the capital squares peacefully.[17] When the new prime minister Ahmed Ghozali took over, he too negotiated with the FIS to bring the crisis to an end. He agreed to organize "free and clean" parliamentary elections within six months and amend the electoral laws that led to the strike. In return, the FIS called off the demonstrations (Roberts 1994a: 469; Willis 1996: 178–180; Quandt 1998: 56–57). When the government began to arrest the radical elements that were at the forefront of clashes with security forces, the FIS leadership did not object too vigorously.[18] The escalation in violence and rhetoric came after security forces expanded their arrests to include mainstream FIS activists and took "provocative" measures against Islamists. On 25 June 1991, the army began to take down banners that read "Islamic Commune" from FIS-controlled town halls.[19]

After the arrest of its principal leaders, the FIS took additional measures to ensure it remained a legitimate actor in the system. In July 1991 it held its *al-wafa* (loyalty) conference in Batna to sort out its strategy in the aftermath of the June events. At least three tendencies emerged during the conference. One group, led by Said Gushi, a founding member of the FIS, believed that Algeria was not ripe for transformation into an Islamic state. Therefore, the FIS should not seek to rule but instead should limit itself to a secondary role of preaching. Gushi wanted the FIS to take a more conciliatory tone toward the authorities and to participate in dialogues with the regime scheduled for the end of July. In other words, the Gushi group wanted to retreat to a social reformist strategy that would shun politics for the time being to protect the legality of the FIS.

Another group led by the "Afghans" Said Mekhloufi and Qameredin Kharban wanted to boycott the elections to exert pressure on the regime to release FIS leaders and repeal the biased electoral laws. This group believed that the FIS controlled the street and therefore could mobilize more demonstrations against the regime.

The third group, led by Abdelkader Hachani, did not want the withdrawal of the FIS from the political arena or a boycott of the elections. Instead, it wanted to continue with the electoral path but was uncertain of the appropriate course of action to take. Hachani's immediate objective was to expand the membership of the FIS consultative council to counter the influence of the Gushi group and quiet the radical elements that threatened to unleash repression against the organization. Hachani succeeded in raising the number of members from thirty-eight to fifty. Many of the new members were not part of the FIS founding committees, which led Gushi to resign.[20]

Furthermore, during the conference, the FIS froze the membership of five consultative council members, including Said Mekhloufi and Qameredin Kharban.[21] The FIS issued a public communiqué announcing the decision to freeze the memberships, thus signaling to the regime that it would not tolerate those who advocate militancy and violence (Charef 1994: 117–118; al-Tawil 1998: 40–41; Qawas 1998: 107–110).

In addition to these measures, which were clearly intended to balance the demands of the retreatists with those of the militants, the FIS's new provisional leader, Hachani, moderated the party's tone after June and did not organize rallies until it was made legal to do so again.[22] When armed Islamists killed three policemen in November 1991 in an attack on a border post in Guemmar, the FIS was quick to distance itself from the attack and condemned it. Hachani accused the military of facilitating the attack to discredit the movement and added, "the FIS operates within legality" (Charef 1994: 221; al-Tawil 1998: 44).

Finally, although the FIS publicly declared its intention to boycott the national elections scheduled for December 1991, it prepared for them and participated in them. According to Rabeh Kebir, Hachani wanted to stay on the electoral path all along. However, the FIS wanted to "deflect the attention of the regime to the possibility of our non-participation as we gathered our ranks and prepared for the elections and determined the nominees."[23] Abdelkarim Ghamati, a member of the FIS consultative council, maintained, "we wanted to participate in the elections, but we did not want the regime to know this so as to put pressure on it to release FIS preachers" (al-Tawil 1998: 43–44). The FIS won 188 seats out of 430 national assembly seats in the first round of the elections and was poised to win an overwhelming majority of seats in the second round of voting.

The aforementioned measures and developments indicate that the FIS was not simply a militant party. Its strategy from 1989 to 1991 can be best characterized as calculated tactical militancy within an overall accommodative orientation. It was not a revolutionary party that aimed to build an Islamic state at any cost and irrespective of the means. In other words, unlike the radical groups that wanted to overthrow the system through armed struggle and shunned democracy as un-Islamic, the FIS was clearly against revolutionary violence in this period. The FIS used its populist militancy to ensure success within, not at the expense of, the newly instituted system of party politics that benefited it the most. When its militancy threatened to lead to intensive repression, the FIS began to accommodate the regime.

Rabeh Kebir, reflecting on this period, states, "the FIS did not wish to gamble with the fate of the people [by attempting to take power]. . . . Perhaps we made a mistake when we did not make it our intention to topple the regime. If we had planned for it we could have succeeded . . . but we did not know what the days ahead hid for us."[24]

Exclusion and Rebellion in Algeria 1992–1997

A bloodless military coup in January 1992 put an end to the electoral process. The military did not just seek to deny the FIS the ability to dominate the national assembly; it sought to exclude the party from politics altogether. After the dissolution of the national assembly and cancellation of the elections, the High State Committee (HCE) declared a state of emergency, suspended the FIS, and closed down its headquarters.[25] In March, the FIS was formally dissolved and this decision was confirmed by the Supreme Court the following month. In July, a military court sentenced Abassi and Belhaj to twelve years in prison. In

November, the state empowered authorities to close down charitable and cultural organizations associated with the FIS, and more than 300 councils controlled by the FIS were dissolved.[26]

The FIS leadership initially sought a political solution to the crisis. In the immediate aftermath of the coup, the FIS attempted to rally the FLN and Socialist Forces Front (FFS) to its side by taking a united stand against the new leadership and challenging the constitutionality of the HCE. When the FIS was banned, it appealed to the Supreme Court to reverse the ban. In the first half of 1992 some FIS leaders—Abdel-razak Rejjam, Rabeh Kebir, Anwar Haddam—made appeals for a political solution based on, inter alia, the release of prisoners, relegalization of the FIS, and return to elections.[27]

Many FIS activists, however, did not share the moderation of the leadership and began to clash with security forces all across the country. Initially, these clashes were spontaneous expressions of anger, but they soon became premeditated attacks against police stations and individual security officers. Islamists organized militias and began to hold meetings to unify the ranks of the emerging armed movement (Mortimer 1996; Willis 1996; Burgat and Dowell 1997; al-Tawil 1998).

The armed movement initially coalesced around the radical groups that had opted to stay outside of the FIS apparatus from 1989 to 1991. During that time, these groups were marginal in the movement and were deliberately pushed aside by the FIS after June 1991. The radicals only gained prominence after the coup put an end to the FIS's electoral option.

Three reasons explain why the radicals, especially the GIA, succeeded in significantly expanding their ranks following the coup.[28] First, the radicals appeared to have been right all along in their assessment of the electoral process and the Algerian regime. Their argument has always been that if Islamists wish to establish an Islamic state, they must prepare for jihad. However, whereas opponents of revolutionary violence within the FIS could successfully argue after June 1991 that the electoral option made jihad unnecessary, it could not credibly do so after the coup. As former FLN leader Abdelhamid Mehri (1997: 5–6) explains, "when the [electoral] experiment was aborted it boosted the extremist wing that claimed that democracy is a game in the hands of the regime and the regime will cancel democracy if it is not in its interest."[29]

Second, the failure of the FIS to declare and organize for armed jihad immediately after the coup gave the radical groups an opportunity to attract FIS activists who were initially not committed to a jihadist strategy but were seeking a commensurate response to the coup (Martinez 2000).

As Qameredin Kharban maintains, "the hesitation of the [FIS] in declaring jihad was a mistake that led to other grave mistakes, one of which is the [GIA]."[30] Third, the radicals were the most prepared for armed struggle given their experience in Afghanistan and the Bouyali group, and therefore constituted a ready-made nucleus around which FIS activists could rally.[31]

The State's Strategy of Repression and Marginalization

The military regime had a combined strategy of political repression of the FIS and dialogue with other political parties and civic associations in an effort to establish the new leadership's legitimacy. In April 1992, the HCE established the National Consultative Council—an interim advisory body without any formal legislative powers, composed of sixty prominent Algerian personalities—to replace temporarily the disbanded parliament. In October 1993, the Commission on National Dialogue was established to organize a National Reconciliation Conference, which was intended to bring Algeria's political parties together to arrive at a consensus over post-HCE institutions (Roberts 1995: 255–257; Mortimer 1996: 31–32). In May 1994, a new quasiparliamentary body was created, the National Transition Council, which consisted of 175 seats to be filled by state-appointed representatives of political parties (including HAMAS and the MNI, but excluding the FIS), professional associations, and trade unions.

However, all these efforts failed to win the military regime the legitimacy it was seeking, principally because the major parties—FIS, FLN, and FFS—along with others refused to recognize the legitimacy of the new institutions. Instead, they called for the reinstatement of the electoral process and inclusion of the FIS in national dialogue. The military regime, however, refused to include imprisoned FIS leaders in the National Reconciliation Conference held in January 1994. As a result, none of the major political parties attended (al-Rasi 1997: 385–387; Mortimer 1996: 32).

The failure to halt the Islamist insurgency through repression led some within the military regime to adopt a three-prong strategy vis-à-vis the Islamists from 1994 to 1995. This strategy entailed continued repression of the armed insurgents; dialogue with other political parties, including HAMAS and MNI; and negotiation with the FIS. Chief executive and later president Liamine Zeroual engaged political parties and imprisoned FIS leaders in a series of dialogues intended to bring the crisis to a halt. In February 1994 Zeroual called for a National Dialogue Conference to include all concerned parties "without exception," thus signaling a willingness to talk to the FIS.[32]

Subsequently, Zeroaul dismissed his prime minister, Redha Malek, and interior minister, Salim Saadi, both of whom publicly opposed dialogue with the FIS. Both Malek and Saadi constituted part of a faction known as the "eradicators"—those who wished to eradicate the Islamists through military measures. The eradicators include the influential retired general Khaled Nezzar, General Arabi Belkhair, chief of staff Major-General Mohammad Lamari, Chief Major-General Benabbas Ghezaiel, and military security chief Major-General Muhammad "Tawfiq" Mediene.

Zeroual, on the other hand, along with generals Muhammed Betchin, al-Akhal Aiyati, Ahmed Salih, Ali Tounisi, and Muhammed Ben Shershal constituted part of a faction known as "conciliators"—those who wished to end the crisis through negotiations and political concessions. The conciliators also included the FLN (until 1996) and the FFS (Roberts 1994c; Mortimer 1996; Qawas 1998: 202–203). These moves set the stage for a series of dialogues between Zeroual and various FIS leaders inside and outside of prison.

These negotiations, however, failed to bring the insurgency to an end. Although the precise demands of the interlocutors varied from one negotiation to another, the salient point of disagreement was whether a declaration of a cease-fire on the part of the FIS would precede or follow the release of FIS leaders from jail. The FIS leadership wanted a cease-fire declaration to follow their release from prison and consultation with the entire Islamist leadership, including some in the armed groups. The regime wanted a unilateral cease-fire declaration to precede the release of FIS leaders from prison. (For more on these initiatives, see Chapter 4.)

In addition to failed dialogue with the FIS, the regime did not succeed in drawing the major political parties—the FLN and FFS—into bilateral and multilateral dialogues. Instead, these parties, along with the FIS, opted to hold their own dialogues under the auspices of the Sant'Egidio community in Rome. These dialogues produced a national contract outlining the principles and procedures necessary for real reconciliation.

The regime, however, rejected the national contract and instead sought legitimacy through presidential elections, which were scheduled for November 1995. In response, the parties that participated in the

Rome dialogues, with the exception of the FIS, organized a rally on 9 June 1995, which was attended by approximately 10,000 people, to reiterate the demands made in Rome and express opposition to the upcoming presidential election (al-Rasi 1997: 439–440).

The presidential election of 1995 was intended to give a semblance of pluralism, as the regime permitted Nahnah, the leader of HAMAS, to compete against Zeroual for the presidency. When Zeroual was elected, his prime minister, Ahmed Oyahya, appointed two HAMAS representatives to ministerial positions and appointed ex-FIS member Ahmed Merrani as the head of Ministry of Religious Affairs.[33] These moves were clearly intended to highlight the regime's willingness to tolerate moderate Islamists. The formal inclusion of Islamists, however, was hardly enough to placate the insurgents, especially given the FIS's electoral victory in 1991.

The state's failure to end the violence through repression, negotiations, and presidential elections resulted in a new three-prong strategy toward the insurgency: repression, constitutional and electoral reforms, and expansion of formal inclusion of Islamists while excluding the FIS. Rather than strike a deal with the FIS, the military regime opted for constitutional and electoral reforms to rebuild an institutional framework and reestablish legitimacy for the state. In November 1996, a new constitution was approved in a national referendum.[34]

This constitution significantly weakened the national assembly vis-à-vis the already powerful executive, and it institutionalized the exclusion of overtly Islamist political parties. Article 42 recognized the right to form political parties but forbade associations from organizing on a "religious, linguistic, racial, gender, corporatist, or regional" basis. An electoral law adopted in February 1997 further prohibited the use of slogans or propaganda based on Islam, Arabism, or Amazighism (Articles 3 and 5). HAMAS and the MNI had to drop references to Islam and changed their names to the Society of Peace Movement (MSP) and al-Nahda respectively (Rashid 1997: 72–74; al-Rasi 1997: 478–484; Quandt 1998: 128–134).

The military regime also decided to continue with its policy of marginalizing the FIS. Following constitutional and electoral reforms, the state organized national and local elections in June and October 1997. Similar to the presidential election in 1995 and constitutional referendum in 1996, these elections were plagued with charges of fraud and vote rigging (Roberts 1998), but this did not stop the various parties from taking their places in state institutions.

In the national elections, the pro-government parties—the newly created (in March 1997) National Democratic Rally (RND) and the FLN under a new leadership—won 219 of 380 seats (about 57 percent), while the unofficially Islamist MSP and al-Nahda won a total of 103 seats (about 27 percent).[35] In the local government elections the pro-government parties won about 72 percent of the departmental seats and 77 percent of the communal seats, while the Islamist parties won approximately 9 percent of the departmental seats and 20 percent of the communal seats (Quandt 1998; Roberts 1998).

The 1996 reforms and 1997 elections were intended to create a system of formal pluralism whereby various political parties, including some with an Islamist orientation (but not former FIS leaders), would be given procedural access to the system but denied any substantive power over policymaking. A weakened national assembly and an all-powerful executive branch allowed the military to exert its influence over the system, as it had done prior to 1989, by its ability to advance and hinder candidates for the position of the president, where real institutional power lies in the Algerian polity. (For political exclusion in the post-1997 period, see Chapter 4.)

In short, the rebellion of Algerian Islamists in 1992 was not inevitable. While the FIS engaged in radical rhetoric and tactical repertoires prior to 1992, it was not a violently insurgent movement bent on revolution. Political exclusion of Islamists from 1992 to 1997 was the main impetus for mass revolt.

The FIS justified its jihad strictly in terms of fighting for the people's right to choose their representatives. In an open letter addressed to all Algerians, Madani Mezraq, the national commander of the AIS, argued that "the youth had no choice but resisting the aggressors and fighting for the sake of regaining the rights of the oppressed [mustadh'afeen]."[36] Responding to charges of terrorism, Rabeh Kebir rhetorically asked: "Who is the bearer of violence that must be condemned? Is it not the military tyranny that violated the constitution and trampled on the law and pursued state terrorism? Did the Islamic Salvation Front not enter elections twice in a legitimate manner . . . and not rely on any violence?"[37]

Even the undemocratic and uncompromising Ali Belhaj points to the 1992 coup as the real cause of violence. In one of the letters issued from his prison cell, he eloquently sums up the impact of institutional exclusion and repression on the Algeria Islamist movement: "We made a promise to ourselves to proceed the peaceful path in our political struggle to reach power as long as the regime abided by that path. Our goal is the creation of an Islamic state according to the choice of the Muslim Algerian people and through the ballot box. . . . But as soon as the [FIS] won, the tyrannical regime launched a coup against the choice of the people, stopped the electoral course, and opened concentration camps and prisons to the innocent."[38]

Secular groups and prodemocracy advocates had every right to be concerned about the FIS's contradictory rhetoric and the veiled threats of some of its leaders prior to 1992. The political exclusion of the FIS, however, only exacerbated matters by discrediting the democratic process, giving credence to proponents of violence, and precipitating violent insurgency that continues to this day.

Exclusionary Politics and Islamist Rebellion in Egypt

Similar to Algeria, the Islamist revolt in Egypt was partly a response to the politics of exclusion that served to delegitimize the ruling regime and the accommodative Islamists who insisted on working through state institutions. After a period of institutional accessibility, the Egyptian ruling regime embarked on a policy of deliberalization in the early 1990s, which contributed, at least in part, to the legitimization of Islamist violence.

During the mid-1980s, in an effort to shore up its legitimacy, the regime of Husni Mubarak permitted political liberalization, which allowed Islamists to play an indirect role in electoral politics. The most notable measure of liberalization was the expansion of opposition forces in the National Assembly (Zaki 1995; Korany 1998). Whereas in the 1979 People's Assembly only 32 out of 372 seats went to the opposition (almost 9 percent), in 1984 the opposition took 58 seats out of 448 (almost 13 percent) and in the 1987 elections it reached 100 out of 458 seats—a little more than 22 percent (Zaki 1995: 80).

During those years, the state acquiesced to the participation of the Muslim Brotherhood in parliamentary and local government elections. The MB was not given the status of a party, but it was able to form alliances with legal opposition parties, including the secular New Wafd in 1984 and the Labor and Liberal Parties in 1987 (Auda and Ibrahim 1995). In 1984, the MB won eight seats, while in the 1987 election it took thirty-six seats, making it the leading opposition force in parliament. In exchange for this access, the MB consistently and unequivocally reaffirmed its commitment to pluralism, gradualism, and nonviolence (Rubin 1990; Mubarak 1995).

The Muslim Brotherhood in Parliament

The participation of the MB in parliament did not result in an obsequious opposition. On the contrary, the MB was in the forefront of challenging the ruling party and government through parliamentary questioning of state ministers, especially the minister of interior. It also insisted on the application of Islamic law, and it was relentless in demanding respect for democratic freedoms and human rights, an end to mass arrests and torture in detention centers, and electoral reforms to ensure a fair and effective democratic process (Radhi 1990/1991; al-Tawil 1992).

The MB was able to push through a number of reforms through parliament, such as expanding religious content in the education curriculum, increasing the hours of religious programming on radio and television, and censoring materials deemed inappropriate for television, including "500 objectionable hours from some soap operas" (Korany 1998: 53). However, the MB made it a point not to question the legitimacy of President Mubarak or his ability to rule. As a matter of fact, the MB supported the renomination of Mubarak for president in 1987. Their criticism, instead, targeted the ruling party and government ministers, as well as particular policies.

The MB justified its use of the parliamentary arena on the grounds that it allowed the group to disseminate its message and influence the rulers of Egypt. For example, in defending the MB's alliance with the traditionally secular New Wafd in 1984, the MB general guide Omar Tlimsani (1985: 195–196) argued: "The opportunity was granted to raise God's word from atop the highest legislative platform. So what should we do given that we possess no party with which to enter [parliament] through the path of elections? We could not nominate ourselves as independents because that is not legally permitted. We have a large popular base. If the MB does not benefit from it, then others will." Tlimsani (1985: 209) later added that the election of 1984 "was an opportunity of a lifetime; if the MB let it slip from its hands it would have been considered foolish."

Similar remarks were made by MB leaders following the 1987 elections: "Our entry into the People's Assembly does not mean our acceptance of the current situation, but we entered the assembly for the purpose of changing this situation and advancing Islamic law *(sharia)*."³⁹ Mustapha Mashhur, the fifth general guide of the MB, gave five instrumental reasons for participating in the electoral process:

1. Through the prominent parliamentary platform and immunity granted to its members, the MB could clarify the meaning of its slogan "Islam is the Solution," which is one of the means of commanding the good and prohibiting the forbidding.
2. Through the parliamentary platform the MB could hold the government and the ruling party accountable for their policies as well as attempt to persuade them to adopt an alternative path. If the MB does not succeed it still benefits because it lets the people know its position while exposing its opponents.
3. Participating in elections is akin to public education, for it allows the people to hear the message of the MB during campaigns.
4. Participating in elections is akin to a public referendum on the slogan "Islam is the Solution," thus allowing the MB to gauge its public support.
5. Through election campaigns and parliament, the MB could discover its opponents and what they hide in their hearts. It also allows the MB to discover the supporters of the movement who are willing to defend it with their pens and tongues.⁴⁰

The fact that the MB was allowed to raise issues of utmost sensitivity—application of the *sharia,* torture in prisons, the lack of real democracy—and that many parties began to modify their political programs to appeal to the MB gave added credence to the claim that participation in parliament, limited as it was, was better than waging war in the streets against the formidable forces of the state.

The Radicals Reject the Parliamentary Strategy

Despite the expansion of system accessibility, the state continued to deny Islamists substantive access to the levers of power. The Egyptian polity continued to be dominated by the executive. The president continued to be the supreme chief of the armed forces and the various intelligence services, as well as the head of the government and the ruling party, and to appoint the top officials of the ruling party and choose the party's candidates for elections. His powers to appoint ministers, dismiss parliament, and legislate by decree when parliament was not in session were undiminished (Springborg 1989; Zeid 1996).

Just as important, the obsequiousness of the ruling party did not lessen. The governing party adopted all the policies of the government and the decrees of the president without questions, amendments, or objections. Not once did the legislature successfully vote down a government or a minister during the 1980s (Qandil 1995a).

The formal inclusion of Islamists in the political system during the 1980s did not placate the radicals, who viewed the MB as an instrument of the regime. Aboud Zumur, leader of the Jihad group, chided the MB for failing to secure a political party by pointing out that "whereas France, Germany, and Italy permit the formation of a religious party, Egypt is proud of the fact it does not permit such a party" (quoted in Ahmed 1995: 109). The radicals accused the MB of legitimating the regime and dividing the Islamist movement. In a Jihad group document entitled *Falsafit al-Muwajaha* (The Philosophy of Confrontation), Tariq Zumur, a leader in the organization, wrote: "The goal of permitting Islamists to enter the People's Assembly is nothing more than an attempt to drag a wide section of the youth behind a course of action in which the path [of the movement] is lost and its goals concealed. The presence of Islamists inside the regime's legislative assembly bestows upon the regime legitimacy it never dreamed of. The mere direction of Islamists toward the ballot box guarantees the fulfillment of [the state's] goal" (quoted in Mubarak 1995: 355).

Aboud Zumur echoed this view in an interview: "The government carefully responds to some of the limited demands of Islamists inside of the [People's] Assembly to fulfill its containment conspiracy to the point of convincing Muslims that there is a possibility of applying Islamic law through the assembly" (quoted in Ahmed 1995: 287). Ahmed (1995: 287) nicely sums up the effect of merely formal inclusion of the MB on Islamist radicalism in Egypt: "The inability of the MB to achieve substantial political gains during the two parliamentary experiences of 1984 and 1987 resulted, on the one hand, in a loss of support for the MB and, on the other, an intensification of the jihadist's criticism toward it. It also consolidated the jihadist's conviction in their rejectionist position toward parliamentary work and predisposition toward greater reliance on violence."

The Jama'a rejected the accommodative path and opted to organize a social movement based on a loosely structured network of social organizations. It split from the Jihad group in 1984 partly because Jihad insisted on clandestine work for the violent overthrow of the regime. While the Jama'a was not opposed to violence and militancy, it believed that the Islamic state must be created through a revolutionary Islamic mass movement, not imposed by a military coup. Consequently, it began to expand its ranks in the cities of upper Egypt—Asyut, al-Minya, Beni Swayf, Souhaj, Qina, Aswan—and the shantytowns on the periphery of greater Cairo—Imbaba, Ain Shems, Boulaq al-Dikrour, al-Amraniya.

The Jama'a pursued a dual strategy of social reformism and direct militant action to win over adherents and build a mass movement capable of revolutionary mobilization at a future date. Specifically, the Jama'a possessed its own networks of mosques through which it established social services to aid the poor and cultivate the group's legitimacy in towns and villages (Mubarak 1995: 260–262). In addition to social reformism, the Jama'a believed in direct militant action justified by the Islamic precept of "commanding the good and prohibiting the forbidding." Such actions included the disruption of musical festivals and wedding ceremonies, destroying video clubs, attacking beer deliveries and bars, and segregating men and women in the universities and the neighborhoods.

Yet despite its antistate rhetoric, the Jama'a did not launch any notable attacks on the state during the 1980s. Instead, much of the violence by the Jama'a hit at "soft" targets. In 1987 there were three assassination attempts against prominent personalities: al-Nabawi Ismail (former minister of the interior), Hasan Abu Basha (former minister of the interior), and Makram Muhammad Ahmed (the secular editor-in-chief of *al-Musawwar* magazine). All three aborted assassinations were not the work of the Jama'a or Jihad groups but that of a splinter group known as Najiun min al-Nar (literally, "Survivors from Hell Fire").

By the end of the 1980s, the Islamist movement was divided between an accommodative wing led by the MB, which was eager to play a political role through the heavily circumscribed institutional channels of the state, and a marginal radical wing led by the Jama'a, which was concentrated in the towns and villages of upper Egypt and some of the suburbs of greater Cairo, and which limited its violence to nonstate targets.

Political Exclusion in Egypt 1990–1995

The rebellion of Islamists in upper Egypt coincided with the political deliberalization of the Egyptian polity in the 1990s (Salama 1994; Kienle 1998). The number of political parties did increase in the early 1990s—by 1994 there were thirteen parties—as Nasserists, Marxists, conservatives, liberals, environmentalists, and even Islamists were allowed to organize parties for formal institutional participation.[41] However, the MB, one of the major political forces in society, faced greater restriction on its ability to play even a limited role in the political arena.

The 1990s began with the state issuing Electoral Laws 201, 202, and 206 of 1990 to replace Law 188, which was deemed unconstitutional by the Supreme Court. These laws adopted a system of individual candidates as opposed to party lists, which is what the opposition wanted. However, Law 206 also redrew (or gerrymandered) the voting districts in such a blatantly unfair way as to privilege the ruling NDP candidates (al-Shourbaji 1994; Auda and Ibrahim 1995).[42]

These new laws did not satisfy opposition groups who, again, were not consulted when the laws were formulated. They, including the MB, decided to boycott the 1990 parliamentary elections.[43] As a result, in 1990 only seven seats went to the official opposition, less than 2 percent. If we add to those the estimated eight seats that went to independent Islamist candidates and the twenty-three seats that went to independent candidates from the New Wafd, secular Labor, Liberal, and Nasserist Parties (a total of thirty-eight seats, a little over 8 percent), we still have a parliament that is proportionally less representative of the opposition than the 1979 one, which allotted the opposition almost 9 percent of the seats (Zaki 1995: 94–96).

The 1995 elections brought no improvement to opposition representation, but for entirely different reasons. The opposition, including the MB, did not boycott the 1995 elections. However, prior to both rounds of the election, the state carried out a wave of arrests against hundreds of MB representatives and cadres to prevent them from running an effective campaign, indeed to block them from putting forward candidates altogether.[44] Days before the election, the state sentenced fifty-four leading MB members to prison terms ranging from three to five years (al-Shawkabi 1995; Campagna 1996). As a result, only one of the 150 MB candidates made it to the People's Assembly, and he was removed in 1996 for being a member of an illegal organization (Ibrahim 1998).

Consequently, the 1995 parliament only had sixteen representatives of the opposition, less than 3 percent, while the NDP secured 317 out of 444 seats—71.5 percent (Mustapha 1995). The remaining seats went to independents, many of whom rejoined the NDP after taking their seats. When the figures are added up, the sum indicates that the political opposition was less represented in parliament during the 1990s than it was during the 1980s.

The lack of opposition forces in the national assembly during the 1990s meant that the legislature was in effect nothing more than a legal secretary to the executive—putting its orders into proper legal form and doing so with due speed and no questions asked. One clear example of this subservience is Law 100 of 1993. This law was intended to regulate the professional associations' elections, supposedly to make them more representative. This measure was largely seen as a way to counter the hegemony of Islamists in professional associations (al-Shourbaji 1994). The law stipulates, inter alia, that at least 50 percent of syndicate members must cast a vote for the election results to be upheld.[45] This law was a significant obstacle given the traditionally low voter turnout in syndicate elections, which rarely exceed 10 percent (Fahmy 1998).

Hearing the news that such a law was under consideration, the opposition demanded a say in its formulation; some professional associations organized conferences to insist on having a voice in the process. The government, however, denied that such a law was in the making. On 15 February, however, the law was proposed in parliament. It was discussed by a parliamentary committee and enacted on 17 February, two days after it had been proposed. The speed with which a controversial law passed the legislature is a striking example of legislative collusion with the executive against the opposition (Owen 1994: 188–189; Qandil 1995b: 190–191).

The exclusion of the MB was not limited to the institutional and professional arenas. In 1993, President Mubarak called for a "national dialogue" (hiwar al-qawmi), which convened in July 1994. The MB and other Islamist organizations were not allowed to participate due to their illegal status. Other parties boycotted the dialogues, thus depriving the proceedings of genuine legitimacy (Cassandra 1995: 17). During this period, the state began to harass midlevel MB cadres and leaders through periodic arrests and internment on the grounds that they constituted an illegal organization intent on overturning the regime (al-Shawkabi 1995; Ibrahim 1998: 139–144).

Radicals Challenge the Efficacy of Moderation

The stagnation of institutional politics and exclusion of the MB in the early and mid-1990s appeared to confirm what the radicals had suspected all along: Islamists could not advance their cause through institutional channels. To be sure, the radicals did not oppose the moderate strategy of the MB on instrumental grounds only; they saw democracy as heresy because it put the will of the people on par with the will of

God (see Chapter 5). However, to the extent the moderate MBs appeared ineffectual and the political system delegitimized, radicals felt secure in their revolutionary convictions and could easily make their case for violence.

In one communiqué, the Jama'a rhetorically asked "what has the Muslim Brotherhood, since its inception until now, achieved of the goals and objectives of Islam, the hopes and needs of the Muslims, and the tasks and requirements of the age?" It added, "what is astonishing is that every time the MB rushes to issue its statements of moral condemnation, denunciation, and disavowal of all that is jihad—it calls it terrorism—the more the government redoubles its constraints against it and strikes it non-stop."[46]

Talat Fouad Qasim, one of the prominent leaders of the Jama'a, rejected MB's parliamentary strategy on the following grounds: "We view the regime's confrontation with the Islamists as one of stages: at first comes [the confrontation with] the Jama'a al-Islamiya, and then comes the turn of the MB. [The regime] will not permit [the MB] to enjoy its seats in parliament and in the syndicates."[47] The Jihad group chided the MB strategy on similar grounds. In its publication *al-Mujahedin* (The Holy Fighters), the Jihad wrote: "All the peacefulness and gradualism upheld by the [Muslim] Brothers during their political struggles, and their work through the regime's legitimate, legal [channels] did not save them from being handcuffed, tried in front of military courts, and dragged to prisons. All the while their preachers declare that they will not be provoked and will not attempt confrontation."[48] As the insurgency developed, Islamists in the Jama'a issued communiqués calling on the youth to abandon the "fake democratic" path and urged them to "join the ranks of the holy fighters for the sake of uprooting the unjust and tyrannical state."[49]

The institutional exclusion and growing harassment of Islamists by the state, especially those who advocated working through the system, gave credence and legitimacy to the claims of radicals. Islamist rebellion in Egypt coincided with greater political exclusion and regime delegitimation.

Inclusion and Exclusion in Comparative Perspective

The experiences of Algeria and Egypt during the 1990s highlight the deleterious effect of institutional exclusion on Islamist strategies. In both cases, the closure of institutional channels to the Islamist opposition contributed to the delegitimation of moderate strategies of contention and expansion of radicalism in the movement.

How does the recent history of Algeria and Egypt compare with other countries that have encountered strong Islamist movements? The experiences of Jordan, Pakistan, and Tunisia offer insight on the extent to which institutional inclusion and exclusion are sufficient to explain accommodative and rebellious strategies in Islamist movements.

Jordan

The Islamist movement in Jordan has historically been divided between an accommodative tendency led by the Jordanian Muslim Brotherhood (JMB) and a radical one led by groups such as Hizb al-Tahrir al-Islami (Islamic Liberation Party) and Jayshu Muhammad (Muhammad's Army). The JMB has been the dominant organization, while the latter two have been marginal players within the movement (Milton-Edwards 1996). Along with these two tendencies, Jordan has witnessed a third Islamist strategy, which shuns overt political participation and confrontation. This strategy is rooted in informal social networks of charitable and cultural organizations that aim to influence personal behavior through preaching and modeling Islamic conduct (Hammad 1997; Wiktorowicz 2001).

It is widely recognized that the institutional inclusion of the JMB and its relatively friendly relationship with the ruling regime since its inception in 1945 have contributed to the relative moderation of the Islamist movement there (Shadid 1988; Krämer 1994; El-Said 1995). The JMB's ideological opposition to socialism, communism, and Arab nationalism (especially Nasserism) during its formative years made it a useful ally of the Jordanian monarchy, which felt threatened by these ideologies (Hourani 1997; Boulby 1999). Consequently, the Jordanian monarchy granted the JMB legal and political space, as well as institutional access principally through the Ministry of Education (Gharaibeh 1997a; Robinson 1997).

Despite the decline of Arab nationalism and the rise of fundamentalism as a formidable opposition force in the Arab world during the 1970s and 1980s, the Jordanian regime did not turn against the JMB. Whereas some secular regimes like that of President Anwar Sadat in Egypt repressed Islamists when they grew in power and influence or when they no longer served their purpose as a counterweight to leftists, the Jordanian monarchy continued to grant the JMB legal status and a degree of institutional access.

Similar to Algeria, Jordan embarked on liberalization in 1989, largely in response to the "bread riots" that took place in the spring of that year. Parliamentary elections were held and Islamists running as independent candidates won thirty-two of eighty seats. Although parliamentary participation did not yield Islamists substantive power, mainly because real power rested within the institution of the monarchy, JMB deputies felt that they had made a palpable gain by having the opportunity to work closely with the government and other political parties, formulate significant legislation, and familiarize the government and the public with its views (Gharaibeh 1997b: 49–50; Ayadat 1997).

This inclusion of the JMB did not lead to a docile opposition. On the contrary, the JMB raised sensitive criticisms that touched on Jordan's alliance with Western states, peace with Israel, and administrative corruption. Nevertheless, the JMB did reaffirm its commitment to democracy and rejection of violence, and it never questioned the legitimacy of King Hussein (Ayadat 1997; Boulby 1999). As Robinson (1997: 388) points out, "Jordan's policy of political inclusion before and during its democratization program led to the creation of an integrated, establishment-oriented and moderate Islamist movement."

The relative moderation of the JMB was influenced by the regime's strategy of channeling all Islamist contention toward the institutional arena while strictly prohibiting extra-institutional protest or mass mobilization, like that seen in Algeria between 1989 and 1991. As Wiktorowicz (2001: 31) explains, "the state only permits organized political parties, which are regulated at the Ministry of the Interior. Political content in other venues of organizational work is suppressed."

The state also seeks to maintain strict control over mosques, Islamic associations, and charitable works to ensure that these avenues do not turn into clandestine Islamist networks. Such regulation takes place through legal codes and administrative hurdles and is strictly supervised by the authorities. This strategy effectively applies the "carrot-and-stick" approach. As long as Islamists do not seek to exert power outside of the "proper" channels of political participation, which generally favor the ruling elite, Islamists are given legal and institutional space. Those who seek to circumvent conventional institutions encounter repression by the ubiquitous *mukhabarat* (secret services).[50]

The success of the JMB in the 1989 elections, and its opposition to sensitive policies, concerned the ruling regime and induced greater restrictions on its political participation during the 1990s. However, unlike Algeria and Egypt, the state did not proceed to deny Islamists institutional access or curtail their legality. Instead, the regime opted to limit the influence of the JMB through legal and electoral manipulations (Gharaibeh 1997a). As a result, the 1993 parliament saw a significant decline in the number of Islamist members. Only sixteen of the thirty-six Islamic Action Front candidates were elected (the IAF is the unofficial party of the JMB). This was half the total of the 1989 elections. Yet, despite electoral restrictions, the IAF "won more than three times as many seats as the runner-up party" (Robinson 1997: 380).

Tensions between the movement and the JMB grew during the late 1990s mainly because of electoral manipulations, circumscribed political influence, and peace with Israel. In 1997, the IAF boycotted the elections because of dissatisfaction with the 1993 electoral laws and, consequently, only four Islamists were elected as independents. The second Palestinian intifada (uprising) in 2000 further exacerbated relations between the JMB and the regime. The JMB has been active in calling for an end to peace with Israel, which is a sensitive foreign policy demand, and has led some mass demonstrations to that end.

In response, the regime has imposed new restrictions on public protest and postponed elections to avoid having "demagogues" benefit from regional instability.[51] Yet despite their mutual frustrations, the JMB and its unofficial party continue to enjoy the cover of legality and the potential of institutional access. As a result, the JMB continues to adhere to the "red lines" that have been drawn by the regime and negotiated over time.

Pakistan

Similar to Jordan, the Islamist movement in Pakistan, led by the Jama'at-i Islami (JI), has enjoyed a degree of institutional access and, consequently, has developed an accommodative orientation toward the political system. However, since the 1990s, Islamist violence has increased in Pakistan and a "jihad culture" has developed to the detriment of domestic and regional stability. The rise in Islamist militancy in Pakistan highlights the fact that institutional inclusion is an insufficient guarantee against radicalism and violence.

Since its creation in 1941, the JI has been a vociferous proponent of Islamization in politics and society, especially during the rule of Ayub Khan, Zulfikar Ali Bhutto, and Benazir Bhutto. Although the JI is a political party, it is also a social movement with a large base of support among the urban lower-middle classes (Eickelman and Piscatori 1996:

110). Its opposition, however, has not been of the revolutionary type. On the contrary, the JI and other Islamist parties, such as the Jama'at-ul Ulema-i Islam (JUI) and Jama'at-ul Ulema-i Pakistan (JUP), have participated in electoral politics despite their failure to secure major electoral successes (Nasr 1994). To be sure, the JI has engaged in episodic violence and extra-institutional militancy, especially through its student wing, Islami Jamiat-i Tulabah (IJT), but its prevailing repertoire has been peaceful contestation through legal institutional channels (Ahmad 1991; Hussain 1994; Lawrence 1998).

The relative moderation of the JI was influenced by two mechanisms of institutional inclusion: judicial review and elite alliances. Prior to the rule of General Mohammad Zia-ul-Haq in 1978, the JI relied on judicial review to contest attempts at repression and marginalization. The relative autonomy of the judiciary in Pakistan has afforded the JI institutional means by which to counter state policies deemed deleterious by the JI.

Four episodes of repression during the developmental years of the JI could have possibly resulted in its radicalization if it had not been for its ability to challenge and succeed in overturning governmental policies through the courts. In 1950, after charging the JI with undermining national security, the government unleashed repressive measures that resulted in the arrest of Mawlana Mawdudi, the founder of the JI; the confiscation of party funds; and the closing of its offices. In 1954, a military court under martial law rule sentenced Mawdudi to death. In 1964, Ayub Khan's government sought to emulate Egypt's repression of the Muslim Brotherhood by arresting JI leaders, confiscating JI property, and closing down its offices. In 1967, once again JI leaders were arrested for challenging the legitimacy of the government.

In each of those instances, the JI went on to appeal the government's repressive policies through the independent judiciary and was able to reverse them. Each time, JI leaders were spared and the party was able to continue with its mission. According to Nasr (1997: 139): "The judiciary's continued ability to check the abuse of power by the executive, although intermittent, has nevertheless been crucial to the openness of Pakistan's politics and to the political enfranchisement of Islamic parties such as the Jamaat. In fact, without the intercession of the judiciary, it is quite likely that the state would have effectively excluded the Jamaat and other Islamic parties from the political process."

In addition to judicial review, the inclusion of Islamists in government has helped moderate the JI since the late 1970s. Prior to the rise of

Zia-ul-Haq in 1978, the ruling regimes sought to marginalize Islamist parties by denying them substantive power while co-opting their message (Hussain 1994; Nasr 1994; Esposito and Voll 1996). This policy failed, however, especially during the last year of Ali Bhutto's rule. Islamist and other parties accused Bhutto of electoral fraud and launched a campaign to oust him, which was the prelude to Zia's coup.

Zia altered the balance of power by adopting an Islamist ideology largely as a cover for his military rule (Mayer 1993; Lawrence 1998). More significantly, Zia gave the JI bureaucratic and ministerial positions, as well as greater influence over the military. According to Nasr (1997: 146), Zia sought to regulate the power of Islamists by "actively encouraging the inclusion of Islamic parties, such as the Jama'at, in the political process and by opening to them new avenues of activity."

The inclusion of Islamists, however, did not result in the complete subordination of their interests, as evinced by their persistent calls for a return to party pluralism (Esposito and Voll 1996: 122). Ironically, the JI insisted on a return to democracy, a system it once shunned as inferior to "Islam," mainly because it saw Zia's increasingly unpopular policies as hurting its image (Nasr 1994).

The post-Zia period, which began in 1988, saw Islamist politics institutionalized within a system of party politics, alliances, and opposition. Interestingly, the inclusion of Islamists in the political process has led to a gradual decline in their electoral support since 1985. As Nasr (1997: 153) points out: "[The JI's] continued participation in the political process has forced costly compromises, policy changes, and alliances on the [JI] and its Islamic allies. These have tamed the revolutionary zeal of Islamic forces and damaged their popular appeal. . . . Participation in the political process has averted radicalization of Islamic movements, and has also successfully restricted them to a small niche in the electoral arena."

The institutionalization of the largest organization in the Islamic movement, however, has been paralleled by the rise of a "jihad culture" and a concomitant increase in sectarian violence and Islamist militancy in Pakistan during the 1990s (Stern 2000). According to one estimate, sectarian violence in Pakistan, including violence between Sunni and Shi'a Muslims, resulted in 1,371 deaths and 3,272 injuries between 1989 and June 2002.[52] In 2001 and 2002, Islamists massacred sixteen Christian worshipers during church ceremonies in Battawalpur, Pakistan, and a suicide bomber blew up a bus filled with foreigners in Karachi, killing ten people. This violence is attributed to a number of small groups, including Sipah-i-Sahaba, Sipah-e-Muhammad, and Ahle-Hadith.

The ascendance of violent militants is not due to an inherent tendency toward radicalism within the Pakistani Islamist movement. Rather, it is a product of particular state policies that acquiesce to radical organizing to promote regional aims. Specifically, the Pakistani governments from Zia-ul-Haq onward have sponsored and trained violent militants in order to advance insurgencies in Afghanistan and Kashmir (Chellaney 2001/2002). As a result, a special relationship has developed between Pakistan's Inter-Services Intelligence (ISI) and militant groups. This relationship has given militants prominence and yielded material and financial resources with which to wage "jihad" (Ahmed 2001/2002).

The policy of aiding violent militants received the support of the U.S. Central Intelligence Agency (CIA) during the 1980s because of its interest in rolling back Soviet advances in Afghanistan. Saudi Arabia also sponsored the rise of militancy in the region by funding the struggle in Afghanistan through Pakistan's intelligence services and promoting madrasahs (religious schools) that were breeding grounds for jihadists. Pakistani militants, therefore, were rewarded for their militancy both internally and internationally, despite their violent "excesses" at home.

Whereas in Jordan political inclusion of Islamists was accompanied by strict regulation of extra-institutional activism, in Pakistan political inclusion of Islamists was supplemented by near complete freedom for violent militants as long as their violence promoted regional aims.[53] It is no surprise, therefore, that those war-hardened militants returning from Afghanistan and Kashmir would have contributed to the radicalization of Islamist discourse and tactics in Pakistan since the 1990s.

Tunisia

The case of Tunisia differs from Algeria and Egypt in an important way. Persistent political exclusion of Tunisian Islamists did not produce rebellion. On the contrary, the Islamist movement responded to institutional exclusion and repression by attempting either to accommodate the regime or to retreat from confrontation. The case of Tunisia demonstrates that institutional exclusion is an insufficient cause of rebellion; additional variables, such as the nature of state repression, are needed for a complete explanation of why Muslims rebel.

Like many Muslim societies, Tunisia experienced a resurgence of Islamism in the 1970s and 1980s. Islamist groups developed during this time with a social base largely made up of young students in the technical fields, teachers, and low-level civil servants (Waltz 1986; Hermassi

1995). In the 1970s, the movement was largely composed of apolitical social reformers and cultural critics who published books and articles, lectured at mosques and universities, and held conferences. With the exception of a small group known as the Islamic Liberation Party, none of these groups prepared or sought to challenge directly the secular state, despite the existence of single-party rule dominated by a secular elite. There were repeated clashes between Islamists and Marxists at the universities in the 1970s, but these clashes hardly went beyond sporadic confrontations and rarely challenged the authority of the state.

The movement took a political turn after the 1978 urban riots and the Iranian revolution the following year (Burgat and Dowell 1997; Shahin 1997; Hamdi 1998). In 1981 the most prominent Islamist organization, the Islamic Tendency Movement (MTI), sought to form an official party. Its program was characterized by moderate reformism that stressed legalism, pluralism, and nonviolence. When the MTI was forbidden to organize as an official party and was repressed between 1981 and 1984, it basically retreated from the political arena and concentrated on building a social base in the universities.

The period between 1986 and 1987 witnessed a rise in Islamist militancy against the state regime, including a plot to assassinate President Habib Bourghiba in 1987 and a few incidents of violence against symbols of secularism.[54] However, such violence and plotting never reached such a level of rebellion as witnessed in Algeria or Egypt. On the contrary, it quickly subsided with the rise of Zayn al-Abidin Ben Ali in a bloodless coup in 1987. From 1987 to 1991, the MTI reaffirmed its commitment to legalism, and it even sought to accommodate the state by changing its name to al-Nahda (the Renaissance) in 1989 to comply with election rules that forbade parties from organizing around religion (Krämer 1994; Hamdi 1998).

The promise of institutional access through electoral politics contributed to the relative moderation of al-Nahda in the late 1980s. The latter indirectly participated in the April 1989 parliamentary elections through independent candidates and won 14.5 percent of the national vote and up to 30 percent in major cities (Eickelman and Piscatori 1996: 133). Yet despite its decent showing, the Islamists failed to win any seats due to electoral rigging. The strong showing of the Islamists led Ben Ali to deny al-Nahda official recognition.

Beginning in late 1990, the government unleashed a campaign of repression after charging the Islamists of plotting to topple the regime and engage in violence, a charge that was hardly convincing to outside

observers. By 1991, Islamist organizations were completely dismi
(Hamdi 1998). Krämer (1994: 218) sums up the state's policy toward
Islamism in this period:

> By 1992, the situation in Tunisia had reached a deadlock. In spite of all
> moves and concessions made over the previous decade, and more
> specifically since Ben Ali's coming to power in November 1987 (the
> recognition of Tunisia's specific identity, of democracy, pluralism, the
> Personal Status Law), the Islamic movement was denied legal recog-
> nition. Caught between a government bent on destroying its most pow-
> erful critic and opponent, and a radicalized membership despairing of
> gradualist strategies of integration into a system that seemed deter-
> mined to reject them, the moderates had been effectively marginalized.

In the early 1990s, there were a few episodes of Islamist violence
and clashes in response to state repression, but since that time the
movement has retreated from the political arena (Hamdi 1998). Thus,
instead of responding militantly to a consistent policy of exclusion, the
Islamist movement in Tunisia more often than not sought to dispel
charges of subversion and fanaticism made against it by reaffirming its
commitment to legalism, pluralism, and incrementalism. Accommodation and retreat, not rebellion, was the response of Tunisian Islamists to
institutional exclusion. The case of Tunisia suggests that mere political
exclusion is not enough to unleash rebellion. We need to incorporate
additional variables to provide a necessary and sufficient explanation of
why Muslims rebel. The following chapter discusses the impact of state
repressive policies on Islamist strategies and shows how in places like
Algeria and Egypt specific state repressive policies combined with
political exclusion to produce the insurgencies of 1992.

Conclusion

The experiences of Algeria, Egypt, Jordan, Pakistan, and Tunisia allow
us to derive some conclusions concerning the impact of system accessibility on Islamist strategies. In four of the cases—Algeria, Egypt, Jordan, and (to a lesser extent) Pakistan—institutional inclusion at different periods in their histories has contributed to nonviolent strategies of
contention. Although Islamist radicalism was not eliminated in those
countries, it was effectively pushed to the margins. (Pakistan since the
1990s has been a notable exception.)

In Algeria, institutional inclusion from 1989 to 1991 resulted in the formation of official political parties that sought to work through the system, despite espousing contradictory rhetoric and engaging in non-revolutionary mass mobilization. When extra-institutional militancy threatened to unleash a major crackdown on the dominant Islamist party and endangered the electoral path, the leaders of that party toned down their rhetoric and avoided further mobilization in order to remain as legitimate actors in the system. Rebellion broke out only when the avenue of electoral politics was blocked by a military coup and suppression of Islamist parties.

Islamists in Egypt were never given the freedom afforded to those in Algeria, but the 1980s witnessed the "backdoor" entry of Islamists into institutional politics. The dominant Islamist organization accommodated the state regime and played by the rules. The radical wing did grow during this period, but it was partly marginalized by a policy of Islamist incorporation. When this policy was gradually reversed during the 1990s, Islamist violence dramatically increased. To be sure, those who rebelled were always opposed to peaceful participation in the system. However, political exclusion in the 1990s gave their rejection of democracy "empirical credibility" in that it made the moderates look foolishly ineffective.

In Jordan, institutional pathways were more or less open to Islamists, despite the lack of substantive access to the levers of power. This policy of inclusion was combined with a state strategy of institutional channeling that strictly prohibited extra-institutional mobilization while granting limited access to administrative and political bureaucracies. The "carrot-and-stick" approach has contributed to the moderation of Islamist politics despite recurring Islamist dissatisfaction with the government's domestic and foreign policies.

Pakistan's Jama'at-i Islami, which is the largest organization within the Islamist movement, has developed an accommodative stance within the political system, despite its radical roots and rhetoric. At several historic junctures, the potential for violence and insurgency was present, but the movement relied on judicial review and electoral politics to advance its aims.

System accessibility in Pakistan, however, has not eliminated militancy and violence in the Islamist movement. State and international sponsorship of violent militants in Pakistan during the 1980s for the purpose of promoting regional aims has negated the moderating influence of political inclusion on the movement. The case of Pakistan suggests that while political inclusion may have averted mass rebellion by Islamists at critical junctures of state-movement interactions, mere inclusion is not sufficient to ensure accommodative, nonviolent behavior. Institutional inclusion must be accompanied by clear and enforceable rules of acceptable political conduct, similar to Jordan's "carrot-and-stick" approach. Otherwise, political inclusion may embolden radicals, grant them national legitimacy, and expand their financial and material resources.

If political inclusion is not a guarantee against violence, the evidence from Tunisia suggests that institutional exclusion does not necessarily produce rebellion. Similar to economic deprivation, institutional exclusion of Islamists abounds in the Muslim world. Countries like Iraq, Syria, and Libya, to name a few, have consistently blocked institutional avenues to Islamist and non-Islamist opposition forces. Yet rebellions are not as frequent as one would expect. Political exclusion of the Egyptian MB during the 1990s may have strengthened the hand of the radicals, but it did not push the MB to rebel or even support the insurgency of the Jama'a. On the contrary, the MB was in the forefront in condemning the violence of the jihadists, even if it raised concern about the state's policy of repression.

Institutional exclusion may be a contributing condition for rebellion, but it is not *sufficient* to induce mass insurgency. In the next chapter, I incorporate the variable of state repression, particularly reactive and indiscriminate state repression, to present a necessary and sufficient explanation of why Muslims rebel.

Notes

1. A political system could be considered "open" to opposition in general but "closed" to particular groups. For example, the German polity since 1945 has been democratic, but it does not permit fascist organizations to access state institutions. Thus, from the perspective of fascist groups the system is "closed."

2. Rabeh Kebir, an activist in the 1980s and a future leader within the Islamist movement, points out that Bouyali was viewed as a holy fighter in the movement. However, he did not receive material support because the preachers he solicited believed the time for armed struggle was not nigh. See part 4 of an interview with *al-Wasat*, 5 July 1993.

3. This information is largely derived from Mubarak's (1995: 137–139; 1997: 316–317) interviews with Talat Fouad Qasim, who was one of the leaders of the Jama'a in al-Minya during the 1970s and the future leader of the group in the 1990s.

4. The Jihad group was responsible for the attempted assassination of Prime Minister Aatif Sidqi and minister of the interior Hasan al-Alfi in 1993

(Mubarak 1995: 410). In that year, they began organizing 800 activists into numerous cells under the title of Tala'i al-Fateh al-Islami—the Vanguards of Islamic Conquest (*al-Hayat*, 18 March 1999).

5. Violence between 1992 and mid-1994 was largely concentrated in the Asyut region, especially in Dairut. According to some estimates, in 1992 there were only three incidents of violence in Aswan, three in al-Minya, and two in Souhaj. In 1993 there were no incidents of violence in al-Minya or in Souhaj (Mubarak 1995: 405–406). In 1995, out of 182 incidents of violence, 130 of them were in al-Minya, 16 in Asyut, 10 in al-Qina, 3 in Aswan, 5 in Souhaj, 4 in Beni Swayf, and 10 in Cairo (*al-Hala al-Diniya fi Misr* 1995: 190). In 1996, out of 97 incidents of violence, 59 were in al-Minya and 18 in Asyut, 8 in Souhaj, 7 in Beni Swayf, 2 in Giza, and 1 each in Cairo, Suez, and al-Qina (*al-Hala al-Diniya fi Misr* 1998: 240). In 1997, out of 51 incidents of violence, there were 31 in al-Minya, 8 in Asyut, 6 in Qina, 2 in Cairo, 2 in Beni Swayf, and 1 each in al-Gharbiya and al-Munoufiya (*Taqrir Misr al-Mahrousa wal-Aalam,* 1997, 1998: 687).

6. *MEI,* 4 November 1988.

7. *MEJ* chronology for 1989.

8. Abassi was an activist in al-Qiyam in the 1960s and one of three leaders to be arrested for organizing a mass demonstration in November 1982. He was subsequently imprisoned for two years. Ali Belhaj was imprisoned from 1983 to 1987 for supporting the Bouyali group. He was also a clergy in al-Sunna mosque at Bab al-Oued in the capital and organized the 10 October demonstration during the 1988 riots (Shahin 1997: 129–132).

9. The program went on to outline some of the goals of the FIS, which included "ending autocratic rule by adopting *shura* (consultation); eliminating political, economic and social monopoly by adopting equality and the principle of equal political, economic and social opportunities"; "reforming the judicial system to return to the judiciary its independence and empower judges as proscribed by Islamic law"; and "guaranteeing the nation's freedom and its right to express its will." The complete content of the Islamic Salvation Front political program can be found in *al-Thawra al-Islamiyya fi al-Jazair* (Cairo: Dar Yafa lil-Dirasat wal-Abhath, 1991, 6–13).

10. See similar statements by Abassi in interviews with *al-Hayat,* 28 June 1990, and *al-Huwar al-Dawli,* January 1990.

11. Quoted in Ali (1996: 269). For more on the views of Belhaj on democracy see Al-Ahnaf et al. (1991: 85–99).

12. The tract can be found in al-Sheikh (1993: 87–96).

13. Prime Minister Sid Ahmed Ghozali put the figures at 55 killed, 326 injured, and 2,976 arrested.

14. Critics accused Islamists of imposing violently their morality on others, especially women. On 11 April 1990, during the month of Ramadan, Islamists in Algiers attempted to forcibly prevent a concert from taking place. This incident, among others, put the FIS on the defensive (*MEI,* 27 April 1990). On a previous occasion, Abassi promptly denied any involvement in an attack on a Blida courtroom believed to have been carried out by a group known as the Sunna wal Shari'a (*ACR* 1989–1990).

15. In the communes the FIS earned 54.3 percent of the votes while in the departments it earned 57.4 percent (Willis 1996: 393–395).

16. *MEI,* 22 June 1990.

17. Hamrouche met with Abassi and Belhaj at their request on 29 May 1991 to try to come to an agreement over FIS demands. Hamrouche refused to give in to their demands, but he verbally agreed to allow the demonstrators to peacefully occupy the First of May and Martyrs' Squares. Hamrouche later testified that he opposed the intervention of the military in the FIS-occupied areas (Willis 1996: 214). Belhaj (1994: 137) points back to this incident as proof of the military's bad intentions. In one of the letters he wrote in prison, Belhaj rhetorically asked "is it not the army that gave orders to fire at demonstrators in the First of May and Martyrs' squares after the protest areas were agreed upon with the former prime minister Hamrouche?!"

18. Indeed, some radicals accused FIS leaders, who were in constant contact with government mediators, of informing on the radicals. These charges were particularly aimed at Said Gushi, a founding member of the FIS and critic of the general strike (Qawas 1998: 131; al-Tawil 1998: 31).

19. In a published interview, Abassi points to this incident as the reason for violence after the situation calmed down by mid-June (Ayyashi 1993: 150). Also, the military prohibited people from converging on Bab el-Oued and Kouba mosques to pray, as they had done regularly during the past two years (*MEI,* 12 July 1991).

20. This information is largely derived from part 5 of Rabeh Kebir's interview with *al-Wasat,* 12 July 1993.

21. During this conference, some accused Mekhloufi, who authored the tract on civil disobedience, of pushing the movement toward an unnecessary confrontation with the regime and went as far as to argue that he was an *agent provocateur.* The other three to have their membership frozen—Benazouz Zibda, al-Hashami Sahnouni, and Muhammed Karrar—were advocates of retreat from politics.

22. In August 1991, Hachani publicly reaffirmed that the FIS "cannot arrive in power other than through free and proper elections." Furthermore, although the FIS declared its intention to boycott and prevent the elections from taking place, it declared it would do so "within the framework of the law" (Rouadjia 1995: 93–94; Willis 1996: 222). The state of siege was lifted in 29 September and the first FIS rally since the June events was held on 4 October. The FIS held another peaceful march of 300,000 on 1 November and a rally on 22 December. It is worth noting that the FIS dispersed its rallies and mass march over a period of three months and did not organize demonstrations during the state of siege, despite the incarceration of its leadership.

23. See part 5 of interview with *al-Wasat,* 12 July 1993.

24. Ibid.

25. The High State Committee, which consisted of a five-member collective presidency, assumed executive powers after Chadli's resignation in January 1992.

26. *MEJ* chronologies for 1992; *MEI,* 4 and 18 December 1992; and *al-Hayat,* 29 October 1992.

27. It was not until late 1992 that some FIS leaders began publicly calling for jihad, and not until 1993, after the emergence of the GIA, did it begin to organize seriously an armed wing (al-Tahiri 1992; Willis 1996; al-Tawil 1998; Martinez 2000). In January 1993, Rabeh Kebir (in an interview with *al-Hayat,* 11 January 1993) stated that the FIS had yet to declare jihad but would do so if the regime maintained its repressive policy.

28. It is widely recognized that the GIA dominated the battlefield in the center of Algeria—Blida, Algiers, Boumerdes, Medea—and had presence in the west and, less so, in the east. In May 1994 the GIA managed to draw the Islamic State Movement (MEI) and prominent FIS activists such as Muhammad Said, Abderrazak Rejjam, Yousuf Boubras. After 1995, internecine struggles led to major splits in the GIA (Labat 1995; Willis 1996; al-Tawil 1998).

29. Ben Hajjar, the commander of the Rabita al-Islamiya lil-Dawa wal Jihad (the Islamic League for Preaching and Holy Struggle, LIDD), which joined the GIA in 1994, maintained that those who opposed the electoral option were few prior to 1992. But when the FIS was "hit twice" (June 1991 and January 1992), these extremists were the only leaders left to guide the movement (interview in *al-Hayat,* 5 February 2000, 8).

30. Published interview with Kharban (al-Tawil 1998: 103). Many FIS activists were angered at the hesitation of the leadership in the immediate aftermath of the coup. Some went so far as to argue that FIS leaders should be tried for their mistake.

31. It is difficult to estimate the number and influence of Algerian "Afghans" in the initial rebellion. At least one group that formed in 1991, led by Mansour Meliani (a former activist in the Bouyali group), was made up mainly of "Afghans." For an excellent account of the Algerian Afghans, see the series of seven articles by Muhammed Muqadem entitled "Rihlet al-Afghan al-Jazaireen: Min al-Jama'a ila Tanzim Al-Qaida" (The Journey of the Algerian Afghans: From the [Armed Islamic] Group to Al-Qaida), *al-Hayat,* 23–29 December 2001.

32. *al-Hayat,* 9 February 1994.

33. Zeroual received 61 percent of the votes, while Nahnah came second with 25.6 percent (Willis 1996: 395). Although many observers recognized that the elections were not entirely fair, the high voter turnout (reported at 75.5 percent) led many to conclude that they were successful in giving Zeroual some legitimacy, especially since the FIS, AIS, and GIA called for a boycott of the elections (al-Rasi 1997: 442–443; Mortimer 1997: 232; Roberts 1998: 21). More importantly, the FLN, FFS, and MNI conceded that it was a mistake on their part to boycott the elections (*MECS* 1995). Merrani broke with the FIS leadership in June 1991 and was later expelled from the party.

34. There were repeated charges of government vote rigging during the referendum, but the constitution was adopted anyway. *IHT,* 30 November 1996.

35. After consistently opposing state efforts to exclude the Islamists from 1992 to 1995, the FLN from 1996 onward abandoned its support for dialogue with the FIS and took a pro-government position. This change in policy was the outcome of a "coup" within the FLN whereby Abdelhamid Mehri, the secretary-general of the FLN since 1989 and proponent of dialogue with the FIS, was ousted in favor of Bouallam Benhamouda, who opposed the national contract (al-Rasi 1997: 470–471).

36. The letter was issued on 1 April 1995. See the text in al-Tawil (1998: 303–304).

37. *al-Hayat*, 26 August 1994. Kamal Qamazi, a principal leader in the FIS, also attributes the violence in Algeria to "the coup against the people's choice" that forced Islamists to take up arms (see his interview with *al-Hayat*, 12 January 2000).

38. The letter is addressed to the Independent Dialogue Committee and is dated 23 November 1993 (Belhaj 1994: 135–158).

39. Quoted in *al-Taqrir al-Istratiji al-Arabi*, 1988, 1989: 512.

40. In *al-Liwa al-Islami*, June 1987.

41. The Amal (Labor), Ahrar (Liberal), and Umma (Islamic Nation) parties are classified as Islamists. The first two adopted this orientation in the mid-1980s largely to draw the MB into an alliance, while the latter formed explicitly with an Islamist agenda. These parties, however, did not command sufficient support to enter the parliament in the 1980s independent of an alliance with the MB.

42. In the 1990s the NDP continued to receive financial subsidies by the state and maintained its monopoly over radio and television. During election campaigns the NDP dominated the news while the opposition was given few slots in the media to air their views (Kienle 1998; Korany 1998).

43. The boycott, however, did not prevent members of the opposition from running as independents. Approximately forty-five MB and Labor candidates participated in the election. The majority of the independent candidates, however, were NDP members who failed to secure the nomination of their party (Zaki 1995).

44. For an account of the interference encountered by the MB candidates and cadres, see "Democracy Jeopardized: The Egyptian Organization for Human Rights Account of Egyptian Parliamentary Elections, 1995," EOHR (December 1995).

45. If the 50 percent threshold is not reached, then new elections are held but this time only 33 percent is needed for the results to be deemed valid. If the one-third threshold is not reached, which is a likely outcome, then the head of the syndicate and the head council maintain their positions for three months until the general association is called on to cast a vote. In February 1995 the law was amended to add that a judicial committee would supervise elections (Ibrahim 1998: 117–120).

46. See communiqué in *al-Hayat*, 8 August 1995.

47. *al-Hayat*, 30 March 1993.

48. Quoted at length in *al-Hayat*, 28 January 1996.

49. *al-Hayat*, 11 November 1995. See similar comments by Muhammed Shawqi al-Islambouli in an interview with *al-Wasat*, 15 February 1993, and by Omar Abdel Rahman in an interview with *al-Hayat*, 18 March 1993.

50. Wiktorowicz (2001: 45–82) does an excellent job of detailing the mechanisms by which the Jordanian authorities manage the activism of Islamists to ensure that their influence does not extend beyond mere formal representation in state institutions.

51. *MEI*, 14 June 2002.

52. Institute for Conflict Management, South Asia Terrorism Portal (www.satp.org). The *IHT*, 27 April 2002, cites a figure of 2,000 people killed in

sectarian violence since the 1990s. For specific episodes of anti-Shi'a violence, see "Country Review: Pakistan 2001–2002," *Country Watch Reports* (2002: 20).

53. After the events of 11 September 2001, Pakistan has faced growing pressure from the United States and India to dismantle the network of militancy it spawned during the previous decade. General Pervez Musharraf has taken steps to arrest known militants and banned several groups. However, there are serious doubts about the ability of the authorities to control the militants (*NYT*, 9 January 2002).

54. In 1986 the MTI began to organize an armed wing to counter any possible repression in the future. The military wing decided to prepare a coup against Bourghiba in late 1987 after the latter sought to impose harsher sentences against Islamists. However, Prime Minister Ben Ali became aware of this plan and initiated a preemptive coup against Bourghiba (Hamdi 1998).

3

Repression and Rebellion

T he reality of state repression in the Muslim world is a daunting one. Few Muslim countries can genuinely claim that they abstain from overt or covert repression of their citizenry. Curiously, few works on Islamism address with theoretical and empirical due diligence the impact of state repression on Islamist strategies. The nature of state repression equals in importance the degree of system accessibility in shaping the strategic orientation of Islamist movements. It is a palpable and often tragic way for a movement to gauge the tolerance limits of the system.

By *state repression* I refer to any action taken by the authorities that "raises the contender's cost of collective action" (Tilly 1978: 100). It includes "restrictions on the rights of citizens to criticize the government, restrictions on the freedom of the press, restrictions on the rights of opposition parties to campaign against the government, or, as is common in totalitarian dictatorship, the outright prohibition of groups, associations, or political parties opposed to the government" (Wintrobe 1998: 34). It also includes mass arrests, judicial and extrajudicial executions of political activists and their supporters, torture, and secret abductions commonly known as "disappearances."

In this chapter, I draw on theories of repression to explain how reactive and indiscriminate state repressive policies contribute to mass Islamist rebellion. Islamist rebellions are often defensive reactions to overly repressive regimes that misapply their repression in ways that radicalize, rather than deter, movement activists and supporters. The cases of Algeria and Egypt are examined in light of this theoretical discussion, with subsequent expansion of the comparative scope to Kashmir, the Philippines, Chechnya, and Tajikistan.

71

Explaining the Repression-Rebellion Nexus

Assessing the impact of repression on movement behavior is as difficult as it is important. Theoretically, there is little agreement regarding the logical consequences of state repression on movements' strategies and tactical repertoires. Some observers contend that repression increases the cost of collective action as to make it unlikely.[1] Others maintain that repression generates additional grievances that motivate further mobilization to punish an "unjust" opponent.[2]

These two perspectives have largely been rejected on empirical grounds; there are many instances where repression both quells and provokes insurgency.[3] Attempts to solve the repression-rebellion puzzle have led some scholars to investigate how varying levels of repression—too much or too little repression—are likely to induce dissent or hinder it.[4] Others look to the timing of repression,[5] its perceived illegitimacy,[6] the institutional context under which it is applied,[7] its targets,[8] the consistency of its application in relation to accommodative strategies,[9] or a combination of these variables.[10]

In the following sections, I focus on the timing and targeting of repression and argue that they are particularly important for explaining the outbreak and scale of Islamist rebellions. By selecting the timing and targeting of repression as my primary focuses, I do not suggest that the other variables are not relevant for explaining Islamist rebellions.[11] However, the timing and targeting of repression provide the most theoretical leverage to explain mass rebellions across the cases I am investigating. Plainly, these two variables come close to being necessary and sufficient to explain rebellion under conditions of institutional exclusion.

Timing: Preemptive Versus Reactive Repression

The *timing* of state repression refers to whether repression is applied preemptively or reactively. Repression is *preemptive* when it is applied before aggrieved activists are able to organize and mobilize disparate supporters and sympathizers around a common goal. Repression is *reactive* when it is applied in the ascendant phase of the protest cycle, after activists have had an opportunity to organize otherwise small and isolated groups for collective action. Preemptive repression seeks to strike at the movement before it has had an opportunity to gain organizational momentum, while reactive repression seeks to demobilize an already organized and politically active segment of the population (Brockett 1995).

Preemptive repression will likely discourage rebellion by Islamist movements. Preemptive repression denies activists the opportunity to expand material and organizational resources rapidly and thus disempowers supporters and sympathizers who may wish to act but see no feasible means to effect change. A movement encountering repression at every attempt to acquire resources might garner a great deal of sympathy and tacit support from a large segment of the population. However, preemptive repression also makes it difficult for people to act out on their anger because it creates uncertainty as to the size and nature of commitment in the movement. Uncertainty, in turn, will force activists to become cautious and will deter supporters from backing radical groups who may appear overzealous or ahead of their time. "In the absence of organizational mobilization and support," explains Khawaja (1993: 67), "potential activists are more likely to keep their anger and grievances to themselves, fearing retributions by authorities."

Brockett (1995: 132) illustrates this contention with reference to peasant immobilization in Guatemala in the mid-1960s and Nicaragua in the mid-1970s. The peasants in both cases, despite encountering widespread and arbitrary murders, shied away from revolutionary groups because the latter were "small and isolated from other political forces." Peasant support for revolutionaries only came when political space for organized collective action opened during the mid and late 1970s, facilitating the rise of a number of support groups and social networks.

Moreover, insurgency, especially in a highly repressive context, involves high-risk activities that require committed and trustworthy participants. "Recruitment is less risky when the recruiter can trust the recruit, and vice versa" (Della Porta 1988: 159). Commitment and trust beyond the core activists involved in initial organizing, however, usually develop through the actual process of mobilization. To induce rebellion on a mass scale, prior mobilization is necessary because it is in this phase that activists and supporters will become acquainted with each other, gauge the level of commitment and numerical support in the movement, and develop bonds of friendship and camaraderie in organized settings (Opp et al. 1995; Pfaff 1996). As McAdam, Tarrow, and Tilly (2001: 132) explain, "beyond a very small scale, every actor that engages in claim making includes at least one cluster of previously connected persons among whom have circulated widely accepted stories concerning their strategic situation: opportunities, threats, available means of action, likely consequences of actions, evaluations of those consequences, capacities to act, memories of previous contention, and inventories of other likely parties to any action."

Many studies point out that the strongest incentive for recruitment into high-risk activities is through friendship ties with someone who is already in the movement (Gerlach and Hine 1970; Snow et al. 1980; Della Porta 1992; McAdam and Paulsen 1993). Preemptive repression, by depriving activists of the opportunity to interact repeatedly with other activists and supporters through mobilization, isolates militants from their potential supporters, raises doubt as to the size of their support, and precludes the cultivation of high levels of commitment and trust across the movement.

Reactive repression, on the other hand, predisposes opposition movements toward rebellion. States that repress movements after a period of mass mobilization and organizing give these movements a chance to gauge their numerical support, develop trust and bonds of camaraderie among activists, and acquire material resources through the expansion of membership financial and material contributions. Thus, activists encountering repression will not only experience additional grievances, but also command resources with which to fight back. If commitment and support are deemed high prior to repression, then supporters will feel empowered to join insurgent organizations, act on their grievances, and take a chance to bring about change (Klandermans 1984; Opp 1988; Lichbach 1995; Kurzman 1996).

In addition, to the extent that reactive repression constitutes a mortal threat to established movement organizations and cadres, the likelihood of rebellion increases. Reactive repression that seeks to eradicate an organized and mobilized movement will encourage activists and supporters to seek a halt to the loss of resources accumulated over time. If inaction entails continued losses, then there will be a greater inclination toward risk to mitigate losses (Berejikian 1992: 652–653; Gordon and Arian 2001: 196).

In such circumstances, a movement organization might choose to fight back "even though it may be expected to accomplish little more than a continuation of the present situation or even a mere reduction of the expected deterioration" (Kriesi et al. 1995: 40). In describing the poor people's movement in Iran, Bayat (1997: 163) points out that "extrakinship mobilization and campaigning do not usually develop under repressive conditions, unless the actors feel a common threat to gains." Goldstone and Tilly (2001: 182) similarly observe that of the popular mobilization during the French Revolution was defensive in inception, responding to threats of growing danger, not a matter of groups seeking change and seizing growing opportunities to achieve it." Thus, the combination of opportunities for insurgency created by the availability of organizational and material resources due to prior mobilization, on the one hand, and the threat to those resources and personal well-being due to reactive repression, on the other, portends rebellion in social movements.

Preemptive repression, in contrast, prevents the accumulation of organizational resources by constantly obstructing efforts at mass organizing. Consequently, movements with limited material and organizational resources have fewer incentives to protect these resources in the face of repression. Where no movement gains have been made due to preemptive repression, retreat, not rebellion, is the likely outcome.

Targeting: Selective Versus Indiscriminate Repression

Targeting refers to the range of "state enemies" encompassed under repressive measures. Does the state target only the leaders and core activists of the movement, or does it also target supporters, sympathizers, and anyone suspected of involvement with the movement? State repression is *selective* when it only targets the leaders and core activists of the movement. However, it is *indiscriminate* when repression expands to include supporters, sympathizers, and ordinary citizens suspected of involvement in the movement (Mason and Krane 1989).

Selective repression predisposes the broader movement toward non-militancy, while indiscriminate repression pushes it toward rebellious strategies. Selective repression signals to supporters and sympathizers that only "troublemakers" will be punished and, therefore, those who keep their distance will not become victims of repression. In contrast, indiscriminate repression antagonizes hitherto inactive supporters and sympathizers, and it intensifies the moral outrage of activists. Although selective repression could result in moral outrage and thus expand the legitimacy resources of the movement, indiscriminate repression is likely to do so many times over. Whatever moral outrages are committed by the militants of the movement will be seen as the "natural" response to indiscriminate repression. A movement with such legitimacy resources will feel empowered to act militantly if other organizational and material resources are at hand.

In his study of liberation theology movements in Latin America, Smith (1991) points out that brutal repression, which targeted political parties, labor unions, and students, as well as Catholics engaged in pastoral activities, facilitated the development of insurgent consciousness and made possible the diffusion of "injustice frames" that motivated insurgency. Similarly, Gurr and Goldstone (1991: 334) and Kiernan (1996: 20–25) offer evidence that the U.S. military's punitive bombings of Cambodian and Vietnamese villages suspected of aiding rebels drove many peasants into the ranks of revolutionary armies.

Indiscriminate repression may explain why the violently militant Shining Path movement in Peru was able to expand significantly in size during the 1980s, despite a relatively democratic system that permitted left-wing and Marxist political parties to participate. The state "applied military force in an often indiscriminate manner, thus alienating local, usually peasant populations" (Palmer 1995: 301).

Furthermore, indiscriminate repression may push occasional activists and known supporters of the movement to seek the protection of radical groups. In her study of left-wing terrorism in Italy during the 1970s, Della Porta (1995b: 118) notes that "many of the new members of terrorist organizations were in fact members of radical groups who joined terrorist organizations in order to have logistical support while evading arrest."

Similarly, Davis and Hodson (1982) and May (2001) show that many Guatemalan villagers joined guerrilla groups because the latter came to be viewed as the only remaining source of defense against government-sponsored massacres of innocent campesinos. Mason and Krane (1989) correlate the expansion of the base of peasant support for the El Salvadoran FMLN during the late 1970s with the escalation of indiscriminate repression by government-sponsored death squads. Horne (1977: 104) shows that the French policy of "collective responsibility" during Algeria's war of independence (1954–1962) expanded the membership of the revolutionary National Liberation Front (FLN).

In sum, "armed insurgencies result from *the violent suppression of the peaceful political activities of aggrieved people who have the capacity and opportunity to rebel*" (Goodwin 2001b: 37). If state repression is reactive and indiscriminate, it will likely induce rebellion. If, on the other hand, state repression is preemptive and selective, it will likely deter mass rebellion. In the following sections, I show how patterns of reactive and indiscriminate state repression contributed in turning Islamist protest and sporadic violence into mass insurgencies in several Muslim countries.

Repression and Rebellion in Algeria

In January 1992, Algeria's military elite suspended the democratic process and unleashed a campaign of repression with the intent to suppress the Islamist opposition. This repression came after three years of Islamist organizing and mobilization, which culminated with a landslide victory for the Islamist party. Unlike other countries in North Africa and the Middle East—Libya, Tunisia, and Syria—the Algerian government extended Islamists the right to form official political parties and participate in local and national elections, which gave them space for mass mobilization in the early 1990s. By the time repression came in 1992, Islamists had much to lose if they did not fight back, and, more importantly, they had organizational resources and popular legitimacy with which to resist repression.

Reactive Repression

Islamist organizing and mobilization between 1989 and 1992 allowed activists in various parts of the country to develop bonds of trust in the movement. In the communes, for instance, the Islamic Salvation Front organized functional cells and neighborhood committees that sponsored activities related to mosques, relief and emergency, and schools. Furthermore, the FIS organized a trade union (Syndicate Islamique du Travail) that included a number of professions—education, tourism, telecommunications, and transportation. The FIS also organized a number of associations such as the League of Islamic Universities and Intellectuals, the Islamic Youth Association, and the Association of the Children of Martyrs (Lamchichi 1992: 102; al-Darif 1994: 199; Labat 1995: 186).[12] The discipline with which Islamists conducted some of their marches and mass prayers indicates the extent of coordination that had developed within the movement since 1989.

In addition, Islamists organized social services—medical clinics, youth clubs, and market cooperatives—that allowed Islamist activists to work together regularly. It also put these activists directly in touch with their communities, which facilitated the development of links with potential recruits. As one observer put it, "at its height the FIS could mobilize hundreds of thousands of people in the space of a few hours."[13] These links also meant that Islamists could draw political and material support from their communities in times of need.

Moreover, state repression came after Islamists were allowed to gauge their numerical support time and again. During the 1980s, the Islamist movement was preemptively repressed because it was not allowed to organize demonstrations or rallies. Consequently, it was so fragmented that Islamists were "unaware whether or not other (Islamist) groups were developing in other regions of Algeria."[14] Elections, rallies, public prayers, and demonstrations in the early 1990s empowered Islamists because it allowed them to measure their popular support repeatedly and realistically. During the May–June 1991 demonstrations in central Algiers, the FIS was able to mobilize 30,000 supporters in one day.[15]

Islamist mobilization came as part of an overall increase in public and union activism after 1989. For example, Algerians witnessed an average of 2,148 strikes for each year between 1989 and 1991, as compared to an average of 877 strikes for each year between 1979 and 1988 (Benamrouche 1995: 48–52). As Mortimer (1991: 583) points out, during the period of political openness, especially 1990, "marches, demonstrations, and rallies became virtually daily occurrences."

The fact that the FIS could bring out hundreds of thousands to march under its banners and millions to vote for it meant that the Islamists commanded legitimacy and could rely on the active participation of their members and supporters. Thus, when repression came, Islamists had the organizational networks and means with which to fight back.

In addition to banning the FIS, the military threatened the material and physical well-being of Islamists. In February 1992, it opened five detention centers in the Saharan desert to hold Islamist activists rounded up since the coup. Thousands of Islamists, including 500 FIS mayors and councilors, were detained between January and March 1992. FIS supporters were forbidden from organizing demonstrations and gathering outside of mosques before or after prayers. Following the cancellation of the elections, riot police were stationed in Islamist strongholds every Friday to prevent after-prayer demonstrations. In October, special courts that were banned under the 1989 constitution were brought back and tougher sentences for "terrorists" were instituted. Finally, in December, the Ministry of Religious Affairs ordered the destruction of all unofficial mosques.[16]

As the conflict developed, Islamist violence induced more repression. In 1992 and 1993 a total of 166 Islamists were sentenced to death, mostly in absentia.[17] Arrests without trial continued unabated, and random searches of suspected militants became normal occurrences. But the gravest development since 1993 has been the almost daily killings of Islamists either through extrajudicial manhunts or clashes during searches.[18]

Between 1994 and 1995, the military, equipped with new counterinsurgency supplies, intensified its war against the insurgents in order to "terrorize the terrorists."[19] In February 1994 security forces killed the third commander of the Armed Islamic Group (Groupe Islamique Armé, GIA), Cey Murad Ahmed (alias Jafa al-Afghani or Sayf Allah). In September 1994 they scored another victory by killing the fourth commander of the GIA, Cherif Gousmi, along with three of his senior lieutenants.[20] In February 1995, under very suspicious circumstances, security forces killed at least ninety-six Islamists who purportedly sought to revolt inside Serkadji prison in Algiers.[21] The biggest success for security forces came in March 1995, when they ambushed GIA militants in Ain Defla, killing at least 300 in clashes that lasted for a week.[22]

The state took additional security measures to put down the insurgency. In 1995 the state began (unofficially) to form citizen militias, especially in secluded regions, as a way to expand the fight against insurgents. Armed militias began to emerge as early as 1993, including the Self-Defense Organization, Free Algerian Youth Organization, and the Amazaghi Youth Organization. These groups were purportedly responsible for "secular violence" against Islamists and proponents of dialogue with the FIS. Although the government denied sponsoring citizen militias, at the end of 1995 it officially promoted the Groupes de Légitime Défense (GLD), commonly known as "patriots," and legalized them in January 1997.[23]

Furthermore, the regime began to coordinate with bordering states, especially Tunisia, to patrol borders jointly and take measures to prevent the movement of arms and rebels.[24] The Algerian regime also sought commitments from Morocco and Egypt to help Algeria in its fight against terrorism (Zartman 1997: 216–217). Finally, although the number of death sentences between 1994 and 1995 decreased from the previous period (forty-six capital sentences, most of which were in absentia), stories of torture, disappearances, and extrajudicial killings continued to emerge.[25]

The regime combined repression with an amnesty law that sought to entice insurgents to surrender with the promise of reduced sentences. Those sentenced to death were to receive a reduced sentence of fifteen to twenty years imprisonment, while those sentenced for life were to receive a reduced sentence of ten to fifteen years in prison. Others were to have their sentences cut in half. The amnesty law did not result in many defections and was generally recognized as a failure.

Indiscriminate Repression

State repression in the 1990s was indiscriminate. Beginning with the events of June 1991, the military embarked on mass arrests that resulted in thousands of detainees.[26] In addition, scores of individuals were fatally wounded during the crackdown that followed the June disturbances, with perhaps as many as 300 people killed according to the Algerian League of Human Rights.[27]

In the immediate aftermath of the coup, the authorities arrested Islamists en masse, irrespective of whether they were violent militants or mere supporters of the movement. Many bearded Muslims wearing the *kamis* (which is a sign of heightened religiosity) were subject to harassment and arrest to the point that many ceased to grow a beard or don traditional Islamic dress (Martinez 2000).

Accurate arrest figures are unavailable, but estimates range from 6,000 to 30,000 interned in desert camps.[28] By 1996, according to an Algerian human rights organization, there were 116 prisons with 43,737 prisoners, half of whom were accused of terrorism. Between July and November 1997, President Liamine Zeroual released approximately 7,000 prisoners. In 1999, Abdelaziz Bouteflika freed 4,000 prisoners with the goal of releasing a total of 15,000 by the end of the reconciliation process that began during that year.[29] The release of such a large number of prisoners during and shortly after the insurgency highlights the fact that many of those imprisoned hardly constituted an imminent threat to the state. To the thousands imprisoned we must add the thousands of "disappeared," many of whom were Islamist supporters or outwardly religious persons.[30]

In addition to mass arrests, repression against FIS-controlled councils in 1992 affected thousands of people beyond the core activists and leaders. By the end of 1992, the state had dissolved 853 FIS-controlled communal councils and 32 FIS-controlled departmental councils. Mus'ad (1995: 257) maintains that if one assumes that each of these councils employed twenty people with FIS leanings, then we can conclude that the authorities had dismissed 17,700 people from their jobs in a very short period. It is uncertain how many of those dismissed took up arms against the state, but it is reasonable to argue that such indiscriminate repression drove some to the camp of the radicals.

State repression after the coup did not distinguish between peaceful demonstrations and violent militancy. The state of emergency imposed on 9 February 1992 forbade all forms of protest. Mustapha Karatali, the commander of al-Rahman militia, which joined the GIA in 1994, claims that on 7 February 1992 the FIS organized a peaceful demonstration but the regime responded with brutality. Many people were killed and arrested.[31] A "national peaceful march" scheduled by the FIS for 14 February 1992 was canceled after the authorities prohibited it and deployed heavily armed paratroopers along its proposed route.[32] FIS supporters were also prevented from demonstrating after Abassi and Belhaj were sentenced to twelve years of imprisonment in July 1992.[33] As Abdelkarim Ghamati, a member of the FIS Provisional National Executive Bureau, explained: "The crisis cell in the [FIS] discussed the issue of demonstrations and the possibility of rallying people, as happened in Iran, to take to the streets to confront the military and remain in its face until it returned to the people its choice by reversing the coup. But the cell rejected this idea because lives were going to be lost. We recognized that the regime would not hesitate to kill the people if they conducted demonstrations or gatherings."[34] The indiscriminate nature of state repression appeared to give Islamists few alternatives to fighting back.

The state's policy of rapid and widespread repression aimed to crush the movement in one fell swoop. However, as Martinez (2000: 48) explains, "the perverse effects of that strategy began to appear from 1993: a number of FIS voters, who had adopted a wait and see attitude then, now became, under the impact of repression, sympathizers of or participants in violence against the regime." Martinez cites many stories of ordinary supporters of the FIS (and even some neutral observers) feeling compelled to lend a supporting hand to the rebels, if not take up a gun, in response to unjustifiable repression toward relatives, friends, and neighbors. Some of those interviewed were not particularly religious, but the sense of moral indignation at arbitrary harassment and outright torture of suspected militants led them to join the armed movement.

Ahmed Bin Aicha, the AIS commander in the western region, points out that "when we were threatened with death, we had no other choice but to take up the gun."[35] Ali Jeddi, another prominent FIS figure, contends that the cancellation of the electoral process and the "unprecedented repression" that followed are the main reasons why the FIS turned to armed opposition, "the option of last resort."[36]

Reactive and indiscriminate repression of Islamists in Algeria in the context of political exclusion contributed to widespread rebellion. The perceived injustice of the coup gave Islamist violence legitimacy. The mortal threat posed by state repression against Islamist organizations and cadres gave supporters of the FIS additional incentive to fight back. The indiscriminate application of repression meant that FIS sympathizers could not guarantee their security through neutrality. Extensive organizational networks developed during the period of political openness, activist and community links forged through local activism, and the realistic self-assurance that stemmed from prior mobilization successes and victory at the polls guaranteed that the Islamists would fight back.

Repression and Rebellion in Egypt

Similar to Algeria, reactive and indiscriminate repression against al-Jama'a al-Islamiyya in Egypt contributed to its rebellion in the 1990s. During the mid-1980s, President Husni Mubarak pursued a dual policy of toleration and isolation toward Islamists. The Muslim Brotherhood was given some political space for institutional and professional activism, while the Jama'a was contained in its upper Egypt strongholds and on the periphery of greater Cairo where it supposedly could do little harm to the central government (Springborg 1989). Throughout the 1980s and early 1990s, the state prohibited Islamists from organizing mass political parties or mobilizing demonstrations. However, the authorities tacitly allowed the Jama'a to conduct social and political activities in its strongholds with relatively little interference. This strategy failed to prevent the outbreak of Islamist rebellion, but it did succeed in containing the insurgency.

Reactive Repression

The Jama'a was able to establish "liberated zones" in some of the towns of upper Egypt and greater Cairo (Cassandra 1995; Bakr 1996; Abdo 2000). In the Asyut city of Dairut, the Jama'a controlled approximately 150 mosques, and in some neighborhoods it imposed complete control. In the mid and late 1980s the Jama'a began to expand its organizing into the shantytowns and peripheral areas of Cairo—Ain Shems, al-Zawiya al-Hamra, Imbaba, and Boulaq al-Dakrour. As one Jama'a activist in Imbaba relates: "Our work was conducted and expanded without any provocations or intervention from the security apparatuses, which gave us a better opportunity to grow. After a short while the Jama'a al-Islamiya became an influential force in Imbaba and everyone took it into account" (quoted in Mubarak 1995: 247).

The Jama'a set up roving bands that often engaged in "forbidding vice"—segregating the sexes, preventing girls from engaging in sporting activities at schools, and breaking up concerts (Ramadan 1995: 241). Its activities against the Copts also went largely unpunished as long as they did not rise to an "alarming" level—one that would attract national and international press attention. This was especially true in Dairut where there were repeated incidents of sectarian violence.[37]

The Jama'a branches regularly held conferences around their mosques and employed their own security guards to protect them. These conferences were often overtly political and critical of the state and "enemies" of Islam. As Mubarak (1995: 257) points out: "The Islamic Group was the only political force in Egypt that conducted mass conferences without acquiring a security permit as the law declares, not to mention the repetition of slogans, declarations and words that represent a violation of and a challenge to the law. Meanwhile, security men—at that time—could not come near conference areas for fear of clashing with the Jama'a paramilitary groups that were given the task of 'protecting' the conferences."

The Jama'a was permitted to enforce its own laws through threat and force at the universities of upper Egypt, as they had done in the 1970s (Springborg 1989: 228). This policy was in line with the broader policy to allow greater restrictions on secular conduct in upper Egypt to ensure social peace. For instance, "five governorates prohibited the sale of liquor, although it is not generally prohibited by law" (Auda 1994: 394).

The policy of turning a blind eye to Islamist violence had its limits. Eventually, the dynamic of violence resulted in escalations that would necessitate state intervention to reassert authority and contain the power of Islamists. However, as Mubarak (1995: 382) explains: "By the time the state intervenes to protect its prestige it is too late. For [the Islamic] group feels a great sense of confidence in its ability to confront the state, which gave it an opportunity to develop, consolidate its strength, and expand to a level where it can impose its authority on the citizens of the region and, indeed, on police officers."

The acquiescence of the state to Islamist activism in upper Egypt also extended to their social services. The Jama'a organized social welfare services out of their mosques to help their impoverished communities.

These activities included distributing meat and rice during religious holidays and passing out school supplies and clothing to poor families in the beginning of each school year. They also set up "reconciliation committees" to mediate conflict in neighborhoods on the basis of Islamic laws. These activities were known to the local authorities because the Jama'a made it a point to publicize them to increase its legitimacy among the people (Mubarak 1995: 260–265; Bayat 2002: 12).

Islamist voluntary associations were also more widespread in rural regions than in urban centers. For example, the Islamist associations constituted 56.8 percent of voluntary organizations in al-Minya and only 21.8 percent in Cairo for the years 1989 and 1990 (Qandil 1995b: 166). The main reason for this imbalance is the spatial autonomy of the rural areas from the central government. As Sullivan (1994: 92) explains: "Urban organizations in particular feel the pressure of government, since the national bureaucracies are close in proximity and, in Egypt as in most developing counties, urbanization precipitates a concern by the central government for the stability of urban centers. In these cases, urban governments are less likely to permit strong religious community organizations that would displace the secular, political institutions by supplying the services that the government is not able to or willing to provide."

This policy of permissiveness was acceptable to the regime as long as Islamists limited their activities to upper Egypt and their violence to low levels. However, the expansion of militant Islamists into greater Cairo and increasing Islamist violence during the late 1980s and early 1990s resulted in a dynamic of violence and counterviolence that eventually contributed to mass repression and rebellion. Ironically, Springborg (1989: 241), one of the foremost experts on Egypt, argued that "the government strategy of dividing and ruling the opposition [during the 1980s] was clearly beginning to bear fruit." In the 1990s the Egyptian regime reaped what it sowed, Islamist insurgency.

Indiscriminate Repression

In 1990, the state assassinated Ala Muhyi al-Din, the official spokesman of the Jama'a, which led the group to form an armed wing by unifying some of the security groups that were involved in protecting Islamist conferences. The Jama'a assassinated Rifat al-Mahjoub, former speaker of parliament, in retaliation for the killing of Muhyi al-Din.

The assassination of al-Mahjoub led the state to carry out a massive sweep in Asyut, Cairo, and Beni Swayf, among other places, which resulted in hundreds, if not thousands of arrests.[38] The crackdown on Islamists, however, did not fully develop until mid and late 1992, two years after the initial crackdown and six years since the resurgence of Islamist organizing and violence in 1986. What appears to have initiated the crackdown were the March 1992 clash between Muslims and Christians in Manshiyat Nasir in upper Egypt, where at least thirteen people were killed; the assassination of the prominent secular intellectual Faraj Fuda in June 1992; and the attacks on tourists that began in June 1992.

In May 1992 the state deployed approximately 2,000 soldiers in the Asyut district of Dairut to impose a curfew after a series of demonstrations and clashes between Islamists and the police. A month later, a state of emergency was declared in some areas of Asyut. In December 1992 the state sent approximately 16,000 soldiers to "liberate" Imbaba in greater Cairo. In January 1993, 8,000 soldiers participated in searches for Islamists in Masarah, Dairut, Sanaba, Manshiyat Nasir, and Dairut al-Sharif. In April 1993, an additional force of 5,000 soldiers was deployed in Asyut.[39]

These attempts to uproot Islamists from their strongholds came too late. According to one Egyptian strategic analyst: "Since the emergence of the phenomenon [of violence] in Egyptian society in 1991, and even until 1993, it is possible to say that the security apparatus had no strategy. It dealt with events individually without linking them together [and without forming] a single political agenda to deal with [Islamist violence]."[40] Another observer maintains that the "liberation" of Imbaba in late 1992–early 1993 was the beginning of a comprehensive state strategy against Islamist violence. However, by 1993 the Islamist insurgency was well under way.[41]

State repression was aimed at not only the hard-core militants of the Jama'a and Jihad groups but also their supporters, families, and virtually anyone who had a beard with a trimmed moustache (a sign of religiosity).[42] The number of people arrested in the 1990s, especially when compared to the late 1980s, indicates that the state threw its net widely.[43] Between 1992 and 1997 more than 47,000 people were arrested, a number that is surely greater than the number of active militant Islamists (see Table 3.1). It was only in 1998 and 1999 that the state released more than 7,000 of these prisoners due to the cessation of violence.[44]

In addition to mass arrests, the authorities began to engage in "hostage-taking" whereby the relatives, especially the wives, of suspected militants were detained until the latter turned themselves in to the authorities.[45] Those arrested were regularly mistreated and, worse, tortured. As

Table 3.1 People Arrested in Egypt, 1992–1997

Year	Number Arrested
1992	9,429
1993	17,785
1994	6,812
1995	4,119
1996	5,101
1997	4,392
Total Arrested	47,638

Source: The data for the period 1992–1994 was collected from Ahmed (1995: 299–305); the 1995 figure was taken from Abulala (1998); the 1996 figure was taken from *al-Hala al-Diniya fi Misr* (1998: 241); the 1997 figure was taken from *Taqrir Misr al-Mahrousa wal-Aalam, 1997* (1998).

suggested previously, torture was not a new phenomenon in Egypt. What distinguished it in the 1990s was its indiscriminate application.

The number of death sentences and executions reached unprecedented levels. In April 1999 the Egyptian Organization for Human Rights reported that 1,001 civilians were prosecuted in front of military courts since 1992. These courts issued ninety-four death sentences, sixty-seven of which were carried out.[46] Also, in the mid-1990s the state increasingly adopted a shoot-to-kill policy as evinced by the decline in the number of Islamists injured and the increase in the number of Islamists killed in confrontations with the police and military (see Figure 3.1). Furthermore, the Egyptian government undertook a number of international agreements to capture and extradite suspected militants to Egypt.[47] By 1999 these agreements resulted in the capture and extradition of Islamists from Afghanistan, Albania, Bosnia, Bulgaria, Chechnya, Kuwait, Libya, South Africa, Sudan, and Yemen.[48]

The fact that repression was reactive meant that radical Islamists had an added incentive to defend the material and organizational resources they had accumulated during the 1980s. As the documents and statements of Jama'a activists indicate, its branches began their struggle against the state not as an attempt to topple the regime but as a way to stop mass arrests, torture, and the takeover of private mosques. Bakr (1996: 199–200), who interviewed a number of Jama'a activists in Asyut, sums up their stated justifications for violence in the order in which they were often repeated:

Figure 3.1 Islamists Killed and Injured in Egypt, 1992–1997

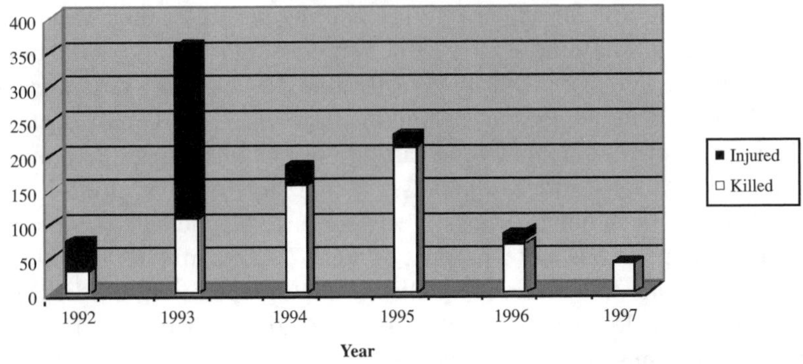

Source: Abulala (1998); *al-Hala al-Diniya fi Misr* (1998); *Taqrir Misr al-Mahrousa wal-Aalam, 1997* (1998).

1. The government's procrastination in applying Islamic law
2. Fulfilling God's commandment to uphold the good and prohibit the forbidden
3. The government's policy of violently ousting the Jama'a from its mosques and incorporating these mosques into the Ministry of Endowments
4. The abuse that has become a habit for the regime
5. The assassination of Jama'a activists and leaders
6. The government's nonrecognition of the Jama'a and its right to preach
7. The reliance on military courts
8. The continuous and systematic use of torture against the Jama'a
9. The government's accommodation of "the enemies of Islam"

In one of its documents, "Concerning the Current Situation Between the Islamic Group and the Egyptian Regime," the Jama'a cites the following reasons for the increase in violence since 1992: (1) The storming of mosques controlled by the Jama'a; (2) the execution of some of the leaders of the Jama'a; and (3) torture of Jama'a members under arrest. The document goes on to say that the Jama'a operated peacefully and limited its activities to holding conferences, distributing leaflets, and sponsoring protests and strikes.[49]

In a document entitled *Hata Mata* (How Long) issued in July 1991, the Jama'a gives as its main reason for resorting to violence the imprisonment of Islamists and their "torture and the torture of their wives and mothers that has become a daily habit in police branches and in the buildings of the central state security investigators."[50] In another report, issued in 1999 to explain the reasons behind the insurgency, the Jama'a declares: "The armed operations that were carried out by our units in the previous years took place because of the presence of a large number of the Jama'a members in prison due to arrests. Their presence behind bars was the reason for the operations, not a product of them."[51] Ibrahim (1995: 412–413) aptly sums up the effect of indiscriminate repression on Egyptian Islamists: "The logical consequence of the randomness in applying security measures in some areas was to create tensions between the public and police agencies. In the midst of conducting a sharp confrontation with some of the Islamic groups, these agencies did not receive the sympathy of the public, which did not provide them a truly helping hand. . . . The politics of arresting the wives and relatives of fugitives and taking them as hostages aided in inculcating the spirit of revenge between security agents and [the Islamic] groups."

Selective Repression Against the Muslim Brotherhood

Unlike the previous period when the state distinguished between moderates and radicals, in the 1990s the state officially promoted the view that the Muslim Brotherhood (MB) and the jihadists are two sides of the same coin (Ibrahim 1995: 404–405). The MB and the Jama'a, the regime argued, engaged in role distribution (tawzi'a adwar) to achieve their goal of destabilizing and toppling the regime.[52]

The regime did not really believe its own rhetoric as evinced by the limited arrests against the MB and the relatively light sentences meted out against its leaders. The arrests were usually against few individuals at a time. Moreover, most of those arrested were released within a short period. Those who were brought to trial were either acquitted or sentenced to between three and five years, which is the sentence for belonging to an illegal organization, not violent activism or abetting terrorism (Ibrahim 1998: 127–144). Nonetheless, the policy of lumping together the MB and the radicals meant that no Islamist was safe from arrest and prosecution.

Several developments help explain the reversal in state policy toward the MB. First, during the 1980s and early 1990s, the MB refused to adopt a quiescent role in parliament. Instead, it raised controversial issues—the persistent use of torture in detention centers and the lack of real democracy and political freedoms in Egypt. These issues touched on the legitimacy of the state and "limited the positive effects of the strategy of delicate balance" promoted by the regime since 1984 (Auda 1994: 393).

Second, the MB threatened the balance of formal party politics by dominating the legal political parties through which it entered parliament. In the 1987 "Islamic Alliance" that brought together the MB with the Labor and Liberal Parties, the MB was able to set the terms of the alliance. It successfully excluded Marxists and Nasserists from the alliance list and enticed the Labor Party to amend its political program to appeal to Islamists. When the alliance won seats in parliament, the MB took thirty-eight of the sixty seats won by the alliance (Auda and Ibrahim 1995: 310, 318).

Third, the MB threatened to expand its influence in civil society as evinced by its prominent, and often dominant, role in professional associations. Since the mid-1980s the MB played a greater role in professional syndicates. These associations constituted an important vehicle through which Islamists were able to embarrass the regime by raising sensitive issues concerning the Muslim world, including the Bosnia, Afghanistan, and the Palestinian-Israel conflicts (Qandil 1992, 1995b, 1996). The state was aware of the MB's strategy and sought to counter it by imposing restrictions—Law 100 of 1993—on Islamist activism in the syndicates.

Finally, and perhaps most important of all, the toleration of the MB in the parliamentary arena did not result in the complete containment of the radical wing of the movement. Thus, there was little need to maintain an accommodative stance toward an organization that did not contribute to the marginalization of violent opposition.

The crackdown on the MB in the mid-1990s raises the question, why did the MB not rebel or support the rebellion of the Jama'a similar to how the FIS supported the jihadists in Algeria? One of the key differences between Algeria and Egypt is that state repression against the MB since 1995 was selective. The state targeted the midlevel leaders of the movement and some of the core activists (al-Shawkabi 1995). The numbers of those arrested in 1995 hardly reached the levels witnessed by the Jama'a or the FIS in Algeria (see Table 3.2).

Most of those arrested were invariably released in a short period, with the exception of ninety-six people who faced trial in military courts between September 1995 and May 1996. However, of those ninety-six, thirty were acquitted and sixty received sentences ranging

Table 3.2 Muslim Brotherhood Leaders and Activists Arrested, 1995

Month	Number of Arrests
January	27
February	0
March	17
April	2
May	14
June	0
July	228
August	50
September	8
October	35
November	457
December	95
Total Arrested	933

Source: Ibrahim (1998: 126–137).

from one year suspended sentence to three years in prison. None were sentenced to more than five years imprisonment (Ibrahim 1998: 139–144). In other words, whereas in Algeria Islamists belonging to the FIS were herded into prisons by the thousands, state repression against the MB in Egypt was discriminate and measured.

While the MB faced greater political exclusion, the organizational and physical well-being of its core leadership was not threatened, which was not the case in Algeria. The MB in Egypt continued to operate its social services and legally challenge the state on key repressive measures. Although greater harassment and restrictions prevented the MB from exerting influence in both the political and professional arenas, MB leaders continued to appear in public, their offices were left relatively untouched, and many of their cadres at the universities were spared persecution. In Algeria, Abassi and Belhaj, the two principal leaders of the movement, were sentenced to twelve years in prison. FIS councilors were stripped of their office and many were imprisoned in the crackdown following the 1992 coup. Activists were picked up en masse and subjected to a brutal desert confinement.

In conclusion, the significant expansion of Islamist violence during the 1990s coincided with reactive and indiscriminate repression against Jama'a activists. The acquiescence to militant organizing and low-level violence in upper Egypt and some of the districts of greater Cairo during the mid-1980s allowed the radicals to garner material, organizational, and identity resources with which to mobilize people. Reactive and indiscriminate repression that effectively began in 1992 and ⌐⌐ at the infrastructure of the Jama'a gave the group added incentive to mobilize in order to protect the gains of its movement.

Islamist rebellion, however, was limited in scale largely because the ruling regime in Egypt was more selective and measured in its repression of the MB. Unlike the military regime in Algeria, the Egyptian regime spared the traditionally moderate MB the persecution it meted out against the Jama'a. MB cadres were not arrested by the thousands, nor were they subject to the torture and extrajudicial killings faced by the Jama'a. The leaders of the MB were permitted a degree of liberty not given to FIS leaders in Algeria. Hence, selective repression of the MB partly explains why the latter did not join or support the rebellion of the Jama'a. (In Chapter 5, I will discuss additional factors that precluded an MB–Jama'a alliance during the 1990s.)

Repression and Rebellion in Other Parts of the Muslim World

The contemporary histories of Algeria and Egypt point to an important link between repression and rebellion. In both countries Islamists rebelled not merely because they were aggrieved or excluded from political participation but because they felt their organizational and physical survival was threatened by overwhelming repression. In both instances, insurgency was a defensive reaction to protect organizational gains and personal lives against predatory states, not an aggressive strategy to topple a secular order. The nexus between repression and mass insurgency is borne out by the experiences of numerous other Muslim societies, including Kashmir, the southern Philippines, Chechnya, and Tajikistan. In all these regions, reactive and indiscriminate repression either precipitated rebellion or legitimated Islamist violence and made it worse than it needed to be.

Kashmir

One of the most tragic and potentially devastating conflicts in the Muslim world has been taking place in the region of Kashmir. Tens of thousands have been killed and injured since armed insurgency broke out in 1989, and thousands more have been made refugees due to expansive violence against civilians. The conflict persists to this day and has a potential to unleash a nuclear conflagration between India and Pakistan, two states that have fought three wars over Kashmir and have contributed to the continuation of the conflict there.[53]

The state of Jammu and Kashmir (henceforth Kashmir) has been a contested region ever since India and Pakistan were partitioned in 1947. Kashmir is a predominantly Muslim region that acceded to Indian control after independence. Although the state has been granted "special status" by New Delhi, manipulation of its internal politics has fostered frustration and alienation among Kashmiri Islamists and nationalists, many of whom insist on separation from India and the right either to join Pakistan or to lead an independent state. Pakistan has fed these aspirations through arms and shelter, but it would be a mistake to treat Pakistan as the sole or most important driver behind separatist struggles. As Ganguly (1997: 38) explains, "the singular political tragedy of Kashmir's politics was the failure of the local and the national political leadership to permit the development of an honest political opposition." India, as much as Pakistan, is responsible for the outbreak of armed rebellion in Kashmir.

Institutional exclusion and indiscriminate repression were the precipitating factors in the outbreak of rebellion in the late 1980s. In 1986, a number of Islamist political parties organized themselves into the Muslim United Front (MUF), which opposed the dominant National Conference Party after the latter allied itself with the Congress Party in a pro–New Delhi union. Many Kashmiris viewed such an alliance as a betrayal of their aspirations for independence and a humiliating show of subservience to New Delhi.

The MUF called for Islamic unity and noninterference from the Indian central government in preparation for the March 1987 regional elections. The MUF was poised to win a large number of seats. However, due to preelection arrests of some of its cadres as well as blatant vote rigging, the MUF won only four of the forty-four seats it contested (Ganguly 1997; Schofield 2000). "The rigged election was the beginning of the end," writes Singh (1995: 103); "most of the youths who had acted as election agents and workers for the MUF candidates were now determined to fight for their rights differently. They had no choice but to pick up the gun."

Many militants in the nationalist Jammu and Kashmir Liberation Front (JKLF) and Islamists in the MUF began to engage in sporadic violence against government officials, representatives of the National Conference Party, and the minority Hindu communities. This violence gained greater organizational coherence by 1989, as strikes, demonstrations, assassinations, and bombings became endemic. However, according to Singh (1995: 115), "things were still not so bad that they could not have been brought under control by an efficient and credible government."

The regional and central governments responded to the violence of separatists with indiscriminate repression. Former governor Shri Jagmohan was brought back to administer the state in 1990, which was "the worst mistake the central government could have made at the time" (Singh 1995: 131). Under Jagmohan's reign, the civilian populations increasingly endured arbitrary searches, mass arrests, and torture at the hands of counterinsurgency services (Puri 1993). "Every youth in Kashmir came to be regarded as a potential militant," writes Schofield (2000: 143). On the first day of his tenure, more than one hundred peaceful protesters were killed when police fired at them as they were crossing the Gawakadal Bridge.

The Gawakadal massacre was a turning point in the conflict because it galvanized popular support for the rebels and discredited the possibility of peaceful resolution to the crisis. As Singh (1995: 132–133) explains, up to that point "Kashmiris could have accused India of political repression, of denying them their right to self-determination, of keeping them forcibly within the Indian Union, but nobody could have accused India of human rights violations."

Human rights organizations reported the now-familiar gross violations of extrajudicial killings, disappearances, collective punishments against villages suspected of harboring rebels, undisciplined shootings, summary executions, torture, and rape during cordon-and-search operations.[54] These policies legitimated rebel violence and strengthened the resolve of hitherto uncommitted activists, many of whom joined or supported armed militants to take revenge against military excesses. "The militants had the support of doctors, lawyers, teachers, judges, retired officials and even policemen" (Singh 1995: 166). The net result of Jagmohan's policy of indiscriminate repression during the initial phase of the insurgency was eloquently stated by a local official: "what Jagmohan did in five months [the militants] could not have achieved in five years" (quoted in Desmond 1995: 6).

As the insurgency developed, the repressive policy intensified, continuing well into the late 1990s. In 1992 the government began to implement what appeared to be a "catch and kill" policy.[55] The state also began arming local auxiliary forces—"village defence committees"—to combat rebels. This policy polarized civilian populations and gave local armed groups the authority to exercise unregulated repression.[56]

The cycle of violence and counterviolence aided in the expansion of more radical Islamist groups such as Hizb-ul Mujaheddin, Harkat-ul Ansar, Jaish-e Muhammad, and Lashkar-e Toiba. All four effectively marginalized the traditional leadership of the separatist movement, led by the JKLF (Davis 1995). To be sure, these groups have benefited from Pakistani financial, political, and military backing, as well as from an influx of Afghan-trained militants who are engaging in a self-declared international jihad. Without such support, many of these groups would have either succumbed to repression or withered away in exile.

However, it would be a mistake to view the Kashmir conflict as a product of foreign interference, India's claims notwithstanding. At its roots, the Kashmir crisis reflects a broader pattern that is, unfortunately, common in the Muslim world. This pattern consists of political exclusion combined with reactive and indiscriminate repression. As Ganguly (1997: 31) explains, Kashmir was the only state in democratic India where "elections were routinely compromised. . . . After years of frustrated attempts at meaningful political participation, and in the absence of institutional means of expressing dissent, resort to more violent methods became all but inevitable."

If institutional exclusion did not make insurgency completely inevitable, the indiscriminate repression of an organized movement did. Repression failed to wear down the insurgents during the initial phase of the rebellion. On the contrary, human rights abuses against suspected militants increased the legitimacy of the rebels and inculcated feelings of revenge in the general populous. As Singh (1995: 238) concludes: "It is this complete disregard of the human rights issue that has helped keep the freedom movement alive. The way Kashmiris see it is that no matter how badly their own militant leaders behave they never behave as badly as the Indian security forces. The result is that India has lost its moral authority." Persistent indiscriminate repression by India's security forces continues to inspire rebellion in Kashmir today.[57]

Southern Philippines

In 1972 a separatist rebellion by Muslims broke out in the island of Mindanao in the southern Philippines. The rebels were led by the Moro National Liberation Front (MNLF), which formed a year earlier to demand independence for the 5 million Muslim inhabitants within the southern Philippines (George 1980). Since that time, violence between the armed rebels and the authorities has escalated, claiming thousands of lives and spawning violent groups that continue to wage war against the government today.

Like Kashmir, Egypt, and Algeria, the insurgency of the MNLF was encouraged by reactive and indiscriminate repression that drove thousands of uncommitted persons into the camp of the militants. The roots of the conflict date back to both the transmigration policies of the Philippine government, which brought Catholic migrants into the majority Muslim south, and the national integration policies, which sought to incorporate the Muslim south as part of one Filipino nation.

These policies combined with social differentiation, economic inequality, and outright racism to produce widespread grievances on the part of Muslim intellectuals (Majul 1988). The separatist movement was begun in the 1960s by dissatisfied young Muslims who "experienced firsthand the magnitude of anti-Muslim bias in the national capital," writes McKenna (1997: 57), adding that the "Christian Filipinos who controlled the Philippines state regarded all unhispanicized citizens as impure and marked Philippine Muslims as especially untrustworthy because of their long history of mutual enmity."

However, mere grievances were not sufficient to produce mass rebellion. It took outright physical threat to the lives of ordinary Muslims in the early 1970s to produce rebellious organizations with popular support. In 1968, the Muslim (later Mindanao) Independence Movement (MIM) formed in response to the summary execution of Muslim recruits within the Philippine army in an incident that came to be known as the Jabidah massacre (Majul 1985). The Ilaga, Christian armed militias, engaged Muslim militias, known as the "Black Shirts," in sporadic communal violence that eventually escalated into outright massacres against the opposing communities (Majul 1988; Turner 1995). "Most commonly, Christian gangs assaulted Muslim farmers and burnt their houses, and Muslim gangs retaliated in kind against Christian farmers," explains McKenna (1998: 149). These acts resulted in countless lives lost, hundreds of homes burned, and over 100,000 refugees by the early 1970s (McAmis 1974; Majul 1985).

The inability of the state to protect Muslim populations and the acquiescence of local Christian authorities with the Ilaga gave impetus to the formation of the more radical MNLF, which replaced the hitherto small and ineffective MIM. According to Chalk (2002: 189), the decision to rebel was partly driven by "the increasingly explicit support given by the Philippine Army to the Christian *Ilaga* campaign aimed at purging Islam from Minadano." McKenna (1998: 154) points out in relation to episodes of violence in the Cotabato Valley that "when Muslim noncombatants were attacked by Ilaga gangs, the Philippine constabulary was invariably slow in coming to their defense. Most distressing to Cotabato Muslims was the ample circumstantial evidence implicating the Philippine constabulary in Ilaga terror."

The MNLF demanded independence for Muslims through armed struggle. However, violence remained sporadic until the Philippine state declared martial law in 1972, marking the beginning of a ban on political organizing and the brutal and indiscriminate crackdown on suspected militants. Repression included summary execution of alleged MNLF rebels, mass arrests and collective punishments against villages, and air bombardments of heavily populated rebel positions, as well as torture and disappearances.

Prior to the declaration of martial law, separatist sentiments remained relatively unpopular. By the mid-1970s, however, the MNLF had as many as 30,000 members (McAmis 1974; George 1980; Majul 1985). According to McKenna (1998: 156, 183, 191), "The imposition of Martial Law was, in fact, the proximate cause, not the consequence, of an armed Muslim insurgency against the Philippine state." He adds that "virtually all of [the fighters] reported that they had joined the rebellion to defend themselves and their families against the Philippine government . . . [while others joined] in order to defend themselves and other Muslims against the Ilaga and the military." Moreover, the insurgents received tremendous support from the Muslim population, who began to view them "as their primary protectors from the murderous hostility of the military."

As the conflict developed, armed groups with an even more radical Islamist orientation than the nationalist MNLF emerged. The most notorious are the Moro Islamic Liberation Front, which commands approximately 15,000 men, and the Abu Sayyaf group, which has ties to Osama bin Laden and commands approximately 1,000 supporters (Chalk 2002). Today, southern Philippines continues to witness "residual" violence associated with these armed groups that emerged within a context of repression.

Chechnya

Perhaps no place has witnessed such reactive and indiscriminate repression as Chechnya did in the mid-1990s. Bombings of civilian cities and villages, brutal interrogation at filtration centers, and recurring human rights violations by undisciplined soldiers contributed to rebellion in Chechnya between 1994 and 1996. Tens of thousands have been killed and injured and countless others have disappeared in the fighting. Like other rebellions, more radical factions with Islamist (or "Wahhabi") orientation have emerged and perpetrated terrorist outrages that persist to this day.

Chechnya declared independence from Russia in November 1991, just as the Soviet Union collapsed, communism was discredited, and the Russian Red Army was disorganized and demoralized. It was a period of tremendous opportunity for a Chechen nation that has had a long and bloody history of confrontation with Russia. Memories of mass deportation and genocidal violence during the Stalin era were engrained in the national consciousness of Chechens (Dunlop 1998; Gall and Waal 1998).

The fact that other former Soviet republics such as Estonia, Latvia, and Lithuania successfully sought independence gave Chechen nationalists hope that they too could secede from the Russians (Splidsboel-Hansen 1994). The mass rebellion that broke out in 1994 was not inevitable, however. As many analysts of the region testify, it was a series of mistakes on the part of Russia that turned the conflict between the obdurate and increasingly unpopular Chechen president Jokhar Dudayev and Russia into a mass insurgency in the mid-1990s.

Initially, the Russians rejected Chechen claims of independence but neglected to respond seriously to the Chechen challenge. Given his preoccupation with more pressing concerns following the collapse of the Soviet empire, Russian president Boris Yeltsin did no more than declare a state of emergency and dispatched a small force of 600 Interior Ministry troops to the rebellious republic few days after its declaration of independence.

With no clear orders on how to proceed, the Russian forces quickly withdrew and by June 1992 almost all of the Russian armed forces had left Chechnya. In the process, Chechen separatists acquired large numbers of Russian arms, tanks, planes, and artillery, partly through a negotiated deal with the Russian military and partly through seizures of arms and illegal purchases from opportunist Russian soldiers (Dunlop 1998: 167–168; Gall and Waal 1998: 112–113). "It was these arms which two and a half years later formed the backbone of the Chechen defence," explains Lieven (1998: 65). Between 1992 and 1994, Chechen armed forces mobilized veterans of the Afghanistan war and set up military training camps. It also created a National Guard, self-defense units, and personal guards armed from Soviet stockpiles (Knezys and Sedlickas 1999: 34–35).

If Russia acted toward the Chechnya question with foolish negligence in 1991, it acted with equally senseless brutality in 1994, as it attempted to displace once and for all the breakaway government of President Dudayev through a military intervention. Russia invaded in November 1994, three years after its feeble attempt to reverse Chechen independence. According to Dunlop (1998: 222), in late 1994, Boris Yeltsin, believing that he could win a quick victory, chose "to resort to Brezhnev (and even Stalin)-era practices: 'black' operations, destabilization campaigns, assassinations, and the installation of 'puppet' regimes."

Initially, Russian forces encountered effective resistance by a small force of Chechen separatists. In response, the Russians responded with aerial bombardments in civilian centers, which resulted in tremendous destruction of property, thousands of deaths and injuries, and a gigantic refugee crisis as tens of thousands were displaced or forced to flee.[58] The overwhelming majority of victims were civilians (Seely 2001). Estimates of the number of people killed just in the first few months of fighting range from 5,000 (Lieven 1998) to 27,000 (Gall and Waal 1998).

What started out as a relatively small force of irregular fighters and National Guard units turned into a rebellion that brought the entire Chechen people against the Russian forces (Gall and Waal 1998: 19). According to Lieven (1998: 301): "The formal Chechen armed forces when the war began numbered fewer than two thousand men. The vast majority of Chechen fighters joined up after the war started, and not in formal military units, but in spontaneously formed groups of relatives, friends and neighbours." The irony is that during the preceding year, the rebellious Dudayev was facing increasing public dissatisfaction with the ongoing criminal anarchy and economic disarray of the republic. He encountered opposition from nearly all segments of society. The invasion turned an unpopular president into a heroic figure representing Chechen pride and resistance to Russia. As Dunlop (1998: 221) puts it, the Russian invasion "was transformed in the minds of a majority of Chechens into a clear-cut national threat."

A nationalist struggle was turned into an Islamist one partly to appeal to the Muslim world for support and partly because Chechen separatists found inspiration in the example of Afghan mujahedin who had resisted the Red Army a decade earlier. As Walker (1998) points out: "It was only after the war broke out that Islam began to become an important theme for the Chechen resistance movement. . . . The war, in short, led to the politicization of Islam—politicized Islam did not lead to war."[59]

As separatist rebels were forced out of Grozny and into the mountains, Russian forces engaged in serious human rights violations and undisciplined excesses that further alienated ordinary Chechens and gave legitimacy to the armed rebels. The most serious violations took place in filtration centers, where Chechen youths were interrogated and, in many instances, tortured.[60]

Villages that were suspected of harboring rebels faced retaliation and collective punishments, including the torching of houses and random killing of inhabitants. In many instances, villages were forced to choose between ousting the rebels, some of whom were outside of the control of village elders, and facing bombardments that could potentially raze entire settlements. "The policy put intense pressure on entire villages and regions, splitting communities into groups who wished to protect their villages and their lives, and those who were willing to see their settlements destroyed in the name of defending them," explains Seely (2001: 269). Most villages were anxious to avoid war, add Gall and Waal (1998: 248), "and if the Russians had acted with any subtlety they could have exploited this very well, but they seemed to prefer General [Alexei] Yermolov's old tactic of complete 'pacification' [which was effectively applied against Muslims in the Caucasus during the early nineteenth century]."

The net result of this policy has been the radicalization of the Chechen public and the legitimization of violence against Russian forces and civilians. One of the most notorious Chechen rebel leaders to emerge during the conflict is Shamil Basayev. He comes from the village of Vedeno, which faced Russian bombardment during May 1994 that resulted in the death of eleven of his relatives. In the spring of 1995, he led a battalion of rebels into the southern Russian town of Budyonnovsk and took around 1,460 hostages and barricaded them in a hospital. A firefight broke out when Russian security forces sought to free the hostages, resulting in 124 deaths (Seely 2001: 276). When interviewed by Russian journalists as to why he undertook this adventure, here is what Basayev had to say: "Before, I was not a supporter of that sort of action, to go and fight in Russia, because I knew what measures and cost it would entail, so I had always refused such things. But when last year we were thrown out of Vedeno, and they had driven us into a corner with the very savage and cruel annihilation of villages, women, children, old people, of a whole people, then we went."[61]

Basayev's statement, self-serving as it may be, speaks to how indiscriminate repression affords legitimacy to Islamist violence even when it is applied against ordinary civilians in the enemy camp.

Tajikistan

Tajikistan, a former Soviet republic, is another blighted Muslim country that has witnessed catastrophic levels of violence and bloodshed as a result of a rebellion that began in 1992 and ended in 1997. Perhaps as many as 50,000 people were killed and more than 800,000 people displaced during the span of five years.[62] Civilians bore the brunt of the mass violence that pitted an amalgam of nationalist and Islamist groups known as the United Tajik Opposition (UTO) against a pro-Communist state regime, which itself was dominated by ethnic groups from the northern and southeastern parts of Tajikistan.

At first glance, the case of Tajikistan appears to support the "poverty breeds rebellion" theory. Tajikistan is one of the most impoverished countries in the world and was the poorest republic within the former Soviet Union. Its economic situation deteriorated further when the Soviet empire collapsed in 1991 (Niyazi 1994; Rashid 2002). However, while poverty undoubtedly contributed to the rise of Islamist opposition, like the other countries discussed in this chapter, the rebellion in Tajikistan also developed out of years of political marginalization and episodes of reactive and indiscriminate repression in the early 1990s.

Similar to the other republics in the former Soviet Union, Tajikistani nationalists, democrats, and Islamists from the Garm-Kartogin and Gorno-Badakhshan regions saw an opportunity to oppose the neo-Communist state leadership supported by an alliance of Khujand and Kulab clans, local Uzbeks, and ethnic Russian settlers. Uzbekistan and Russia also aided the neo-Communist forces against the opposition (Gretsky 1995; Zviagelskaya 2001; Rashid 2002). In the early 1990s, a number of new political forces emerged as the Soviet Union was undergoing perestroika. Chief among these forces were the Democratic Party of Tajikistan (DPT), the Rastakhez (Rebirth) movement, and the Islamic Renaissance (or Rebirth) Party (IRP). The latter espoused a revivalist Islamic ideology, while the former two promoted Western-style liberalism and nationalism respectively (Dudoignon 1997).

Prior to formal independence in 1991, the IRP was not permitted to organize in Tajikistan. As a matter of fact, Islam and Islamic institutions in general were obstructed because they were seen as reactionary and a source of anti-Sovietization policies (Olimova 1999). The ban, however, did not prevent the party from expanding underground. By the time independence came, "the [IRP] was estimated to be the largest [party] after the Communist Party of Tajikistan" (Brown 1997: 88).

Democrats, nationalists, and Islamists organized mass demonstrations in August and September 1991 against the Communist Party in Dushanbe, the capital of Tajikistan. Perhaps as many as 100,000 people joined the demonstrations, which persisted intermittently until May 1992 (J. Anderson 1997: 169). The demonstrators were calling for a constitutional referendum, parliamentary elections, and, eventually, the resignation of former Communist Party chief Rakhmon Nabiev.[63]

By that time, pro-government Kulyabi forces took part in counter-demonstrations. The Kulyabi faction was allied with Khujandi elite from Leninabad, which historically dominated the government. Violence broke out on each side, but it was sporadic and unorganized. Violence escalated in May when President Nabiev used his emergency powers to issue a decree authorizing the distribution of 1,800 automatic weapons among his supporters and created a National Guard made up mainly of Kulyabis (Asadullaev 2001).

Opposition supporters took over Tajik television during the disturbances, which gave Nabiev the pretext to order the National Guard to suppress the demonstrators, resulting in a number of fatalities. When thousands of opposition demonstrators demanded to address Nabiev at his headquarters on May 10, security troops opened fire, fatally wounding fourteen. In an inconsistent move, Nabiev entered into negotiations with the opposition, which resulted in an agreement to disband the National Guard and share power with the opposition.

The pro-government Khujandi-Kulyabi alliance rejected the power-sharing agreement and began waging a violent campaign to oust the opposition. They were supported by Uzbekistan's president Islam Karimov and the 201st Division of the Russian Army, both of whom used the "threat of Islamic Fundamentalism" as a pretext to side with the pro-government alliance (Gretsky 1995).

Paramilitary groups from the Kulyabi forces "began to massacre villagers in the vicinity of Kurgan Tyube who supported the IRP" (Rashid 2002: 103). In September of that year, the rebels forced President Nabiev to resign at gunpoint. By this time, the civil war had begun in earnest as both sides had paramilitary groups with guns, artillery, and armed personnel carriers (Brown 1997: 90–91).

By December 1992, the pro-Communist forces had gained control of the capital. At least 20,000 people were killed between May and December 1992 (Akiner and Barnes 2001). The new government gave ascendancy to the Kulyab faction. Emomali Rahmonov, a Communist leader from Kulyab, became the new president, and he immediately gave key government ministries and the army to Kulyabis. This government moved quickly to silence the opposition and deprive them of legal and organizational standing (Gretsky 1995; Atkin 1997).

The repression that ensued was reactive in nature. As Rashid (2002: 100) points out, when the Soviet Union was collapsing in 1991, the IRP grew organizationally: "No other Islamic movement in Central Asia has ever been given such a chance at mass contact as Tajikistan's IRP was in those years. When the IRP was registered as a political party by the Tajik authorities in December [1991], just a few days after the collapse of the Soviet Union, it already claimed twenty thousand members."

Similar to Algeria, repression in Tajikistan sought to do more than contain the opposition; it aimed to deprive it of all political and organizational existence. The threat was all-encompassing. According to Brown (1997: 93): "From the moment of its establishment in Dushanbe in December 1992, the new government determined to silence, if not physically destroy, the anti-Communist opposition that had briefly dominated the country's government the previous year. The groups that had made up the anti-Communist coalition in 1992—the Islamic Renaissance Party, the Western-oriented Democratic Party, the Tajik nationalist Rastokhez movement, and the separatist Lali Badakhshan—were first suspended and then formally banned by the Supreme Court in June."

Repression against the opposition was also indiscriminate. The violence of the combatants during the civil war was not simply a political struggle for power. As insurgency and repression proceeded apace, many groups saw an opportunity to settle old scores and disputes between the clans. Civilians and entire villages suspected of supporting the opposition were subject to cruel and systematic repression characterized by summary executions, ethnic cleansing, torture, disappearances, looting, and the destruction of homes and personal property.

By early 1993, nearly 100,000 refugees had fled to Afghanistan and adjoining towns seeking protection.[64] An estimated 35,000 homes were destroyed during that period alone.[65] To be sure, the violence was not one-sided; the opposition carried out anticivilian violence and brutalized government soldiers and administrators in their efforts to topple the neo-Communist regime (Gorvin 1997; Rashid 2002). In the final analysis, however, indiscriminate repression by pro-government paramilitary forces was the impetus for rebellion. These forces benefited from the old regime and sought to maintain the provincial hegemony that existed during the Soviet days by violently rejecting the negotiated agreement between Nabiev and the opposition.

Prior to pro-Communist mobilization in May 1992, the opposition's tactical repertoire was that of relatively peaceful mass demonstrations in public squares (Niyazi 1994; Olimova 1999; Olimova and Olimov 2001). The arming of pro-government forces from Kulyab "precipitated the outbreak of violence in Dushanbe that led directly to the civil war" (Brown 1997: 90). The indiscriminate repression pushed the opposition to defend itself through violent means. As Hizomov Mirzokhuzha, former rebel commander with the UTO, put it, "I could never have imagined that I would become a rebel. . . . No one wants to end up fighting, but the life of a person is written—and sometimes, if you don't fight, you are going to be killed."[66]

Between 1993 and 1997, opposition forces formed the UTO and set up bases in Afghanistan, where they infiltrated to launch hit-and-run attacks. The rebels recruited many of their members from the Tajik refugees in northern Afghanistan and received training and logistical support from Afghan fighters and government prior to the rise of the Taliban in the mid-1990s. Other Islamists in Central Asia, especially the Islamic Movement of Uzbekistan, gave material and membership support.[67]

Fighting effectively came to an end in 1997, after four years of on-and-off negotiations between the UTO and the government. A number of field commanders and warlords, however, continue to oppose the peace agreement that gave legality to the Islamist opposition and 30 percent of all government posts to the UTO. This deal was similar to the one negotiated by the opposition with President Nabiev in May 1992.

Conclusion

The experiences of Algeria, Egypt, Kashmir, the southern Philippines, Chechnya, and Tajikistan highlight the deleterious effects of reactive and indiscriminate repression on Islamist movements. In all these cases, Islamist rebellion was a defensive response to brutal and indiscriminate repression that threatened the organizational and physical well-being of Islamists and their supporters. In the context of institutional exclusion, rebellion became a legitimate strategy for countering repressive state policies. While many of these movements had radical wings that espoused violent rhetoric and goals, they were marginal in the movement. Repression gave those radicals fertile soil in which to grow and created the necessary and sufficient conditions for mass-scale recruitment into rebellious organizations.

In Algeria, the Armed Islamic Group (GIA) garnered little support prior to the 1992 military coup and mass arrests that ensued. In Egypt, the violence of al-Jama'a al-Islamiyya was sporadic and nonrevolutionary in nature. The heavy-handed policy of the state, which did not distinguish between core militants and sympathizers, pushed the Jama'a to form an armed wing and launch an insurgency in upper Egypt.

In Kashmir, a history of electoral manipulation combined with the reactive and indiscriminate repressive policies of Governor Shri Jagmohan against Kashmiri nationalists to intensify the turn to separatist violence. In the southern Philippines, the Ilaga militias' massacres in Muslim communities in Mindanao gave impetus to the formation of rebellious organizations to defend the lives and property of Muslims. In Chechnya, indiscriminate bombings of Chechen cities and villages inflamed the Muslim populations and inspired many to volunteer against the invading Russian force. In Tajikistan, the reactive and indiscriminate drive by neo-Communist forces to wrest power from the opposition, and the decimating repression that followed their takeover of Dushanbe, unleashed a civil war and encouraged the shift from mass demonstrations to violent rebellion during the 1990s.

These cases give credence to the theoretical proposition put forward in the beginning of this chapter: when institutional exclusion is combined with indiscriminate repression after an extended period of mass organizing and mobilization, large-scale rebellion is likely to occur.

Moving on from the political environment and the opportunity structures under which Islamist strategies of accommodation and rebellion emerge, the following chapters investigate the mobilization structures and ideological frames of Muslim rebels. Chapter 4 explores how Muslim insurgents organize themselves under conditions of repression, and Chapter 5 focuses on how rebels justify their rebellion against opponents and motivate their supporters to engage in anticivilian violence. The manner in which Islamists organize themselves during rebellion and the ideological frames they advance to justify and motivate violence bear directly on the issues of protracted conflict and expansive violence.

Notes

1. Refer to the works of Snyder and Tilly (1972), Hibbs (1973), Oberschall (1973), Oliver (1980), and Hardin (1982).

2. Refer to the works of Eckstein (1965), Gamson et al. (1982), Goldstein (1983), White (1989), Rasler (1996), and Olivier (1990, 1991).

3. See the excellent survey of the literature by Zimmermann (1980, 1983).

4. Refer to the works of Gurr (1968, 1970), Lichbach and Gurr (1981), Muller (1985), Muller and Seligson (1987), and Muller and Weede (1990). Some of these authors support the "inverted-U" hypothesis, which posits that low and high levels of repression deter dissent, but medium levels of repression incite rebellion. This hypothesis has been challenged empirically by Francisco (1995, 1996) and Lee et al. (2000).

5. Refer to the works of Snyder (1976), Gurr (1986), Tarrow (1989), Costain (1992), and Brockett (1995).

6. See Opp and Roehl (1990).

7. Refer to the works of Gupta et al. (1993) and Gartner and Regan (1996).

8. Refer to the works of Mason and Krane (1989) and Moore (1998).

9. See Lichbach (1987) and Ginkel and Smith (1999).

10. Refer to the works of Della Porta (1995a, 1996).

11. In the course of my doctoral research, I tested the validity of some other variables in relation to my case studies and found that they, indeed, shape the collective behavior of opposition groups (Hafez 2000b).

12. Mus'ad (1995: 239) maintains that in 1989 there were about 12,000 voluntary associations. By 1991, there were 40,000, many of which were religiously oriented. Although these numbers may be inaccurate—it is not clear how she arrives at these figures—other observers have also noted the expansion of voluntary associations throughout Algeria during this period (Qawas 1998; Charef 1994).

13. *MEI*, 13 May 1994.

14. Rabeh Kebir in Part 2 of an interview with *al-Wasat*, 21 June 1993.

15. *Le Monde*, 29 May 1991.

16. *MEJ* chronologies for 1992; *MEI*, 7 February and 20 March 1992; *al-Hayat*, 29 August 1992.

17. *MEJ* chronologies for 1992 and 1993.

18. See *MEJ* chronologies for 1993 and 1994 for an indication of the level of repression. In reading the chronology of events in the first two years of insurgency, I found reports of both Islamist deaths and injuries. However, after 1993, almost all reports were of Islamist deaths only.

19. It was reported widely that in 1994 the French along with the United States and Eastern European countries supplied Algerian forces with up-to-date counterinsurgency equipment, including thermal sensors to modernize Soviet-built Mi-24 helicopters and night vision equipment (*MECS* 1994; *Le Monde*, 10, 11, and 16 November 1994).

20. *MEI*, 7 October 1994.

21. HRW, "Algeria: Six Months Later, Cover-Up Continues in Prison Clash that Left 100 Inmates Dead" (August 1995); *MEI*, 3 March 1995.

22. *MEI*, 31 March 1995.

23. *al-Wasat*, 13 December 1993; AI, MDE 28/11/96 November 1996, MDE 28/23/97 November 1997; *Le Monde Diplomatique*, October 1997.

24. Tunisian forces were allowed to cross into Algeria without prior permission to engage insurgents. Also, Tunisian forces carried out deforestation

operations along the border areas to deprive insurgents of cover (*MECS* 1995: 231–232).

25. AI, "Algeria: 'Disappearances'—The Wall of Silence Begins to Crumble" (3 March 1999); HRW, "Human Rights Abuses in Algeria: No One Is Spared" (1994); HRW, "Neither Among the Living nor the Dead: State-sponsored 'Disappearances' in Algeria" (February 1998); HRW, "Algeria's Human Rights Crisis" (August 1998); *The Independent,* 30 and 31 October and 1 November 1997; *The Observer,* 25 May 1997. Information on the forty-six capital sentences from *MEJ* chronologies for 1994 and 1995.

26. The Algerian League for the Defense of Human Rights put the number of arrested at 8,000 while Prime Minister Ghozali put the figure at 2,976.

27. *MEJ* chronologies June–July 1991.

28. President Muhammad Boudiaf put the number at 6,000, while FIS leader Abderrazak Rejjam put the figure at 30,000 (see *MEJ* chronology for 16 and 23 February 1992). On 12 March 1992, Interior Minister Larbi Belkhair released a report stating that 9,000 had been arrested since the disturbances began in January 1992 (*NYT,* 13 March 1992).

29. *al-Hayat,* 6 July 1999.

30. AI, "Algeria: Who Are the 'Disappeared'?" (3 March 1999).

31. See interview with *al-Hayat,* 8 February 2000.

32. *MEI,* 21 February 1992.

33. *MEI,* 24 July 1992.

34. See interview with Ghamati in al-Tawil (1998: 93–94).

35. Interview with *al-Hayat,* 3 February 2000.

36. Interview with *al-Hayat,* 14 January 2000.

37. EOHR, "al-Mazbaha al-Taifiya bi-Dairut" (7 May 1992). For additional anecdotal evidence of police acquiescence to low-level Islamist violence against the Copts, see the various testimonies of local policemen, Islamists, and human rights officials in Mubarak (1995: 382–386). For a historical and political analysis of anti-Coptic sectarian violence in Egypt, see Ansari (1984b) and Fatah (1997).

38. See *MEJ* chronology for 1990 and *MECS* (1990). These sources do not indicate an exact number of arrests but they do speak of sweeps that resulted in "hundreds arrested."

39. See *MEJ* chronology for 1992 and 1993.

40. See the annual *al-Taqrir al-Istratiji al-Arabi, 1994* (1995: 425).

41. *al-Wasat,* 22 March 1993.

42. See HRW, "Egypt: Human Rights Abuses Mount in 1993" (22 October 1993); AI, "Egypt: Indefinite Detention and Systematic Torture: The Forgotten Victims" (July 1996).

43. In 1987 the state arrested approximately 4,000 suspected militants. In 1988 the number declined to 1,159, while in 1989 it went back up to 2,114. In 1990 the number declined to 955, but in 1991 it went back up to 1,370 (*MEJ* chronology; Ahmed 1995: 299). S.E. Ibrahim (1996: 73) puts the number of arrests between 1982 and 1993 at 25,000. Unfortunately, he does not break down these numbers to show in which years the arrests were concentrated. But another source (Ahmed 1995: 299–300) puts the number of arrests at 9,428 in

1992, and 17,785 in 1993, which suggests that most arrests took place in those two years, not in the 1980s.

44. *al-Hayat,* 27 April 1999. The release of 7,000 prisoners within two years after the end of the insurgency indicates that the state had arrested many people on the mere suspicion of being militants.

45. See HRW, "Egypt: Hostage-Taking and Intimidation by Security Forces" (January 1995).

46. The 19 April 1999 report was quoted in *al-Hayat,* 20 April 1999.

47. Agreements were signed with Russia, Greece, Argentina, South Africa, Uzbekistan, Pakistan, and a number of Arab countries. See *al-Hayat,* 28 December 1998, and *al-Wasat,* 18 January 1999.

48. For an interesting series of interviews with Egyptian Islamists recounting the story of their arrests and extradition from some of these countries, see *al-Hayat,* 22, 23, 24, and 27 March 1999.

49. *Hawla al-Muqif al-Rahin bayna al-Jama'a al-Islamiya wal-Nizam al-Misri.* The document is extensively quoted in Mubarak (1995: 396–398).

50. The document is quoted in *al-Hala al-Diniya fi Misr* (1995: 189).

51. The report is quoted in *al-Hayat,* 31 July 1999. Muntasir al-Ziyat, the prominent Islamist lawyer who defended the radicals during military trials, also argued that state repression—including repeated random arrests, torture, detainment of Islamists' relatives—after years of allowing Islamists to "peacefully" propagate their message was the reason for the expansion of violence (in Aamer 1995: 54–55).

52. These charges were made publicly at the highest levels, including by former interior minister Hasan al-Alfi (*al-Hayat,* 24 November 1995) and President Husni Mubarak (*al-Hayat,* 18 September 1996).

53. "Even More Dangerous in Kashmir," *The Economist,* 19 June 1999.

54. Asia Watch, "Human Rights in India: Kashmir Under Siege" (May 1991); Asia Watch, "Human Rights Crisis in Kashmir: A Pattern of Impunity" (June 1993); AI, "'An Unnatural Fate': Disappearances and Impunity in the Indian States of Jammu and Kashmir and Punjab" (December 1993).

55. AI, "Torture and Death in Custody" (January 1995); HRW, "India's Secret Army in Kashmir: New Patterns of Abuse Emerge in the Conflict" (May 1996).

56. HRW, "Behind the Kashmir Conflict: Abuses by Indian Security Forces and Militant Groups Continue" (July 1999).

57. In the 9 January 2002 *NYT* article, the story of Nazir Ahmed Khan, eighteen, highlights the deleterious impact of torture on ordinary individuals. "The teenager from the village ran off and joined Jaish-e-Muhammad after his father and older brother were arrested and tortured by the police, something that human rights groups say happens with alarming frequency."

58. HRW, "Russia's War in Chechnya: Victims Speak Out" (January 1995); HRW, "War in Chechnya: New Report from the Field" (January 1995); U.S. Committee for Refugees, *World Refugees Survey 2000: Country Report, Russian Federation.*

59. This view is supported by Dunlop (1998: 149), who writes, "it was only in mid-November 1994, when Russian military invasion of Chechnya

appeared increasingly likely, that Dudayev finally proposed that his self-declared independent republic of Chechnya become an Islamic state, introducing *sharia* law and forming an Islamic battalion to counter Russian aggression."

60. HRW, "'Welcome to Hell': Arbitrary Detention, Torture, and Extortion in Chechnya" (October 2000); HRW, "The 'Dirty War' in Chechnya: Forced Disappearances, Torture, and Summary Executions" (March 2001).

61. Quoted in Gall and Waal (1998: 259).

62. *NYT,* 20 October 2000; HRW, "World Report 2001" (5 October 2001).

63. HRW, "Human Rights in Tajikistan: In the Wake of Civil War" (December 1993).

64. AI, "Hidden Terror: Political Killings, 'Disappearances' and Torture Since December 1992" (May 1993); AI, "Human Rights Violations Against Opposition Activists" (October 1993); HRW, "Human Rights in Tajikistan: In the Wake of Civil War" (December 1993).

65. A. H. Richter, Testimony to the U.S. House of Representatives Foreign Affairs Committee, Subcommittee on Europe and Middle East, Washington, D.C., 22 September 1994.

66. *NYT,* 20 October 2000.

67. *NYT,* 3 May 2001; HRW, "World Report 2001"; International Crisis Group, "Central Asia: Islamist Mobilization and Regional Security" (1 March 2002).

4

Exclusive Organizations and Protracted Conflict

slamist rebellions often turn into protracted conflicts despite attempts by international mediators, state actors, and Islamist combatants to find peaceful resolutions to the violence. After years of rebellion and numerous peace initiatives, we continue to witness "residual" Islamist attacks in places like Algeria, Chechnya, Kashmir, the southern Philippines, and Tajikistan.

In this chapter I discuss how exclusive mobilization structures—the formal and informal organizational vehicles through which people engage in collective action—contribute to protracted violence in the Muslim world. Exclusive organizations are likely to thrive in exclusionary and highly repressive political environments that induce activists to seek protection from predatory state repression. However, these organizations, in turn, have an adverse impact on conflict resolution because they encourage competition among rival groups and facilitate the sabotage of peace efforts by more moderate leaders.

Inclusive Versus Exclusive Organizations

In their seminal 1966 article on movement organizations, Zald and Ash Garner (1987: 125–126) define an inclusive organization as one with relatively unrestricted criteria for membership. It usually "requires minimum levels of initial commitment—a pledge of general support without specific duties, a short indoctrination period, or none at all." An inclusive organization "typically requires little activity from its members—they can belong to other organizations and groups unselfconsciously, and

109

their behavior is not as permeated by organization goals, policies, and tactics."

In contrast, an exclusive organization is one that establishes strict criteria for membership. Only those who share a set of beliefs and meet a demanding standard of conduct are accepted as members. An exclusive organization usually "requires the recruit to subject himself to organization discipline and orders, and [draws] from those having the heaviest initial commitments." It not only "requires that a greater amount of energy and time be spent in movement affairs, but it more extensively permeates all sections of the member's life, including activities with non-members." According to Della Porta (1995b: 107), such organizations also "attempt to reduce the claims of competing roles and status positions on those they wish to encompass within their boundaries."

Exclusive organizations tend toward loosely structured groups that command their own resources and commanders. Although these groups may declare nominal allegiance to a leader, they usually "lack common, central leadership, organization and clear-cut procedures for deciding upon a common course of action" (Oberschall 1993: 67).

Repressive Environments
and Exclusive Mobilization Structures

Repressive political environments encourage exclusive, loosely structured mobilization structures. Movements in a repressive environment encounter several constraints they must overcome to be able to effect change. First, there is the problem of government infiltrators, informers, and agents provocateurs who threaten to discomfit the plans of movement groups and destroy the movement from within. To overcome this problem, movement organizations must find ways to recruit only trustworthy activists.

Second, there is the threat of movement decimation by a decisive blow from the security forces. Movements in a repressive environment accumulate material and organizational resources slowly and therefore must be careful not to lose them to state repression. To overcome this problem, movement organizations must find ways to absorb the inevitable blows of state repression without suffering disintegration (O'Neil 1990).

Finally, clandestine activities in repressive systems demand a high degree of group solidarity and cohesion; disunity and discord could bring about the loss of lives. The need to maintain secrecy when conducting movement activities increases the dependency of individual activists on one another. If one activist decides to defect, the whole organization is vulnerable to the defector's subsequent actions. As Crenshaw (1992: 32) explains, "the pressures toward cohesion and uniformity that exist in all primary groups are likely to be intensified under the circumstances of underground life." To overcome this constraint, movement organizations must find ways to forge group cohesion and reduce the possibility of defections.

Exclusive, loosely structured organizations help overcome the constraints generated by a repressive environment. Exclusive organizations that include only the like-minded and regulate the behavior of their activists—limiting their external ties and demanding adherence to a strict mode of conduct—aid in the development of committed activists and group cohesion. Organizers initially dip into the pool of relatives, friends, and neighbors with whom trust is already established (Lofland 1966; Snow et al. 1980; Della Porta 1988, 1992). These recruits are often required to engage in "bridge burning" acts to solidify their dependence on the group and make defection unlikely (Gerlach and Hine 1970).

Under these circumstances, each activist begins to identify his or her needs and interests with those of the group. This pattern has been observed in left-wing movements in Italy (Moss 1997) and the Shining Path movement in Peru (McClintock 1998). In both cases, frequent regulation of behavior created what Della Porta (1995a: 12) terms "spirals of encapsulation," whereby activists' links to the external world were all but completely cut off as intergroup ties matured. The unity of the group becomes bound to shared ideals and heightened emotional camaraderie (Crenshaw 1981; Post 1987).

Exclusive and loosely structured organizations, by breaking up members into smaller units or cells, ensure that the penetration of one group by government informers will not result in the demise of the organization as a whole. Laqueur (1987: 211) notes this type of organizational restructuring in the Provisional IRA that emerged in 1969 as a splinter group from the IRA. Organizationally, it was divided into large units headed by the "army council" and divided into companies, battalions, and brigades. However, after a number of damaging infiltrations, it was reorganized into smaller squads, each containing three to five militants. May (2001: 9) observed a similar pattern in the Campesino movement in Guatemala, where the "most obvious effect of [state-sponsored] violence on internal structure was a movement toward secrecy and clandestine organizations, and away from 'legal recognized' organizations."

Inclusive, formal, centralized organizations make easy targets under repressive systems. According to Koopmans (1993: 654), "Formal organizations make a movement's boundaries clear, its leaders identifiable and accountable, and its strategies more predictable." An organization with a clearly established hierarchy and central authority, once discovered, can be easily dismantled by the state; its leaders will be captured and its functional subsections disbanded. This is essentially what happened with the Peruvian Shining Path, which was a centralized, hierarchical organization firmly controlled by its leader Abimael Guzmón Reynoso (or Gonzalo). After the capture of Gonzalo in the early 1990s, the organization was effectively immobilized and suffered splits (McClintock 1998).

Exclusive Organizations and Protracted Violence

Social movements dominated by exclusive, loosely structured organizations are likely to experience protracted conflict. Exclusive organizations that produce spirals of encapsulation deprive activists of the opportunity to come across competing ideologies. Consequently, such organizations increasingly lose touch with political reality because the lack of countervailing influences denies the organization evaluative mechanisms by which to assess its performance and goals. As Post (1998: 33) explains: "Group pressures are especially magnified for the underground group, so that the group is the only source of information, the only source of confirmation, and, in the face of external danger and pursuit, the only source of security."

Spirals of encapsulation replace external affiliations with in-group associations; the "entrapped" activist increasingly relies on his "comrades" or "brothers" for evaluation. However, an exclusive group often "cannot afford an honest, self-critical appraisal of its theoretical premises and positions; questioning its theoretical assumptions would endanger the group's raison d'être and could activate a destabilizing effect on the group consciousness" (Wasmund 1986: 220). Under such circumstances, objective assessments of the political environment necessary for strategic calculations disappear; groups become increasingly driven by emotive and abstract appeals to justice and retribution (Crenshaw 1992, 1995; Apter 1997; Wieviorka 1997; Sprinzak 1998).

Even if movement leaders attempt to abandon rebellious strategies and reach an agreement with an opponent, they are likely to precipitate movement schisms. Oberschall (1993: 103–104) contends that an exclusive, loosely structured movement "speaks with many voices, each claiming to represent its constituency." Under these circumstances, the "recognition of some, but not other leaders and factions as legitimate spokesmen of the challenger may itself become an additional issue in the conflict, and sometimes becomes *the* principal issue."

Excluded groups will likely seek to undermine the "official" representatives of the movement through timely violence. A recent example of this dynamic is the 1998 bombing of the Omagh shopping center in Northern Ireland by an IRA splinter group calling itself the "Real IRA." The bombing was intended to sabotage negotiations between Sein Fein and the British government. Similar patterns have been observed time and again in the Palestinian-Israeli peace process since the early 1990s.

Loosely structured challengers tend to disperse their resources across the various units, making it difficult for leaders to enforce decisions on the movement's subcommanders. Given that each group is likely to possess its own leader, men, and arms, there is little to stop a group from refusing to abide by decisions deemed inappropriate by the central leadership. Under these circumstances, the state elite will not know exactly who commands the allegiance of the movement and therefore cannot be sure that concessions to an exclusive, loosely structured organization will result in concomitant concessions from the movement. As Gamson (1975: 95–96) concluded some time ago, "a group that had neither bureaucratic structure nor centralized power had very little chance of gaining acceptance [by the establishment]."

In short, protracted conflict is partly a product of exclusive, loosely structured organizations that make compromise through negotiations and concessions difficult. If the political environment encourages the diffusion of exclusive factions, the likelihood of protracted violence is high.

Exclusive Movements and Protracted Conflict in Algeria

The Islamist insurgency in Algeria turned into a protracted conflict despite efforts at crisis resolution since 1994 and a unilateral cease-fire declaration by the Islamic Salvation Army (AIS) in 1997. As the Islamist movement faced sustained political repression from 1992 onward, its mobilization structure became increasingly decentralized. In contrast to the previous period (1989–1991) when the Islamist movement was more or less organized within the Islamic Salvation Front (FIS), which served as an umbrella organization, Islamists after the military coup were divided and subdivided into numerous political and armed camps. In contrast to the FIS's inclusive membership criteria, the groups that formed after the coup became increasingly exclusive, accepting only those who strictly adhered to their views.

The FIS as an Inclusive Mobilizing Force

From 1989 to 1991, Islamist mobilization was more or less organized behind the FIS. Although there were fourteen other Islamist parties, the FIS was by far the most dominant.[1] The inclusive nature of the FIS facilitated its rapid expansion in the movement. The organization made room for less-committed activists. It divided its members into sympathizers, supporters, and activists. Only the active members had to abandon any association with other religious or political groups; to devote some of their time and energy to the activities of the organization, as well as contribute 5 percent of their monthly income to the organization; and to obey the commands of the leadership on order (Labat 1995: 187).

The FIS did not impose obstacles to the inclusion of other tendencies and leaderships in the Islamist movement; its only rule for alliances was that whoever joins the FIS must do so as an individual promoting the broad aims of the organization, not as a representative of other groups.[2] The FIS did reject a broader Islamic alliance with Harakat al-Mujtama al-Islami (HAMAS) and the Mouvement de la Nahda Islamique (MNI) because they saw the latter two as competitors; instead, the FIS insisted on unity under its own banner.[3] Yet despite the refusal to unite with HAMAS and MNI, the FIS remained an inclusive organization as evinced by the composition of its consultative council, which incorporated various tendencies—Salafiyya,[4] Jazaira,[5] Algerian "Afghans," Takfir wal-Hijra,[6] and former Bouyali activists (Labat 1995; al-Tawil 1998). As Rouadjia (1995: 74–75) put it, "the FIS must be considered, in light of experience, as a melting-pot for very diverse factions which have little more in common than Islam and the desire to put an end to a political situation in Algeria."

The inclusive nature of the FIS was dictated by its electoral strategy during the period of political openness. Inclusive membership criteria based on broadly framed Islamist goals did not force movement activists to commit themselves to one group or another. Inclusive organizing allowed the FIS to expand the number of cadres who could help organize its campaigns. A strict membership criterion would have challenged the loyalties of Islamist voters and would have split the movement into numerous factions to accommodate each tendency. As Labat (1994: 105) explained, "The different elements of the party, not having arrived at an understanding as to a precise plan, seem to have chosen a 'least common denominator,' as the only means to bringing them together."

The Rise of the GIA

The inclusiveness of the FIS-dominated movement gave way to fragmentation as Islamists were forced underground in 1992. The militancy of the radical groups, especially the Groupe Islamique Armé (GIA), proved to be attractive to many Islamists in a context of increasing government obstinacy and repression. During 1993 and 1994 the ranks of the GIA steadily grew, not only in the center where it emerged, but also in the western regions of the country (Labat 1995: 308–309).

The radicals, however, did not create an inclusive, centralized organization. Initially, they consisted of small cells of militants who took the initiative to organize themselves for attacks on state institutions and personnel. During 1992 and 1993 they operated in urban centers without overall direction.[7] Although some of the historic leaders of the militant wing made attempts to unify their ranks in a series of meetings in 1992—and were on the verge of doing so in September 1992—fear that other groups might be infiltrated with government agents led some to opt for autonomy (Willis 1996: 268–274; al-Tawil 1998: 104–108). Instead, by the end of 1992 several armed groups emerged—the Islamic State Movement (MEI),[8] the Armed Islamic Movement (MIA),[9] the Islamic Front for Armed Jihad (FIDA),[10] and the GIA.

The growth of the GIA between 1993 and 1994 did not signify greater coordination and control of the armed struggle. The GIA operated as a conglomeration of armed militias dispersed over at least nine zones, each of which was under an appointed *amir* (commander).[11] These militias carried titles such as al-Muhajeroun (the Exiles), al-Furqan (the Holy Quran), al-Itisam (Preservation), al-Shuhada (the Martyrs), al-Istiqama (Uprightness), al-Huda wal-Nur (Guidance and Light), al-Rahman (the Merciful), al-Fateh (the Conquest), al-Rabaniyya (the Divine), al-Haq (the Truth), and al-Muwaqaoun bi-Dima (Those Who Sign with Blood). The size of each of these groups ranged from 20 to 300 militants, led by a commander who was nominally committed to the central leadership.[12]

The structure of the GIA was not based on a system of cells and sectors; rather, it was made up of roaming armed bands, many of whom took refuge in the mountains, where they set up camps in caves and constructed underground tunnel systems for shelter, safe havens, and arms and supply caches. These groups constantly shifted their positions to avoid detection, and if a member of a pack went missing for more than a day, the group would decamp and move to another location.[13]

These groups did not take instructions from the central leadership, other than perhaps a general declaration ordering militants to begin attacking foreigners, for instance. Instead, each group made its own decisions concerning what, when, and where to attack. As subsequent developments proved, when a group did not approve the policies or actions of the central leadership, it declared itself independent of the national commander or pledged its allegiance to another armed group.[14]

The merger of some MEI and FIS leaders with the GIA in May 1994 appeared to produce an inclusive movement. Other FIS leaders, however, rejected this union and formed the Armée Islamique du Salut (AIS).[15] The unity under the banner of the GIA and declared allegiance to Cherif Gousmi, the organization's fourth commander, was based on strict criteria. All the parties involved had to adhere to the Salafiyya tradition and abandon any "innovations."[16] The first article of the unification communiqué declared that the GIA, FIS, and MEI have agreed "to abide by the Book (Quran), the Sunna (traditions of the Prophet) and the Salafiyya tradition" (al-Tawil 1998: 152).

This declaration was a departure from FIS's 1989 political program, which did not declare the FIS to be a Salafiyya party. The opening line of the section entitled "Description of the Islamic Salvation Front" states, "[The FIS] works to unite the ranks of Islamists and preserve the unity of the [Muslim] community." Throughout its program there were no references to the Salafiyya or "righteous forefathers" (al-salaf al-salih). Instead, references were invariably to the Quran and the sayings of the Prophet, something all Islamists would find acceptable.[17]

The exclusive orientation of the GIA was manifested in its behavior toward other opposition groups that did not join its movement. The GIA refused any unity with the political wing of the FIS and made it clear that it was not the FIS's armed wing.[18] Despite symbolically appointing Abassi and Belhaj to its consultative council, the GIA unequivocally opposed the electoral strategy of the FIS and insisted that any unity with the group had to be based on a renunciation of elections, parliaments, and democracy.

When it became clear that the FIS was not going to abandon its demand for a return to the electoral process, the GIA completely broke with it. On 4 May 1995, it issued a communiqué declaring that AIS leaders had one month to get in touch with the GIA to repent and join its ranks.[19] Shortly after, the GIA issued an explicit threat against eight FIS leaders demanding they cease speaking in the name of the Islamist movement.[20] Finally, on 13 June 1995 the GIA issued a communiqué entitled "An Open Letter to Abassi Madani and Ali Belhaj," in which it ousted Abbasi and Belhaj from its consultative council and permitted "the shedding of the blood of those 'blood merchants' inside and outside [Algeria] unless they repent."[21]

The GIA also excluded armed groups that rejected democracy but did not completely adhere to its Salafiyya orientation. In 1995, Jamal Zitouni issued a pamphlet entitled "Hidayat Rab al-Alamin" (The Guidance of the Lord) in which he rejected any alliance with groups such as Hizb al-Tahrir and the Takfir wal Hijra, all of whom are considered radical groups by many Islamists.[22] Zitouni went on to specify the following GIA membership rules: a member had to adopt the Salafiyya tradition; obey the commander on demand; and repent if he at one point or another belonged to the FIS, AIS, HAMAS, MNI, Takfir wal Hijra, the Muslim Brotherhood, the Jazaira, or secular parties.

The pamphlet went on to state that former FIS members who wanted to join the GIA had to "proclaim the banner of the [FIS] a polytheist, democratic banner; repent from political, electoral and democratic activities; and declare their innocence from all calls for dialogue with the apostate tyrants [i.e., the regime]." Those who at one point belonged to Takfir and non-Islamist groups had to sever all ties with them and their members as well as provide information on their activities. Any imam (prayer leader or cleric) who sought entry into the GIA had to "issue a religious edict (fatwa) to motivate jihad." Finally, those who wanted to leave the GIA were considered either apostates, defectors, opportunists, or potential informers and corrupters. Whatever the case, their punishment was death.

The Rise of the AIS

The May 1994 unification of some armed groups under the banner of the GIA was rejected by FIS leadership in prison and abroad as well as by its unofficial armed wing, the AIS. In the following two months the FIS decided to officially declare the formation of its armed wing largely to win back its supporters and offer an alternative to the GIA (Burgat and Dowell 1997: 321–322; al-Tawil 1998: 167–172; Hafez 2000a).

Similar to the GIA, the AIS was a relatively decentralized armed group. The formation of the AIS initially consisted of unifying the armed groups that were loyal to the FIS in the western regions. After the GIA's unification declaration, the AIS declared the formation of the "Western Military Committee" in June 1994 and appointed Ahmed Bin Aicha as its commander. The following month, armed groups loyal to the FIS in the eastern region declared the formation of the AIS "Eastern Military Committee" with Madani Mezraq as its commander. On 18 July 1994, the committees issued a joint communiqué declaring the unification of the eastern and western committees under the joint leadership of Mezraq and Bin Aicha. In March 1995, Mezraq was appointed national commander of the AIS.[23]

The AIS divided Algeria into at least three zones—east, center, and west—and appointed a commander to lead each zone.[24] Moreover, similar to the GIA, the AIS consisted of roving bands of approximately 50–200 militants who took refuge in mountains or "liberated zones." The AIS was not based on a system of sectors and cells, and it is not clear to what extent the individual groups made their own decisions concerning operations. In any case, by 1994 there were at least two sizable armed groups competing for the loyalty of Islamists. The GIA was acknowledged to be the dominant group in terms of numerical support, but the AIS also commanded thousands of supporters.[25]

The FIS and AIS quickly moved to regain hegemony in the Islamist movement. The AIS issued a number of open letters in which it denounced the violence of the GIA and called on armed groups to rally behind the FIS and its armed wing. In one letter, Madani Mezraq urged the holy fighters to join the AIS to wage a jihad that is legitimate, with clear contours and limited objectives. He also urged them to beware of those elements that excommunicate people without foundation or evidence. In an implicit criticism of the GIA's increasingly daring attacks, he reminded the holy fighters that jihad is not suicide, nor is it revenge, adventurism, anarchy, or blind zeal. In another letter that condemns violence against civilians, he states "we fight among men, we do not kill the old, women, or children."[26]

GIA's War Against the Other Armed Groups

Competition between the GIA and AIS resulted in an open war between the armed groups. The AIS initially avoided organizing in the middle of the country, where the GIA was dominant, for fear of sparking confrontation. As FIS leader Abderlkarim Ghamati explains, "The AIS formed an initial organization of approximately fifty individuals in the middle, but the [GIA] threatened to kill them. [Therefore,] we decided not to open the door of battle with [the GIA]."[27]

Azzedin Ba'a, one of the leaders of the MEI who refused to unify ranks with the GIA in May 1994, was killed by the GIA in June 1995.[28] In the following month, the GIA executed one of the original founders of the FIS, Abedlbaqi Sahroui, in a Paris mosque.[29] These two executions were not isolated incidents. There were repeated reports in 1995 of clashes between the GIA and AIS, resulting in the deaths of approximately sixty militants (Willis 1996: 353). After a series of warnings and threats, the GIA explicitly declared war on the AIS on 4 January 1996.[30] Later that month, sources close to the FIS Executive Body Abroad (under Rabeh Kebir) accused the GIA of slaying 140 FIS activists, including 40 commanders.[31]

The GIA also turned on itself as the insurgency developed. In July 1995, Abdelrazak Rejjam and Yousuf Boubras, both former FIS leaders who joined the GIA in 1994, withdrew their group from the GIA after accusing the group of killing the innocent and abducting women.[32] In the same year, the GIA executed approximately one hundred Takfir wal Hijra militants allegedly for refusing to abandon their violence against civilians and "innovations."[33] In November 1995, the GIA executed Muhammad Said, Abdelrazak Rejjam, and others for supposedly seeking to take over the movement and change its Salafiyya orientation.[34]

These executions led many of the groups that constituted the GIA to split. In November and December 1995, al-Rabita al-Islamiyya lil Dawa wa al-Jihad (LIDD) and Larbaa militia declared their independence from the GIA.[35] In January 1996, al-Salafiyya militia also withdrew its support for the GIA.[36] Said Mekhloufi threatened to wage a full-scale war against the GIA if it did not release MEI militants it held captive.[37] Other groups—al-Rabaniyya, al-Shuhada, al-Haq—departed in the beginning of 1996.[38] In July 1996, Zitouni was killed in a trap set by former GIA militants, possibly in revenge for the killing of Said and Rejjam (al-Rasi 1997: 475).

Splits continued well into 1998 as other militias opted to form independent groups, including al-Jama'a al-Salafiyya lil-Dawa wal-Qital (Groupe Salafiste pour la Prédication et le Combat, GSPC), which is one of the most active militant groups in Algeria today.[39] Thus, as the insurgency developed, the armed movement became even more exclusive and decentralized.

A Fragmented Political Movement

In addition to a fragmented armed movement, the political movement splintered into competing camps. The coup and subsequent arrest of the remaining FIS leadership resulted in multiple centers of authority and opened the door for leadership competition. The FIS developed at least five leadership centers: (1) the imprisoned leadership of Abassi Madani, Ali Belhaj, and Abdelkader Hachani; (2) the "crisis cell" and FIS Provisional National Executive Bureau (FIS-PNEB inside Algeria); (3) the FIS Executive Bureau Abroad (FIS-EBA); (4) the FIS Parliamentary Delegation Abroad (FIS-PDA); and, of course, (5) the FIS's armed wing, the AIS (FIS-AIS).

Although the historic leaders of the FIS were in prison, their orders carried weight in the movement and their consent regarding any reconciliation agreement was necessary to give legitimacy to the process. The "crisis cell" and FIS-PNEB were formed in the period between the first round of parliamentary elections and the coup. Suspecting that the military was about to intervene in the electoral process, FIS leaders met to appoint a collective leadership to function as a decisionmaking cell in case of government repression.[40] The cell was responsible for formulating FIS decisions and drafting its communiqués, which were issued and signed by Abdelrazak Rejjam as the official representative of the FIS-PNEB (Mus'ad 1995: 231; al-Tawil 1998: 96–98; Qawas 1998: 163). Many of these leaders came to be known as the internal leadership of the FIS because they operated inside Algeria, sometimes within the armed groups themselves. Some of the prominent representatives from the FIS-PNEB—Muhammad Said, Abdelrazak Rejjam, Yousuf Boubras—joined the GIA in May 1994.

As for the FIS-EBA, it was created in the summer of 1993 as a way to unify the ranks of FIS leaders and create a single voice for the movement. A conference among FIS leaders was held in Tirana, Algeria, to appoint the members of the FIS-EBA. Rabeh Kebir was unanimously voted president of the new body while Abdallah Ans, Qameredin Kharban, and Anwar Haddam were appointed as his deputies.[41] Kebir represented a pragmatic orientation, while his deputies were more militant (al-Tawil 1998: 137–141).

Anwar Haddam headed the fourth leadership camp, the FIS-PDA. Haddam claimed to represent FIS parliamentarians elected in 1991 in an official capacity. Although the Tirana conference clearly empowered Kebir as the official representative of the FIS abroad, this did not prevent

Haddam from speaking on behalf of the FIS and challenging Kebir's authority on several occasions. A clear example of this insubordination was exhibited in the aftermath of the May 1994 defections of FIS-PNEB members to the GIA. These defections received the support of Anwar Haddam, much to the chagrin of Kebir, who was promoting the unification of the AIS.[42]

The FIS-AIS, as indicated earlier, was created to compete with the GIA for the loyalty of militants, in order to give the political wing of the FIS bargaining power vis-à-vis the regime. However, despite regular communication between the FIS and AIS, the latter operated independently when it came to military operations.[43] By 1994 the FIS leadership was effectively fragmented. These five centers of authority, as we shall see shortly, resulted in divergent declarations that made negotiations with the authorities difficult.

The Failure of Peace Initiatives

The exclusive and decentralized mobilization structure of the Islamist movement guaranteed that the task of conflict resolution was going to be an arduous one. The expansion of the radical wing after the election's cancellation posed a serious problem to the FIS. Although the FIS was just as determined as the GIA not to succumb to state repression, it was not entirely opposed to the idea of compromise in order to resolve the crisis. The FIS was willing to negotiate with the state and proffered demands to end the crisis: release of political prisoners, including the leadership of the FIS; rehabilitation of the FIS as a legitimate political party; and the reinstitution of the electoral process.[44] Although these demands were a tall order for the military regime, they nonetheless indicated a willingness to reach a deal through dialogue and negotiations.

The expansion of the radical wing, especially the GIA, would not have been problematic for the FIS had the GIA agreed to pursue FIS aims. The GIA, however, was bent on a total war with the state and rejected any compromise, including the return to the democratic process. In short, the problem for the FIS was that the bargaining chip of armed struggle fell into the hands of those who did not wish to bargain. In order for the FIS to win back its supporters and exert pressure on the regime, it had to compete with the GIA by offering activists a less radical, but nonetheless more effective, option than total war. It had to show that compromise had its rewards.

Overview of Peace Initiatives, 1994–1995

The first negotiations took place in February and March 1994. In February 1994, two FIS leaders—Ali Jeddi and Abdelkader Boukhamkham—were released from prison. Shortly after, Zeroual dismissed two eradicators from the government—Redha Malek and Salim Saadi. In return, Zeroual demanded a call for cease-fire from the released leaders. However, the FIS refused to make such a call until other leaders were released from prison, the Sahara detention centers were closed, and the party was relegalized.[45] The regime rejected the FIS's demands, and the initiative failed.

The second attempt at negotiations met a similar fate. Abassi sent two letters to Zeroual in August 1994 expressing, inter alia, the FIS's commitment to party pluralism and alternation of power through elections. However, the letters added that the military must be removed from politics; the FIS must be recognized; the state of emergency must be lifted; military operations against insurgents must be stopped; political prisoners must be given general amnesty; and the regime must set up a neutral interim government to oversee new elections. The letter stated that it was necessary to give imprisoned FIS leaders the freedom to consult with each other and with leaders in the military field.[46]

Although these were stringent demands, Zeroual transferred Abassi and Belhaj to house arrest and freed three other FIS leaders—Abdelkader Omar, Nureddin Shiqara, and Kamal Qamazi—in September 1994. But that is as far as the process went. Zeroual insisted that the FIS call for a cease-fire, while the FIS insisted that it be allowed to consult the leaders inside Algeria and abroad.[47] After a series of meetings that lasted until October, Zeroual declared the dialogue a failure.[48]

The third round of negotiations fared no better. Abassi, again, sent letters to Zeroual in April 1995 calling for a political solution based on the withdrawal of the military from politics; political pluralism and peaceful alternation of power through elections; rehabilitation of the FIS; cancellation of the state of emergency and amnesty to all political prisoners; and formation of an interim government to oversee new elections, among other demands.[49]

Zeroual responded to this initiative by allowing Abassi to meet other FIS leaders, and he sent his personal aide, General Muhammed Betchin, to work out a compromise. The government even produced a "Document of Principles" that Abassi agreed to in prenegotiation discussions. The document put forward the government position, which declared that the regime aimed to construct a sovereign state and a democratic republic within the framework of Islamic principles. To achieve this goal, the government advanced a number of principles by which all parties must abide: violence must not be used as a method to reach power; the republican and democratic character of the state must be upheld; Islam must be above all party considerations and political bidding; individual and group rights must be respected; democracy, political pluralism, and alternation of power must be affirmed; and the military must be removed from politics and party competition.[50]

The government document, however, did not respond to the FIS's principal demand for the legalization of the party. In response, the FIS put forward its own document that comprised principles and procedures to end the crisis. The principles advanced by the FIS included: Islam is the religion of the Algerian state; the 1989 constitution is the appropriate constitutional framework for the state; political pluralism and the people's right to choose its rulers must be respected; alternation of power through elections must be guaranteed; force as a means to power must be rejected; and the military must be removed from politics.

As for the necessary procedures to achieve the aforementioned principles, the FIS document stated that the political ban on the FIS and the state of emergency must be lifted; consultation among all those whose participation is necessary to make important decisions must be permitted; and all who were harmed during the crisis must be compensated. It also demanded that all prisoners must be released; a neutral government must be appointed to organize new elections; and the effective leadership of the FIS must be freed (al-Tawil 1998: 315–319).

This exchange of documents did not go any further, however, because the regime refused to release FIS leaders from prison until they declared a cease-fire.[51] The FIS insisted that a declaration of a cease-fire would come only after its leaders were released.[52] The regime found this demand unacceptable, and the dialogue was declared a failure.

The Failure of the First Round of Negotiations

Why did the FIS leadership not compromise by declaring a cease-fire before consulting with other leaders in the movement? Why did it insist on the release of jailed leaders prior to a call for a cease-fire? It is difficult to answer these questions with certainty, but one could reasonably argue that the divisions within the FIS and expansion of the radical wing meant that a cease-fire declaration without guarantees of major concessions was not likely to produce a cease-fire, thus highlighting FIS's inability to control the armed movement.

During the first round of negotiations, the FIS was divided over what concessions to make. By 1993, representatives of the FIS-PNEB—Muhammed Said and Abdelrazzak Rejjam—opted for a more militant route than Kebir would have wanted. Rejjam initially set conditions for dialogue in March 1992.[53] By November 1993, however, he declared the "FIS rejects dialogue or reconciliation with the putschist tyranny. . . . We shall not accept any alternative to the Islamic state."[54]

In that same month, Belhaj sent a letter to the Independent Dialogue Committee rejecting any dialogue with the military-organized National Dialogue Commission (scheduled to meet in January 1994) because "those who pushed the country toward destruction, corruption, and devastation cannot be part of reconciliation or agreement." He went on to set conditions for "real" reconciliation, including bringing to justice those responsible for the coup, invalidating all measures taken since the cancellation of the elections, and organizing a televised conference among the major political parties—including the FIS (Belhaj 1994: 157–158).

Rabeh Kebir took a different line in December 1993 by issuing a set of conditions for dialogue with the National Dialogue Commission. While repeating Belhaj's demands for punishing those responsible for human rights violations and canceling all decisions taken since the coup, Kebir dropped the demand to uphold the results of the December 1991 elections.[55]

These divergent demands indicate that, by the first round of negotiations, the FIS leadership needed to get its house in order before it could make a decision for the armed movement as a whole. A conciliatory position by Abassi would not have been respected without the support of Belhaj, who commanded the allegiance of some of the radicals. Just as important, given that by 1994 the Islamist insurgency was in full force and the regime was not successful in winning the support of the FLN and FFS for the exclusion of the Islamists, FIS leaders were not likely to convince the militants to settle for anything less than full rehabilitation of the party and reinstitution of the electoral process. Indeed, the insurgency allowed imprisoned leaders to make substantial demands, especially since the maximalist GIA had not yet united other armed groups under its banner.

However, FIS demands in the first round of negotiations were too much for the eradicators in the military regime, whose consent was essential for any deal to hold up. One primary purpose behind the coup was to deny the FIS legislative power. FIS demands not only implied that the coup and dissolution of the FIS were illegitimate, they also threatened to bring back a process that clearly benefited the FIS the most. The eradicators held commanding positions in the military and were certainly in a position to sabotage any substantial concessions. Zeroual, who was appointed by the military regime, could not make a decision that would split the military in the course of an insurgency.

Zeroual needed the FIS to make a call for a cease-fire and a reduction in violence to strengthen his hand vis-à-vis the eradicators. The FIS, however, could not oblige him. Consequently, the first round of negotiations failed.

The Failure of the Second and Third Rounds of Talks

By the time of the second and third rounds of negotiation, the MEI, FIDA, and some members of the FIS-PNEB had defected to the GIA and received the support of Haddam, the head of FIS-PDA. In order to be able to compete with the GIA for the loyalty of Islamists in the movement, the FIS had to declare officially the formation of its armed wing. Thus, the FIS was already on the defensive by mid-1994 and could not make a decision that could potentially drive more of its supporters into the arms of the GIA.

Just as important, the unification of the armed groups under the GIA meant that the FIS could not make a decision without a commitment from these groups to heed the call for a cease-fire. As Mortimer (1996: 34) put it, "The political leaders of the FIS could ill afford to give an order that the armed insurgents would ignore." An unobserved call for a cease-fire would have sealed FIS's fate as a negotiator; the regime would not have made concessions to a party that had little influence over the armed movement.

Even if the FIS was willing to make major concessions and Zeroual was willing to respond in kind by exerting pressure on hard-liners, GIA violence strengthened the position of the eradicators in the regime by allowing them to argue that any deal with the FIS was destined to be mere ink on paper. The GIA was aware of FIS attempts at reconciliation. Some of its declarations and activities were timed to sabotage any deal in the making and clarify to all concerned that agreements would not put an end to the GIA's violence. The second article of its May 1994 unification communiqué made it a point to declare "no dialogue, no cease-fire, no reconciliation, and no security and guarantee (dhimma) with this apostate regime." The communiqué further declared that "the GIA is the only legitimate organization for jihad in Algeria" and "all mujahedin must join the GIA."[56]

By making these claims, the GIA was sending a clear signal that it would not abide by the orders of any other group, including the FIS. The GIA repeated the "no dialogue, no cease-fire" declaration in a communiqué issued on 13 September 1994, a day after Abassi was released from prison in preparation for negotiations. This time the communiqué added that whoever recognizes an apostate is an apostate.[57]

In addition to its declarations, the GIA did not relent in its violence during times of negotiation. On the contrary, "daily attacks on military, police and civilian targets increased proportionally concurrent with attempts at a political dialogue with the FIS."[58] Islamist violence allowed the eradicators in the regime to argue, not without warrant, that any deal with the FIS would not halt the crisis. The fighting between the GIA and AIS gave additional credence to the claims of the hard-liners.[59]

By the start of the second and third rounds of negotiations, the rejectionist GIA weakened the FIS's bargaining position by allowing the eradicators to challenge the efficacy of negotiations. The only way the FIS could overcome its weak position was to try to establish a single voice for the movement behind the historic leadership through conferences with its political and field leaders. As Kebir put it, "A simple appeal for a truce, even if it comes from Abassi, will not stop the bloodshed. We must gather together all our cadres in both political positions and in the armed groups" (quoted in Willis 1996: 337). But this demand implied the recognition of the FIS and its legitimacy as a political actor on the scene. Such a recognition (whether de facto or de jure) by Zeroual had to be negotiated with the eradicators, who were opposed to any compromise that promised to legitimize the FIS and its leaders.

The best that Zeroual could do to win concessions from the eradicators was to have the FIS call for a cease-fire and see if the armed groups were willing to abide by it. If armed groups agreed to a cease-fire, then the position of the conciliators would have been strengthened vis-à-vis the eradicators and further negotiations may have produced some form of political inclusion. However, as in the first negotiations, the cease-fire call prior to major concessions was unacceptable to the FIS. The hard-liners in the regime used the hard-liners in the armed movement to hinder serious compromise; the conciliators on each side could not act without the effective consent of the hard-liners.

By 1996, Zeroual appeared to have accepted the position of the eradicators by refusing to engage the FIS in any dialogue; he simply demanded that the FIS declare a cease-fire in exchange for amnesty. In 1997 the AIS agreed to call for a cease-fire without any substantial concessions from the regime. The deal was negotiated between Madani Mezraq, the commander of the AIS, and General Ismail Lamari. It did not involve the political leadership of the FIS.[60] As Boukhamkham simply put it, "We were not contacted at all by the authorities."[61]

The decentralization of the armed movement meant that the Islamist movement developed exclusive organizations and spoke with many voices. Dialogue and negotiations could not produce concessions, despite the willingness of some of the combatants to resolve the crisis, because each side of the conflict was constrained by its hard-liners. Moreover, the consolidation of exclusive groups with radical worldviews meant that political initiatives were not likely to end the violence unless these initiatives conceded to the major demands of Islamists. Consequently, no resolution was reached.

Political Exclusion and Protracted Conflict After 1997

The exclusion of the FIS continues well into the 2000s and contributes to the persistent violence that plagues Algeria to this day. In April 1999, Abdelaziz Bouteflika was elected president after six other candidates withdrew in protest of what they saw as predetermined elections. Despite the controversy, FIS and AIS leaders Abassi Madani, Rabeh Kebir, and Madani Mezraq supported Bouteflika's presidency. On 4 June 1999, Mezraq sent a letter to the new president reaffirming the AIS's commitment to "end the crisis and stop the bloodbath." In response, Bouteflika issued a statement promising to give Mezraq's "courageous initiative legal foundations."[62] A few days later, Abassi sent a letter to Bouteflika supporting the efforts of Mezraq. In addition, the FIS made public for the first time a letter issued by Abassi to the armed groups on 5 June 1998 in which he called on them to cease their insurgency and support the AIS's 1997 cease-fire.[63]

In July 1999, the Algerian parliament adopted the Law of Civil Concord (al-Wi'am al-Madani) at the urging of the newly elected president. The law extended amnesty on a case-by-case basis to rebels whose hands were not soiled with blood and who had not raped women or placed bombs in public places. The law also promised to reduce the sentences of those convicted of any of the aforementioned crimes, with the maximum sentence not exceeding twelve years. The law did not affect the AIS, which benefited from a general amnesty due to its 1997 cease-fire.[64] According to government figures, 4,200 AIS rebels took advantage of the general amnesty, and 22 GIA militias comprising approximately 800 rebels agreed to abide by the cease-fire.[65]

The FIS and AIS hoped that the Law of Civil Concord would be a step toward a lasting political solution that would reintegrate Islamists into the political process (even under a party other than the FIS). However, it did not take long for their hopes to be dashed. On 22 November 1999, an unknown gunman assassinated Abdelkader Hachani, who had engineered FIS's electoral victory in 1991. In an interview with *al-Wasat* few days later, Bouteflika made it clear that there was no chance of the FIS returning to the political arena.[66] Since that time, negotiations between the FIS/AIS and the state have not resumed, and the authorities have rejected the legalization of the Wafa Party, which is led by Ahmed Taleb Ibrahimi and is believed to be the heir to the FIS. Although other Islamist parties exist, ex-FIS leaders are prohibited from participating in them.[67]

The AIS unilateral cease-fire and the Law of Civil Concord did not bring violence to an end.[68] In fact, it exposed the extent to which the FIS had been fragmented. While Abassi, Hachani, and Kebir gave their support to the cease-fire, Belhaj continued to withhold his.[69] Some FIS activists abroad have shifted their support to non-GIA armed groups that did not abide by the cease-fire, including al-Baqoun ala Ahd (Those Committed to the Covenant) and al-Jama'a al-Salafiya lil-Dawa wal-Qital.[70] Ahmed al-Zawi and Qameredin Kharbane, both former members of the FIS-EBA, along with Abdallah Ans continue to voice their opposition to the cease-fire through the FIS Coordination Council (FIS-CC), which was created in 1996 to compete with the FIS-EBA.

Many ex-FIS supporters who rejected the cease-fire claim that they have been vindicated by the failure of the Law of Civil Concord, which they argue has turned into a mere "police measure" as opposed to a political alternative to violence and repression. The eradicators within the Algerian military and government, they argue, insist on treating Islamists as representatives of a defeated movement that must accept surrender, not as interlocutors who can play a legitimate role in Algeria's political future.[71]

On 8 February 2002, Algeria's security forces succeeded in killing Antar Zouabri, the sixth commander of the GIA. Under his leadership, Algeria witnessed countless massacres of civilians. His death, however, did not bring about an end to violence. On the contrary, his successor, al-Rashid Abu Turab (his real name is Awkali Rashid), issued a communiqué promising more "blood and blood, destruction and destruction."[72] Random bombings and massacres intensified in the following months.[73] On 5 July 2002, as Algeria celebrated the fortieth anniversary of its independence, a powerful bomb killed thirty-eight people and injured eighty in a Larbaa market south of Algiers.

Exclusive Movements and Protracted Conflict in Egypt

Similar to Algeria, the Islamist insurgency in Egypt turned into a protracted conflict. Attempts at a resolution of the crisis at different junctures and decisive blows against Islamists in the mid-1990s failed to bring the insurgency to a halt. It was only in the late months of 1997, five years after the opening shots of the insurgency in 1992 and ten years since the resurgence of Islamist violence in 1987, that the radical wing declared a unilateral cease-fire.

The Mobilization Structure of Radical Islamists

By 1992 the militant Islamist movement consisted of exclusive, loosely structured organizations that established strict criteria for membership, regulated the behavior of their activists, and distributed decisionmaking powers along various organizational nodes. This was especially the case with al-Jama'a al-Islamiya, the largest and most active militant group during the insurgency.

The Jama'a did not emerge as an exclusive organization in the 1970s, when it first appeared on university campuses. On the contrary, it was an organization that placed few obstacles to membership and made few demands on its members. It was open to all Muslim students on the condition that they abide by Islamic behavior and uphold their religious obligations such as praying five times a day. Members also had to memorize the Quran and some of the prophetic sayings. However, they did not have to sever ties with other groups, adopt clandestine names, or pay dues. As Kepel (1984: 148) points out, the members of the Jama'a "were recruited on a minimalist Islamist basis and in which indoctrination lacked the intensity to which [the leader of the radical Takfir group] subjected his members."

The persistent lack of meaningful political access during the late 1970s and the crackdown on Islamists between 1979 and 1981 resulted in a split within the Jama'a movement. In 1979, some of the more radical Jama'a branches began seeking the political and ideological guidance of organized militant groups. They found it during the summer of 1980 in the inchoate Jihad group, headed by Abdel Salam Faraj.[74] This union did not last, however, as the Jihad group split into the Jama'a, headed by the blind preacher Omar Abdel Rahman, and the Jihad al-Islami, headed by the Jihad group's imprisoned military planner, Aboud Zumur.

The main reason for the split was the divergent organizational orientations of the two tendencies that constituted the Jihad group in 1980. The Jama'a tendency wanted to build a mass movement through public preaching and direct action, especially "forbidding vice" activities. The Jihad group, on the other hand, believed that "forbidding vice" brought undue attention and repression to activists and depleted the resources and energy of the movement. It wanted to form a disciplined clandestine organization capable of launching a decisive strike (or a coup) against the state.[75]

Despite its goal of building a mass movement, the Jama'a during the 1980s developed strict membership criteria. In the 1980s they chided the Muslim Brotherhood (MB) for demanding from it members "no more than adherence to Islam in its widest meaning, that is the mere utterance of the two [obligatory Islamic] confessions" (Mubarak 1995: 222). Furthermore, whereas the Jama'a in the 1970s had its members read the Quran and the sayings of the Prophet (something all Muslims would find unobjectionable), in the 1980s their indoctrination entailed reading the works of the *salafi* scholars Ibn Taymiya and Ibn Hanbal, as well as contemporary Islamist ideologues Abu ala Mawdudi and Sayid Qutb.

Once recruits reached a certain level of indoctrination, they were given the published works of the Jama'a, including their key work *Mithaq al-'Amal al-Islami* (The Manifesto of Islamic Activism). Moreover, in contrast to the 1970s when it was sufficient for Jama'a members to engage only in some of the group's functions, in the 1980s Jama'a members were extensively involved in the movement's activities, as they were obliged to show complete obedience and subordination to the commanders.

Finally, the Jama'a did not only reject the MB and refuse alliances with secular parties, it also condemned other radical groups—especially the Takfir wal Hijra strand—because they did not strictly adhere to its view concerning the nature of the prevailing social order in Muslim societies (Mustapha 1992: 164–166). The Jama'a also did not cooperate with the Jihad group despite the ideological affinity between them.[76]

The Jama'a had two command centers in the 1980s. The first was in Tara prison, where some of its historic leaders, including Karam Zuhdi, Najih Ibrahim, Asim Abdel Majid, Aisam Darabalah, and Ali al-Sharif, were incarcerated for life. The other consisted of leaders outside of prison—Ahmed Abduh Salim (commander in Asyut), Ali al-Dinari (commander in al-Minya), Husni Mahmoud (commander in Souhaj), and Ahmed Abdel Rahman (commander in Ain Shems). Omar Abdel Rahman was the general commander and spiritual leader of the Jama'a.

Decisions taken at a national level had to be approved by the majority of the national consultative council. However, decisions concerning the regions, districts, or specific mosques had only to be approved by the majority of the regional, district, or mosque consultative councils. Any legal Islamic decree (fatwa) had to be approved by Abdel Rahman.

In sum, the organizational structure of the Jama'a in the 1980s combined hierarchy with decentralization—leadership roles were clearly defined, but decisionmaking was dispersed along the four levels of organization: nation, region, district, and mosque.

Radical Fragmentation During the 1980s and 1990s

In the 1980s both the Jihad and Jama'a groups suffered splits. New, even smaller and more localized factions emerged with such names as Najiun min al-Nar (Survivors from Hell Fire), al-Shawqiun (after their leader Shawqi al-Sheikh), al-Samawiyun (after their leader Abdulah al-Samawi), al-Wathiqun min al-Nasr (Those Confident of Victory), al-Khilafa (the Caliphate), al-Hirikiyun (the Activists), al-Amr bil Ma'arouf wal-Nahi an al-Munkar (Commanding the Good and Prohibiting the Forbidden), and al-Qisas al-Islami (the Islamic Punishment).[77] Many of these had no more than a handful of members and were responsible for few operations, usually against "soft" targets—video stores, music festivals, weddings, and Coptic communities.

Perhaps more important than these splits was the organizational restructuring that took place within the Jama'a in 1990 as a result of growing confrontations with the regime. For the first time since its inception the Jama'a formed a clandestine armed wing with its own commander to supplement its *dawa* (preaching) and political wings.[78] Moreover, each region had its armed wing with its own commander.[79]

The military wing was organized into a central leadership, which ordered substantial operations, and a cellular leadership in each of the regions or districts, which acted according to its own exigencies (Mubarak 1995). The various units that made up the military wing were called *kataib* (militias or squadrons).

The Jama'a also developed a dual external leadership. The first consisted of Omar Abdel Rahman, who resided in the United States in the early 1990s and was subsequently imprisoned by U.S. authorities in 1993. The second resided in Peshawar, Pakistan, and included Muhammad Shawqi al-Islambouli (brother of Sadat's assassin, Khaled), Talat Fouad Qasim, and Abdel Akhr Hamad. The three set up an Islamic tribunal in Peshawar to determine the culpability of government officials and pass judgment on them, which usually meant ordering their assassination. The judgment was then put into plan by other leaders abroad, including Rifa'i Ahmed Taha, an activist since the 1970s and one of the first to organize an armed wing, and Muhammad Hamza, fugitive since the assassination of Sadat (Mubarak 1995: 408). In 1989 the external leadership established a newsletter entitled *al-Murabitun* in Pakistan.

In the early 1990s Talat Fouad Qasim moved to Copenhagen, Denmark, where he was given asylum and served as a spokesman of the Jama'a until he was arrested by Croatian authorities in September 1995. After that time the Jama'a leadership abroad was divided between the European wing headed by Osama Rushdie, who was based in Holland, and the Afghan wing headed by Rifa'i Ahmed Taha and Muhammed Shawqi al-Islambouli. Some of the Jama'a continued to look to the imprisoned Omar Abdel Rahman for direction, but the leadership position officially went to Talat Fouad Qasim in 1993. As we shall soon see, the distance between these leaders was not merely geographical.

Failed Reconciliation Initiative, 1993

The diffusion of exclusive, loosely structured organizations in the Islamist movement guaranteed that the Islamist insurgency that began in 1992 would not find a quick resolution. After Islamist violence and state repression escalated to unprecedented levels in 1992, a number of Islamists sought to mediate between the Jama'a and the interior ministry in April 1993. A delegation of approximately twenty-five intellectuals and religious scholars, which came to be known as the "mediation delegation," met with Interior Minister Abdel Halim Musa to suggest ways to end the crisis.[80] One of the participants was Ahmed Faraj, who was an aide to the prime minister (Mubarak 1995: 415–416). A delegation member claimed that Aboud Zumur had expressed in a letter his willingness to end violence and give mediation efforts a chance. The mediation committee suggested the names of five Islamist leaders to head negotiations with the authorities—Aboud Zumur, Safwat Abdel Gahni, Karam Zuhdi, Najih Ibrahim, and Aisam Dirabala (four of the five were in prison).[81]

Islamist demands during this period were not clear. According to one of their defense lawyers, the militants had three demands: (1) the release of all the representatives of Islamist groups arrested in the past ten years; (2) cessation of government propaganda against the Jama'a; and (3) an end to all arrests and repressive measures against the Jama'a. In return, the government demanded that the Jama'a end all attacks on tourism, police forces, and government officials; abandon the idea of toppling the government through force; and cease all contacts with outside forces.[82]

However, according to Ahmed (1995: 301), Zumur actually met with General Abdel Raouf Salih to put forward the conditions for a cease-fire. His demands were the release of Islamist leaders and prisoners, an end to mass arrests and torture, and the return of private mosques to the Jama'a along with a promise that the state would not interfere with their preaching activities. A high-level security official also admitted that Islamists in Asyut, the focal point of the insurgency from 1992 to 1994, were willing to cease fighting if military courts were canceled, Islamic law applied, and Islamists held under unspecified charges released.[83]

During this time, one of the Jama'a leaders issued a communiqué stating that there would be no dialogue with the regime and there could be "no solution to the present situation except by returning to God's wise laws and His rule in all aspects of life. . . . We and all that we command are for the Islamic state."[84] Meanwhile, talk of possible compromise with the Islamists led President Husni Mubarak to dismiss his interior minister, Musa, on 18 April 1993. This move was widely interpreted as disapproval of Musa's conciliatory strategy, which might diminish the prestige of the state (haybet al-dawla).

Two days after Musa's dismissal, the Jama'a attempted to assassinate Safwat al-Sharif, the minister of information. During the same day, the Jama'a abroad issued a communiqué affirming the death sentence previously issued against former interior minister Musa.[85] The following day a communiqué was distributed in Asyut declaring that the

Jama'a promised to "pursue its course against the enemies no matter the cost and consequences."[86] One of the potential interlocutors with the regime, Safwat Abdel Ghani, also declared in a communiqué that "the violent operations in Egypt will not cease and that the battle with the police and the regime will not end" until an Islamic state is established.[87] A month later, however, he reversed his position by restating the same demands put forward by the Jihad group leader as a condition for a cease-fire.[88] This reversal, however, did not prevent Talat Fouad Qasim, the Jama'a leader abroad, to declare: "There is only one decision we demand to be taken: the establishment of an Islamic state. The violent confrontations and battles will continue as long as [the authorities] refuse to apply Islamic law, even if they release all prisoners and give them positions and great sums of money."[89] All these actions and declarations sealed the fate of the mediation delegation, as its members acknowledged with sad resignation.

A Second Failed Initiative, 1994

The second initiative to bring violence to an end came in April 1994, a year after the failure of the first initiative. Following a group conference, Salah Hashim, the commander of the Souhaj branch of the Jama'a, issued a moderately worded statement in which he declared that the Jama'a "does not object to dialogue to solve the crisis." He added, "The Jama'a al-Islamiya denounces violence and the killing of innocent people and calls on both sides to put down arms and abandon violence."[90]

This document, Mubarak explains (1995: 417), indicates a split between the dawa wing, centered in al-Minya and Souhaj, and the military wing in Asyut. The leaders of al-Minya and Souhaj did not want the conflict to escalate and spread to their areas. Prior to mid-1994 most of the violence was in Asyut; Souhaj and al-Minya witnessed only two and three incidents of violence between 1992 and 1993 respectively. However, the decisive blow received by the Jama'a military wing in Asyut in 1994, and the government's new strategy of an all-out war to eradicate the Jama'a in upper Egypt, forced the other branches to mobilize their activists.[91]

Salah Hashim's communiqué came just as violence began to spread to other regions of upper Egypt. Talat Fouad Qasim, however, issued a communiqué denying the statement "that appears to back down from [the group's] firm positions." He went on to affirm that the internal and external leadership of the Jama'a were not divided on the issues of dialogue with the regime or confrontation with the authorities.[92] Similar to the previous initiative, this attempt did not bear fruit. Instead, the decentralized nature of the Jamaʻa allowed it to carry out attacks in other upper Egypt towns even as Asyut "fell" to the government.

A Third Failed Initiative, 1996

The third initiative to end violence came during March 1996. This time it was Khaled Ibrahim, the imprisoned commander of the Aswan Jamaʻa, who issued a communiqué calling on the Jamaʻa to lay down its arms for a year to save the country from the "deluge of blood."[93] This initiative received no response until Muntasir al-Ziyat, the prominent Islamist lawyer who defended the militants of the Jamaʻa and Jihad groups, issued public letters to the groups' leaders inside Egypt and abroad urging them to respond positively to the initiative in order to thwart the "conspiratorial grip of the Zionist, Crusader, and Communist triad."[94]

Similar to earlier initiatives, however, this attempt was largely ignored by the imprisoned leaders and other branches of the Jamaʻa. The only response came from Talaʻi al-Fateh, the reconstituted armed wing of the Jihad group. It issued a communiqué stating its demands for a cease-fire, including a halt to mass arrests, the release of Islamists arrested under state-of-emergency laws, an end to military trials, and a sincere effort to apply the *sharia*.[95] However, the political wing of the Jihad group, headed by Aymen al-Zawahri, issued a communiqué rejecting "this forsaken and insulting initiative."[96]

The Fourth Initiative and the Luxor Massacre, 1997

It was not until July 1997 that an initiative by the historic leadership of the jihadist wing of the movement received a positive response. On 5 July 1997 some of the leaders of the Jamaʻa, imprisoned since Sadat's assassination, issued a unilateral cease-fire.[97] Within a month after the call, more imprisoned leaders, including some from the Jihad group, Hizb Allah, and Najiun min al-Nar, gave their support to the initiative.[98] Finally, Omar Abdel Rahman, the spiritual leader of the Jamaʻa, issued a call from his U.S. prison cell to abide by the initiative.[99]

The widespread support for the initiative, however, did not result in a quick end to the conflict. That August, one of the Jamaʻa units took credit for some operations and congratulated their fighters for killing six people, including four policemen in Manflout. Their communiqué repeated their earlier demands—the release of detainees, an end to military trials, and the nullification of the decisions of military courts.[100] Less than two months later, one of the Jama'a units claimed responsibility for the killing of eleven policemen in al-Minya.[101]

The most gruesome act by one of the Jama'a units, however, was the massacre of fifty-eight European tourists and four policemen in Luxor on 17 November 1997. After a period of confusion over who was responsible, it became clear that it was the work of the Shahid Talat Yasin Hamam militia, one of the military units of the Jama'a. Osama Rushdie, a Jama'a leader in Holland, condemned the massacre in its official publication *al-Murabitun*.[102] This condemnation was followed by another from the imprisoned Jama'a leaders.[103] Shortly after, the head of the military wing, Mustapha Hamza (Abu Hazim), declared his "surprise" at the attack and denounced it.[104]

It is interesting to note that these condemnations came separately from the different figures that constituted the Jama'a leadership. Rather than issue one communiqué, the separate leaders deemed it necessary to issue their own communiqués to make their positions clear, thus highlighting the fragmentation of the organization. More importantly, the "surprise" of the head of the military wing at the actions of some of his militias sheds light on the decentralization of the military wing and the inability of the central leadership to control its units.

Condemnations of the Luxor massacre by leaders inside Egypt did not stop Rifa'i Ahmed Taha, one of the senior leaders of the Jama'a in Afghanistan, to declare his approval of the massacre and deny that the Jama'a had halted its war on tourism.[105] Taha's refusal to support the cease-fire was not just the opinion of one leader. The Jama'a leaders based in Afghanistan were not convinced that a cease-fire was the proper move. This led the historic leaders in Egypt to issue a call to "the Brothers abroad" urging them to abide by the cease-fire. In the same communiqué they acknowledged that the leaders abroad have "ignored the call of our preacher Dr. Omar Abdel Rahman supporting the initiative."[106] It was only in March 1998 that the leadership abroad, excluding Taha, accepted the initiative.[107] Only in November 1998, more than a year after issuing the call for a cease-fire, did the military leaders of the Jama'a accept the initiative.[108]

The various initiatives and their outcomes highlight the difficulties of settling a violent conflict when exclusive, loosely structured organizations proliferate in a movement. In the case of Egypt, the division between an internal and external leadership as well as the division between a military wing and a political wing posed a problem to the regime.

Cease-fire initiatives by leaders who were not in a position to enforce them gave the state little incentive to negotiate. The state could not respond positively to or undertake cease-fire initiatives with people it deemed extremists and terrorists without some guarantees that such initiatives would succeed. For years the state portrayed radical militants as fanatics and criminals. It accused them of being agents of foreign powers, such as Iran and Sudan, seeking to destabilize Egypt and keep it backward. It also attributed to militants venal intentions hidden behind the mask of religion. Many of the leaders of the Jama'a abroad either were convicted of terrorism and sentenced to death or were wanted on similar charges.

After this type of campaign to discredit the Jama'a and its leaders, the state could not simply engage them in negotiations with the mere hope that they could iron out an agreement among themselves to cease hostilities. The regime viewed such a step as inappropriate because it diminished the state's credibility. As a high official in the security apparatus explained, "negotiations with terrorists means their recognition and that is not an option."[109] The Jama'a, on the other hand, could not declare a cease-fire without major concessions by the regime. Fahmi Houwaydi, one of the Islamic scholars who led the mediation delegation in 1993, appropriately expressed the dilemma facing both sides of the conflict: "The extremists will not stop violence from their end without something in return. They want from the government the release of fundamentalists that did not commit acts punishable by law. The government, on the other hand, will not accept their release as long as it cannot guarantee that the extremists will not continue with their violent activities."[110]

In Egypt, the state opted to repress the radicals until they declared a unilateral cease-fire. The militants declared a cease-fire in 1997, only after they were militarily exhausted and their leadership dispersed all over the world or in prison. Once the militants committed themselves to a cease-fire and abided by it on the ground, the state began to take some conciliatory steps toward them.[111]

Protracted Conflicts Across the Muslim World

The rebellions in Kashmir, the southern Philippines, Chechnya, and Tajikistan turned into protracted conflicts for reasons similar to those in

Algeria and Egypt. Repression forced many Islamist groups to organize into exclusive organizations, each with its own leadership, membership, and arms. When attempts were made to settle the conflicts through
peaceful means, those who were excluded from negotiations or did not
wish to compromise sabotaged peace efforts through timely violence.
Even when the combatants succeeded in reaching agreement, radicalized militants continued their jihad despite dim prospects for success
and growing popular dissatisfaction with their violence.

Kashmir

In Kashmir, the rebellion of 1989 was led by the Jammu and Kashmir
Liberation Front (JKLF). By the mid-1990s, however, the JKLF was
pushed into the background by more radical Islamist groups. Ganguly
(1997: 169–171) names eight other militant groups that have competed
with the JKLF, while Schofield (2000: 145–146) cites at least thirteen,
including Hizb-ul-Mujahideen, Harkat-ul-Ansar, and Lashkar-e-Toiba.
These groups command no more than a few thousand militants and
often not more than a few hundred. They continue to fight to this day
despite the repudiation of armed struggle by the JKLF and growing
–discontent with continuing violence. On 13 December 2001, Lashkar-
e-Tobia and Jaish-e-Muhammad carried out a daring suicide attack on
India's parliament, killing scores of parliamentarians and guards. Their
violence unleashed a series of belligerent maneuvers between India
and Pakistan, threatening to precipitate another war between the two
countries.[112]

The relationship between the armed groups is highly competitive
despite their shared goal of achieving independence for the people of
Kashmir. In the early years, the various factions clashed with each other
even as they were waging battle against the Indian state (Ganguly
1990/1991: 65). The groups are split ideologically between those who
seek to join Pakistan and others who want an independent Kashmir
state.[113] In addition, some have been radicalized by the influx of transnational militants who adhere to a pan-Islamist vision that calls for a
total war against "infidels" and "apostates."[114]

These groups lay claim to territories within and around the Kashmir
Valley, from which they have waged operations against the authorities
and increasingly against civilians.[115] In the mid-1990s, the separatist
factions operated under an umbrella organization known as the All Parties Hurriyat Conference (APHC). However, this has not stopped them

from rejecting calls made by the APHC to cease their violence against tourists, foreigners, and other civilians (Schofield 2000: 201–203). Even when some of the militant groups sought to end the conflict through negotiations, others responded with violence in an effort to sabotage peace talks.[116] In August 2000, gunmen massacred Hindu pilgrims and workers in and around the Kashmir Valley to express their opposition to the peace talks under way between Hizb-ul-Mujahideen and the Indian government.[117]

Support from Pakistan has aided in prolonging the conflict and perhaps has become the main lifeline for militants who appear to have lost popular support. Many of the groups that operate today are either based in Pakistan or have benefited from direct military and financial support provided by Pakistan's intelligence services and political parties. In 2002 the Pakistani authorities began to crack down on these militants in an effort to placate international calls to end cross-border terrorism into India.[118] Rebels, however, have stepped up their attacks on Indian civilians in the hope that their violence will undermine efforts to calm tensions between the two beleaguered nations.[119]

Southern Philippines

In the southern Philippines, "residual violence" from the 1972 insurgency persists to this day, as new groups with more radical Islamist worldviews have emerged. These factions include the Moro Islamic Liberation Front (MILF), a splinter organization from the Moro National Liberation Front (MNLF), and the Abu Sayyaf Group (ASG). Both the MILF and the ASG have carried out attacks against the Philippine authorities, foreigners, and civilians in an effort to press their demands for an independent Islamic state in the southern Philippines. The ASG has gone further by rejecting cohabitation with Christians and has perpetrated vicious massacres against Christian populations. It also specializes in hostage-taking and does not hesitate to decapitate its hostages when they fail to secure a ransom. Its links with transnational terrorists has earned it the wrath of U.S. forces, who have begun aiding the Philippine military in neutralizing the group.

The major organization that currently perpetuates the insurgency in the southern Philippines is the MILF. It is estimated to have between 10,000 and 15,000 militants in at least six divisions (Davis 1998: 32–33). The MILF emerged out of a schism that developed within the MNLF in 1976. At that time the MNLF wanted to scale back its demand for full independence to pursue a peace agreement with the Marcos regime. The Tripoli agreement, as it was called at the time, offered autonomy to Muslims in the southern Philippines (Majul 1985: 73). Those opposed to the peace agreement coalesced around Hashim Sala-mat, who challenged the leadership of Nur Misuari, and eventually formed the MILF as a distinct organization bent on fighting for complete independence (Chalk 2002). The loosely structured MNLF facilitated this split. According to McKenna (1998: 157), "The MNLF never controlled all of the rebels fighting the government and was, in fact, a loosely knit group, with the borders between those fighters who were members of, aligned with, or exterior to the MNLF never very clear."

When the Philippine government sought to negotiate directly with the MNLF, the excluded MILF responded with stepped-up attacks to demonstrate its presence and make clear that no peace could be achieved without its consent. For example, when President Corazon Aquino decided to negotiate with the MNLF in Jeddah, Saudi Arabia, in 1987, the MILF warned that it must not be barred from taking part in the dialogue. When talks took place and produced a cease-fire agreement, the MILF launched a terror campaign, striking at government targets and sabotaging power lines, bridges, and government buildings (McKenna 1998: 246).

In 1996, twenty years after the Tripoli agreement was signed, the MNLF accepted the Davao consensus accord, which entailed, inter alia, the complete cessation of hostilities and the formation of the Autonomous Region of Muslim Mindanao (ARMM). Both the MILF and ASG, however, have rejected this agreement. The MILF has engaged in peace talks with the Philippine government, but no real peace appears to be in sight. In August 2001, both parties signed an agreement for the cessation of hostilities.

However, skirmishes persisted, and it appears that some MNLF forces joined the fray, once more, in early 2002.[120] More troubling are the perpetual attacks waged by the ASG, which is "riven by internal tribalism and clanism, tending to function less as a structured political grouping and more as a loose collection of private 'lost commands' motivated purely by greed" (Chalk 2002: 209). The ASG conducts virtually daily attacks in its strongholds of Zamboanga and Basilan, including repeated massacres against Christian populations. All in all, three decades of fighting has cost tens of thousands of lives and there appears to be no peace in sight. Ex-rebels and "lost commands" with competing loyalties, ideologies, and interests continue to hinder efforts at long-term peace.[121]

Chechnya

After a three-year lull in violence, fighting broke out in Chechnya in late 1999 as a result of stepped-up attacks against Russian cities by radical Islamists and Chechen separatists. A series of blasts rocked Russian apartment blocks, restaurants, and shopping centers in southern Russian cities and Moscow itself. Although Chechen rebels have not claimed responsibility for these terrorist outrages, it is widely believed that radicalized separatists and transnational "Wahhabi" Islamists are behind the attacks. Between August 1999 and July 2000, an estimated 2,369 Russians were killed and 6,946 wounded.[122] In response, the Russian army unleashed another campaign of indiscriminate bombardments and human rights violations that has led to international condemnation and perpetuation of anti-Russian sentiments among Chechnya's Muslims (Politkovskaya 2001). The brutality of the Russian response continues to inspire militancy to this day.[123]

The Chechen rebels never constituted a unified movement. Although in the first war, between 1994 and 1996, they professed general loyalty to the rebellious president Dudayev, they comprised exclusive units with their own leaders, men, and arms. The Chechen volunteers were made up of friends and neighbors who "lack a military hierarchy and organization, formal training, formal commanders and tactical doctrine," explains Lieven (1998: 325). He adds, these "units are therefore quite literally 'bands of brothers.'" These groups were generally small and distinct from each other. "Almost every village had its appointed commander, with fifteen to twenty-five armed fighters under him, and up to 100 more in reserve whom he could call up at short notice" (Gall and Waal 1998: 306). Thus, by the time the second war broke out in 1999, there were more than 300 armed groups with a combined strength of 2,500 who were beyond the control of Chechen authorities.[124] The largest of these is the General Dudayev Army, headed by Salman Raduev.[125]

Less popular, but not less dangerous, is a militia of transnational Islamists who were led by Jordanian-born Ibn al-Khattab (killed in 2002) and Dagestani Islamist leader Jadji Bahuddin. Their aim is more than the ouster of Russian forces from Chechnya and establishment of an independent Chechen state (Lieven 1998: 146; Seely 2001: 306). These leaders have been joined by Turkish, Afghani, and Middle Eastern Islamists who want to establish an Islamic union that is much more ambitious and threatening to Central Asian regimes. "Moscow's problem is that it is facing a Chechen opposition which is increasingly diverse and uncoordinated." The Chechen field commanders "are split on political and religious lines."[126]

These armed groups have wreaked havoc in both Chechnya and Russia through indiscriminate violence, wanton acts of terrorism, and outright criminal activities. In addition to the series of bombings against Russian cities, Chechen rebels have carried out suicide attacks against Russian soldiers. They also targeted civilians, Western aid workers, and Chechen administrators.[127] Russia's brutal and indiscriminate military response has not succeeded in subduing such disparate groups and may only aid their cause by alienating ordinary Chechens victimized by such repression.

Tajikistan

In Tajikistan, the government of Emomali Rahmonov entered into negotiations with rebel groups under the banner of the United Tajik Opposition (UTO) in 1994. After pressure from Russia and Central Asian states and under the aegis of the United Nations, the negotiations lasted for three years and a peace accord was finally signed in 1997. However, warlords and militants continue to conduct high-profile political assassinations and other forms of political violence. "Parts of northeastern Tajikistan remain largely under the control of former UTO fighters who have rejected the terms of the peace settlement."[128]

The 1994 negotiations sought to address a number of issues, including establishing principles for national reconciliation, finding solutions to the refugee problem, and achieving a cease-fire. Underlying these issues were two areas of concern: (1) demobilization of armed groups and (2) skepticism over whether the opposition groups could agree among themselves. Since the outbreak of the civil war, rebels within the UTO organized as independent factions that controlled different parts of the country. These groups had diverse loyalties and could reject any agreement that they did not deem satisfactory (Brenninkmeijer 1997: 180).[129] According to Zviagelskaya (1997: 168): "The difficulty in making the ceasefire hold lies, firstly, in the fact that by no means all the armed detachments are controlled by the opposition leaders. The field commanders involved in military action on the border have their own aims."

This was made abundantly clear by the numerous cease-fire violations by the armed opposition. As negotiations were taking place, the UTO and other groups conducted several incursions from northern Afghanistan to attack government positions and Russian border guards. Some of these attacks were part and parcel of the opposition's strategy of consolidating its power during the negotiation process, but groups not interested in reconciling with the state regime also carried out many of these attacks.[130]

As for the ability of the opposition to reach consensus, government officials and their Russian supporters have expressed concern that "the opposition leaders at the talks represented some factions only among a large range of forces with diverging objectives which could never come to a concerted agreement at the talks" (Brenninkmeijer 1997: 195). From the start, the UTO expressed diverse and contradictory perspectives, which reflected the radically different visions of the Islamist, liberal, and nationalist groups that it comprised. More significantly, the subgroups that constituted each of the three opposition tendencies were fragmented and beset by rivalries.[131] IRP militants based in Afghanistan became radicalized by the influx of other Central Asian Islamists into their movement. These militants express pan-Islamist goals that cannot be satisfied through negotiations with the ruling regime.

These obstacles notwithstanding, the combatants were able to achieve a formal peace accord in 1997 and provided the opposition important concessions, including legality and 30 percent of the seats in parliament. Yet despite the signed peace agreement, inclusion of opposition in government, and legalization of the Islamist opposition, "fighting continued as the warlords who had been left out of the agreement continued to mount guerrilla attacks" (Rashid 2002: 91).

Conclusion

The experiences in Algeria, Egypt, Kashmir, the Philippines, Chechnya, and Tajikistan validate the proposition that exclusive organizations contribute to protracted conflicts. In each instance, rebellions gave rise to exclusive groups that competed with each other or else opposed each other over policies, tactics, and ideology. Such loosely structured factions made the task of peacemaking extremely tenuous, as those opposed to peace simply refused to adhere to agreements between the warring forces or, worse, engaged in timely violence to sabotage efforts at reconciliation.

Exclusive organizations made it easy for hard-liners in the incumbent camp to raise doubts about the feasibility of peace with the combatants in Algeria and Egypt. In Kashmir, exclusive organizations with virulently radical ideologies simply ignored the calls of moderates within their movement to seek peace or at least cease engaging in anti-civilian violence that discredits their cause. In the southern Philippines, when the historic leadership finally signed an agreement with major concessions on each side, other groups denounced them and continued their insurgency. In Chechnya, exclusive groups that emerged during the first war with Russia precipitated a second war through terrorist outrages that would shock ordinary Chechens. In Tajikistan, the presence of armed factions with diverse loyalties and interests within the opposition camp undermined the credibility of the opposition and prolonged the negotiations between the government and rebels. Reconciliation was eventually achieved, but despite major concessions to the opposition, violence by radicalized groups has not entirely subsided.

The aforementioned cases reveal an important lesson for the Muslim world. Reactive and indiscriminate repressive policies rarely achieve their intended "decisive blow" or turn into "small victorious wars." When Islamist movements encounter repression, they adjust accordingly. They do so by adopting exclusive mobilization structures that promise to shield them from repression and increase the cohesiveness and loyalty of their members. The common outcome borne out by recent history is the institutionalization of radicalism in the movement and perpetuation of underground careers. Like a shattered vase, it is not easy to put together an Islamist consensus around peace and reconciliation once the movement has been fragmented into numerous exclusive factions. Exclusion and repression are a recipe for protracted conflict, not swift victory.

Notes

1. HAMAS and the MNI, the two major competitors of the FIS, did not win any seats in the first round of the 1991 national elections. Their combined total of votes was 518,790 compared with 3,260,359 votes for the FIS. For the names and leaders of others parties, see Mus'ad (1995: 253–254).

2. The FIS managed to win over many of Jaballah's MNI activists prior to and after the formation of the FIS, including Abdelkader Hachani, Ali Jeddi, Abdelkader Boukhamkham, and Rabeh Kebir. According to Qameredine Kharban, both HAMAS leader Nahnah and MNI leader Jaballah sought entry into the FIS after the June 1990 elections. The FIS consultative council agreed to allow them in as individuals but not as groups. Both Nahnah and Jaballah rejected this condition. The same thing happened with Muhammad Bouslemani, the leader of the Muslim Brotherhood. He was asked to join the FIS but rejected the offer because, as he put it, the MB has too long a history to simply melt into another organization (al-Tawil 1998: 24–25).

3. In September 1990, HAMAS organized a conference that sought to bring numerous parties with an Islamist orientation into an alliance. The MNI agreed to attend but the FIS refused (Charef 1994: 110).

4. The Salafiyya tendency in contemporary Algeria does not represent a set of clear ideas. Rather, it shares a common belief that Muslims should be ruled by an Islamic state organized according to the precepts of the Quran, the Sunna (the traditions of the Prophet Muhammad), and the righteous forefathers (al-Salaf al-Salih). The latter include the companions of the Prophet and the Rightly Guided Caliphs—Abu Bakr, Omar Ibn al-Khattab, Uthman Ibn Afan, and Ali Ibn Abi Talib—and Islamic religious scholars including Ibn Hanbal, Ibn Taymiyya, and Muhammad Ibn Abd al-Wahhab. Contemporary Salafiyya tends to be literalist in its reading of the Islamic tradition and believes Islamic law is a set of religious, social, and economic rules that should be applied in every Muslim society; Islamic law is not subject to change from one place to another. Contemporary Salafiyya should not be confused with the Salafiyya movement of Jamal al-Din al-Afghani and Muhammad Abduh, both of whom were "modernists" who wanted to reform Islamic law by reinterpreting the Quran and the traditions of the Prophet. They are more accommodating of Western institutions and democracy, whereas the contemporary Salafiyya movement generally rejects democracy as an "innovation" and, hence, un-Islamic.

5. The Jazaira (literally Algerianist) is the title given by the *salafis* to Algerian Islamists in the early 1980s. The Jazaira rejects the rigidity of the contemporary Salafiyya movement, especially its belief that Islamic law could be applied in the same manner across the Muslim world—hence the title Algerianists. They are closer to the "modernists" because they believe Islam must be reinterpreted in light of historical transformations and must readapt to different times and places. Also, they tend to be more accommodating of democracy. Many Islamists in this tendency reject the derisive title bestowed upon them. But, much to their chagrin, it gained currency in the movement.

6. Hachemi Sahnouni, another prominent member and fiery preacher of the FIS, was a former member of the Takfir wal Hijra strand.

7. Initially the armed movement was urban-based. It was not until 1994 that the theater of battle shifted to the mountains where many insurgents took refuge after successful state repression in the cities. See *al-Wasat*, 22 March 1993, and Luis Martinez, "L'installation dans la guerre," *La Croix*, 31 May 1997.

8. The MEI was formed in March or April 1992 by "General" Abdelkader Chebouti, a former Bouyalist; Said Mekhloufi, a former member of the FIS

consultative council; and Azzedin Ba'a, a former Bouyalist. Many writers make the mistake of claiming that Chebouti formed the MIA after his release from prison in 1990. This is not the case. Although Chebouti and Ba'a were members of the MIA in the 1980s, the organization they formed in the early 1990s was given the title MEI (al-Tawil 1998: 59–62, 107–108).

9. The MIA was mainly organized in the western regions and consisted of FIS activists and supporters who took the initiative to gather arms and form small groups for attacks against security forces. These groups did not take official organizational structure but merely adopted the title of Bouyali's armed movement. A year after the coup, they began to call themselves the AIS, indicating their loyalty to the FIS, after the latter began unofficially to organize an armed wing.

10. The FIDA is believed to have consisted mainly of Jazaira supporters with connections to FIS leader Muhammed Said.

11. This information is inferred from a GIA communiqué dated 4 October 1994 in which Mahfouz Tajeen, who was the fifth amir of the GIA (for less than a month), listed the names of nine amirs to lead nine separate zones (*al-Hayat*, 5 October 1994). The tradition of dividing Algeria into separate zones, each with its own amir, is not uncommon in the armed Islamist movement. It was done under Bouyali, who divided Algeria into ten zones, and also by the AIS, which divided Algeria into at least three zones.

12. The names and sizes of these GIA groups could be gathered from the series of communiqués in 1996 declaring splits from the GIA and from reports of groups laying down their arms in 1999 (*al-Hayat*, 1 January 1996, 3 and 23 March 1996, 8 June 1999, and 9 and 14 September 1999). In January 2000, twenty-two GIA militias composed of approximately 800 militants—an average of about thirty-six militants per militia—were granted complete amnesty after abiding by the AIS cease-fire call (*al-Hayat*, 12 January 2000).

13. This information is derived from a high-ranking security official interviewed by Camille al-Tawil in *al-Hayat*, 8 June 2002, 10.

14. For example, Mustapha Karatali, the amir of al-Rahman militia, states that when the GIA began to order attacks on the families of security forces, he and his group refused. Also, they refused to allow militants outside their area (Larbaa) from joining their militia despite orders from the central leadership to do so (see interview with *al-Hayat*, 8 February 2000).

15. Muhammad Said, Abderrazak Rejjam, and Yousuf Boubras came as representatives of the FIS Provisional National Executive Bureau. However, they did not inform the imprisoned FIS leadership, the leadership abroad, or the other armed groups loyal to the FIS of their decision to join the GIA (see interview with Madani Mezraq in *al-Hayat*, 26 July 1996).

16. The inclusion of representatives of the Jazaira tendency—Muhammad Said, Abderrazak Rejjam, and Yousuf Boubras—under the banner of the GIA posed a problem to some of the participants, including Said Mekhloufi, who came as a representative of the MEI. Mekhloufi made it a point to stress that the GIA will "follow the salafi path; any deviation from this path is a revocation of the pledge of allegiance" (al-Tawil 1998: 145–154). Subsequent communiqués reiterated that the GIA is a Salafiyya group (*al-Hayat*, 15 September 1994, 21 March 1995, and 14 January 1996).

17. *al-Thawra al-Islamiyya fi al-Jazair: al-Nus al-Kamel lil-Barnamij Asiyasi li-Jabhat al-Inqadh al-Islamiyya* (Cairo: Dar Yafa lil-Dirasat wal-Abhath, 1991, 1–41).

18. Madani Mezraq, the national amir of the AIS, maintains that several attempts were made in 1992 and 1993 to bring the GIA and other groups together to form a unified armed movement under the leadership of the FIS, but the GIA did not respond to these initiatives. Instead, "we began to hear claims that it is not appropriate to fight under the banner of parties, and the FIS should change its name because it contains opportunists" (*al-Hayat*, 26 July 1996).

19. *al-Ansar*, 12 May 1995

20. *al-Hayat*, 10 May 1995

21. *al-Ansar*, 15 June 1995.

22. The pamphlet's complete title is *Hidayat Rab al-'Alamin fi Tabyeen Usul al-Salafiyeen wama Yajib min al-Ahd ala al-Mujahedeen* (The Guidance of the Lord of the Universe in Clarifying the Traditions of the Forefathers and the Requirements of Allegiance Among the Holy Fighters). It is a sixty-two-page pamphlet carrying the name Abu Abdel Rahman Amin and is dated 27 Rabi'a al-Thani 1416/1995.

23. See published interview with Ahmed bin Aicha in *al-Hayat*, 8 June 1996; interview with Madani Mezraq in *al-Hayat*, 26 July 1996; communiqué by Mezraq in al-Tawil (1998: 168–169); and interview with Abdallah Anas, an FIS representative abroad, in *al-Hayat*, 28 March 1995.

24. Interview with Ahmed Bin Aicha in *al-Hayat*, 3 February 2000.

25. Martinez (1997/1998) estimates the number of AIS militants at 7,000 to 8,000. The authorities at one point put the number at 5,000, while those close to the AIS put the figure at 10,000 (*al-Hayat*, 15 July 1999). The minister of the interior put the number of AIS militants who benefited from the 1999 Law of National Reconciliation and the General Amnesty granted to the AIS by President Bouteflika in January 2000 at 4,200 (*al-Hayat*, 20 January 2000).

26. The letters were issued in March and April 1995 and cited in al-Tawil (1998: 298–299 and 303–304).

27. Interview with Ghamati in al-Tawil (1998: 174).

28. The GIA claimed responsibility for his execution in its London-based newsletter, *al-Ansar*, 7 September 1995.

29. The GIA claimed responsibility in 1997 (al-Tawil 1998: 213).

30. *al-Hayat*, 7 February 1996.

31. *AFPI*, 21 January 1996. The FIS and AIS continued to accuse the GIA and former-GIA militias of attacking their activists (see *al-Hayat*, 7 February 1996 and 7 May 1998).

32. *al-Hayat*, 5 July 1995.

33. Although the GIA claimed that they executed them because of their violence against civilians (see GIA communiqué #35 in *al-Ansar*, no. 101, 15 June 1995), the truth of the matter is that there emerged an internal struggle between Jamal Zitouni and Ben Sheeha, the commander of zone four, over the distribution of weapons captured during raids on military targets. Ben Sheeha refused to equally share these weapons with Zitouni, which led the latter to remove Ben Sheeha as commander of zone four and put Mustapha Aqal in charge instead. This resulted in internecine fighting that culminated in the death

of Ben Sheeha along with thirty of his men in the beginning of 1996 (see *al-Hayat*, 26 November 2001, 15).

34. After initially denying the deed, the GIA sent a two-hour videotaped confession of a GIA activist, Abdelwahab Lamara, in which he admitted that he conspired with Said and others on several occasions to take over the leadership of the GIA. In the last attempt, they conspired with the former amir of the GIA, Mahfouz Tajeen, to oust Zitouni and replace him with Said. A day after the "confession," both Tajeen and Lamara were executed (al-Tawil 1998: 240–242).

35. AFPI, 10 October 1997, and *al-Hayat*, 1 January 1996.

36. *al-Hayat*, 3 February 1996.

37. *al-Hayat*, 21 February 1996.

38. See the communiqués issued by these groups in *al-Hayat*, 3 and 23 March and 10 June 1996.

39. In September 1998 this group united militias in zone #2 (Tizi Ouzou and departments surrounding Algiers) and zone #5 (Constantine and East of Algeria) under the leadership of Hassan Hattab, who was a former GIA commander in zone #2 before breaking with the group in 1996. This group opposes both the GIA and AIS (*al-Hayat*, 17 September 1998, 30 April 1999, and 11 May 1999).

40. The crisis cell consisted of Abdelkader Hachani, Rabeh Kebir, Qasim Tajouri, Yakhlif Sherati, Uthman Aisani, Abdelkarim Ghamati, and (later) Abderrazak Rejjam.

41. Kebir established a base in Germany, while Ans established one in Afghanistan (and later Britain), and Haddam established one in the United States (where he eventually was imprisoned).

42. Haddam issued a communiqué in July 1994 congratulating the unification of the armed groups under the GIA (*al-Hayat*, 12 July 1994). A month later the FIS-EBA issued its own communiqué declaring Haddam was no longer part of the FIS (*al-Hayat*, 2 August 1994).

43. Rabeh Kebir repeatedly made this point in an interview with Ahmed Mansour, host of the "Bila Hudoud" (Without Borders) television program aired by *al-Jazeera* out of Qatar on 26 January 2000. Kebir stated that FIS leaders communicated with the AIS via telephone, fax, letters, and messengers. But the AIS did not take orders regarding military operations or targets. Ahmed Bin Aicha admitted in an interview (*al-Hayat*, 3 February 2000) that he never personally met Madani Mezraq, the national amir of the AIS.

44. See FIS communiqué #22, dated 19 March 1992 and signed by Rejjam; FIS communiqué in *al-Hayat*, 8 July 1992; and *MEI*, 1 May 1992.

45. Other concessions demanded by the FIS included a cessation to all repressive measures against the movement, negotiations with the effective opposition in Algeria, and cancellation of all military court verdicts issued since 1992. The FIS claimed that these concessions were promised by the regime, but the regime denied making such promises before any cease-fire declaration. Rabeh Kebir (in an interview with *al-Hayat*, 1 April 1994) claimed that the FIS did not guarantee Zeroual a cease-fire in exchange for dialogue. A cease-fire would only come after FIS political and military leaders had an opportunity to consult each other and agree on a cease-fire. This is corroborated by Abdelkader Boukhamkham (in an interview with *al-Hayat*, 31 October 1999).

46. The contents of the letters are quoted at length in al-Tawil (1998: 179–181).

47. Rabeh Kebir (in an interview with *al-Hayat*, 17 September 1994) claims that the jailed leaders were promised freedom to confer with the rest of the consultative council outside of prison as a first step to resolving the crisis. This is confirmed by Kamal Qamazi, one of the released FIS leaders. But, he added, FIS leaders insisted on other demands, including a televised dialogue among the parties to determine the culprits behind the crisis (*al-Hayat*, 27 October 1994).

48. Zeroual placed the blame squarely on Belhaj because of his alleged contacts (via letters) with Cherif Gousmi, the commander of the GIA. When Gousmi was killed in September 1994, security forces found on his body two letters addressed to him by Belhaj. The letters declared support for the mujahedin and urged him to cooperate with the AIS to put pressure on the regime (Willis 1996: 337–338; al-Rasi 1997: 422; al-Tawil 1998: 183–184). Boukhamkham, however, argues these letters were merely intended to win the confidence of the GIA leader so as to facilitate a political solution (*al-Hayat*, 31 October 1999).

49. *al-Sharq al-Awsat*, 14 July 1995.

50. *al-Hayat*, 13 July 1995.

51. There were also disagreements over the nature of government amnesty to the insurgents and prisoners. The FIS wanted a general amnesty but the government insisted that the prisoners be freed under the "clemency law," which implied they were criminals not political activists. Another disagreement was over whether or not the FIS would be re-recognized as the FIS or under a different name (*al-Hayat*, 23 July 1995; *MEI*, 21 July 1995; *MECS*, 1995: 218).

52. Rabeh Kebir (in an interview with *al-Hayat*, 13 July 1995) confirmed this was the sticking point.

53. See communiqué #22 dated 19 March 1992 quoted in al-Tawil (1998: 100–101). The conditions included the release of all political prisoners, an end to the state of emergency, compensation to victims, resumption of elections, and the opening of a national dialogue with political parties.

54. Communiqué #42 by the FIS-PNEB signed by Rejjam.

55. *MEI*, 7 January 1994.

56. Zitouni repeated the claim that the GIA is the only group carrying the banner of Jihad in his pamphlet *Hidayat Rab al-'Alamin* (1995: 9 and 43).

57. See GIA communiqué in *al-Hayat*, 15 September 1994.

58. *MECS* (1994: 238).

59. According to a source close to Zeroual, the second round of negotiations failed partly because "the FIS has yet to make clear its position toward the GIA." He added, "What is required from those politically responsible in the FIS is to say if the armed wing is under its control or not. Will this wing accept what the [FIS] decides or not?" (*al-Hayat*, 18 October 1994). Similarly, one of the mediators in the third round of negotiations expressed that the government had doubts about the ability of the party to control the insurgents (*MEI*, 21 July 1995).

60. *al-Hayat*, 6 June 1999. The content of the cease-fire agreement has not been made public. What is clear is that there were no promises made to rehabilitate the FIS or reincorporate it into the political process. In an interview

with *al-Hayat,* 28 December 1999, one of the top chiefs of the AIS acknowledged that the cease-fire decision was made on 11 July 1997 by the AIS leadership after a series of contacts with the authorities. He also acknowledged that the decision did not involve any of the political leadership of the FIS. One of the conditions for the cease-fire was the release of Abassi Madani, which occurred on 15 July 1997.

61. Interview with *al-Hayat,* 31 October 1999. According to an AIS leader close to Mezraq, the FIS did not participate in the 1997 negotiations, nor did the AIS demand the reinstitution of the FIS (*al-Hayat,* 29 December 1999).

62. Interestingly, the letter by Merzaq was quoted in parts by Algerian television, which was an unprecedented recognition of the AIS (*al-Hayat,* 5 June 1999).

63. For the letters to Bouteflika and the armed groups, see *al-Hayat,* 13 June 1999.

64. *al-Hayat,* 1 July 1999; *MEI,* 28 January 2000.

65. *al-Hayat,* 12 and 20 January 2000.

66. *al-Wasat,* 29 November 1999.

67. Prior to the May 2002 legislative elections, the Nahda party reported that the ministry of the interior had rejected fifteen candidates in twelve departments because of their former association with the FIS (*al-Hayat,* 30 April 2002).

68. After the declaration of the 1997 cease-fire, there were a series of massacres, some of which targeted FIS supporters. Massacres and violence in general continued well into 1998, 1999, and 2000. Between April and December 1999, i.e., the first eight months of Abdelaziz Bouteflika's presidency, armed groups killed approximately 1,000 people (*al-Hayat,* 31 December 1999). In 2000, official figures put the number of people killed per month at about 300 (according to the International Crisis Group Africa Report, No. 4, "The Algerian Crisis: Not Over Yet," 20 October 2000.)

69. *al-Sharq al-Awsat,* 28 August 1999.

70. Some FIS activists have rallied around Belhaj's line and have denounced Madani Merzaq's cease-fire. They run a newsletter in London entitled *Sawta al-Jabha* (The Voice of the Front), which carries the communiqués of Baqoun 'Ala al-'Ahd and al-Jama'a al-Islamiya lil-Dawa wal-Qital. They compete with another group, also in London, that represents the views of Rabeh Kebir of the FIS-EBA. They publish a newsletter entitled *al-Sabil.*

71. International Crisis Group Africa Report, No. 31, "The Civil Concord: A Peace Initiative Wasted," 9 July 2001.

72. The communiqué was dated 12 February 2002, one day after the appointment of Abu Turab as the head of the GIA, but it was distributed on 28 March 2002 (*al-Hayat,* 1 April 2002).

73. On 18 March 2002, a powerful bomb was detonated in central Algiers. On 30 May 2002, the day of legislative elections in Algeria, twenty-five Bedouins were slaughtered in the village of Sanjas after the GIA promised violence in a communiqué a few days earlier. A month later, thirteen people were killed near southern Algiers by GIA gunmen who entered a bus and started shooting passengers (see *al-Hayat,* 22 March, 16 and 31 May, 15 and 30 June 2002). Violence was also intensified by al-Jama'a al-Salafiyya lil-Dawa wal-Qital

(GSPC) in response to military sweeps in its strongholds. In April 2002, it killed twenty-one Algerian soldiers in a set trap, and in May 2002 the group is said to have executed thirty-one villagers in two separate incidents in Tiarat and killed fifteen more soldiers (*al-Hayat*, 3 April and 3 and 7 May 2002). According to the French Press Agency, from January to July 2002 approximately 810 people were killed in Algeria (*al-Hayat*, 11 July 2002).

74. This unification brought together various small groups regionally located with some of the Jama'a groups in upper Egypt under a new organizational apparatus known as Tanzim al-Jihad (the Jihad Organization) headed by an eleven-member consultative council and the command of preacher Omar Abdel Rahman. This organization was responsible for Sadat's assassination and the October 1981 insurrection in Asyut (Janinah 1988; Hamouda 1989; Moro 1990; Ramadan 1993; and Auda 1994).

75. Muntaser Ziyat, a sympathetic observer of the movement and lawyer of radical Islamists during the 1990s, sheds light on this split in part four of an eight-part series on the life of Aymen al-Zawahri, who heads the Jihad group in Egypt and has become Osama bin Laden's second-in-command. The series is published in *al-Hayat*, 10–17 January 2002.

76. An indication of the increasing exclusiveness of the Jihad and Jama'a groups is their refusal to operate jointly military training camps in Pakistan and Afghanistan (Mubarak 1995).

77. *al-Taqrir al-Istratiji al-Arabi, 1988* (1989: 511); *al-Sharq al-Awsat*, 31 December 1994; Mustapha (1996: 378).

78. The first amir of the Jama'a armed wing was Talat Yasin Hamam, who was killed in April 1994 by security forces. Since then, the military wing has taken the title Kataib al-Shahid Talat Yassin (the Militias of the Martyr Talat Yassin). The fallen leader was replaced with Ahmed Hasan Abdel Jalil, who was killed in November 1994. The latter was replaced by Mahmoud Sayid Salim, who was in turn replaced by Sayyid Adel Rahim Mustapha, who was killed in July 1996. Mustapha Hamza (Abu Hazim) was the last amir of the Jama'a armed wing.

79. This information is inferred from a 1998 communiqué by the Jama'a in which the names of seven military amirs of different regions arrested in the early 1990s were cited as signatories (*al-Hayat*, 2 November 1998).

80. *al-Sharq al-Awsat*, 16 April 1993.

81. *al-Hayat*, 17 April 1993.

82. Ibid.

83. Ibid.

84. *al-Hayat*, 18 April 1993.

85. *al-Hayat*, 20 April 1993.

86. *al-Hayat*, 21 April 1993.

87. *al-Hayat*, 12 May 1993.

88. *al-Hayat*, 11 June 1993.

89. *al-Hayat*, 30 August 1993.

90. *al-Hayat*, 21 April 1994.

91. In April and November 1994 security forces succeeded in killing the leaders of the Jama'a military wing. In that year the state also began its shoot-to-kill

policy; it killed 159 Islamists and injured only 40. In 1993 the state arrested more than 17,000 suspected Islamists, most of whom were from Upper Egypt.

92. *al-Hayat*, 23 April 1994.

93. *al-Hayat*, 8 March 1996.

94. *al-Hayat*, 3, 4, and 5 May 1996. For Ziyat's own view of this episode, see *al-Hayat*, 14 January 2002, part 5.

95. *al-Hayat*, 8 May 1996.

96. *al-Hayat*, 23 May 1996. It is not clear whether the Tala'i al-Fateh remained the armed wing of the Jihad group after 1993. In that year the group suffered a split whereby Yasir Tawfiq Ali al-Siri, based in London, formed a new group called Tala'i al-Fateh al-Jadid and later Tala'i al-Fateh al-Islami. In 1996 this group along with another called Haraket al-Jihad united under the title Haraket al-Jihad-Tala'i al-Fateh-Misr. This merger, however, was of no consequence. The group probably had more words in its title than activists in its ranks.

97. *al-Hayat*, 6 July 1997.

98. *al-Hayat*, 13 July and 7 August 1997; *Malef al-Ahram al-Istratiji*, September 1997: 97–98.

99. *al-Hayat*, 10 August 1997.

100. *al-Hayat*, 23 August 1997.

101. *al-Hayat*, 16 October 1997.

102. *al-Hayat*, 28 November 1997.

103. *al-Hayat*, 3 December 1997.

104. *al-Hayat*, 8 December 1997.

105. *al-Hayat*, 10 December 1997.

106. *al-Hayat*, 1 January 1998.

107. Rifa'i Taha and Aymen al-Zawahri were pictured together with Osama bin Laden in February 1998, after the signing of the first communiqué of the newly created International Front for Combating Jews and Crusaders (*al-Hayat*, 24 February 1998). Subsequent developments proved that the Jama'a leaders abroad were divided. In December 1999, Muhammed Shawqi al-Islambouli issued a statement declaring that he along with Rifa'i Taha had resigned from the Jama'a consultative council in the previous year. Taha also issued a statement that he resigned from the council but affirmed his membership within the group (*al-Hayat*, 3 December 1999). It is not clear what prompted these resignations, but one can reasonably speculate that the two leaders did not approve of the cease-fire initiative of July 1997.

108. Seven imprisoned leaders of the military wing signed a communiqué declaring their acceptance of the unilateral cease-fire (*al-Hayat*, 19 November 1998).

109. *al-Wasat*, 26 April 1993.

110. Ibid.

111. In 1998 the minister of the interior released approximately 6,000 detainees. They were mainly relatives of the Jama'a leaders that signed the cease-fire agreement, ill and old Jama'a members, and activists not involved in violent activities (*al-Wasat*, 28 December 1998). In March 1999 a military court gave twenty-four Jama'a defendants reduced sentences; there were no

death or life sentences issued even though the convictions could have resulted in such punishments (*al-Hayat,* 9 March 1999). In April 1999 the authorities released an additional 1,200 members of the Jama'a (*al-Hayat,* 27 April 1999). In May of that year, in an unprecedented move, a court of appeals reversed the death sentences of three and the life sentences of six Jama'a activists because part of the evidence against the defendants was produced through torture (*al-Hayat,* 23 May 1999). For a similar analysis of the end of the insurgency, see Gerges (2000).

112. "India and Pakistan on the Brink" *The Economist,* 5 January 2002.

113. Raymond Bonner, "In a Paradise Torn by Feuding Giants, Kashmiris Long for Independence" *NYT,* 2 June 2002.

114. Jonah Blank, "Kashmir: Fundamentalism Takes Root," *Foreign Affairs,* November/December 1999; Rajiv Chandrasekaran, "Kashmiris in Middle of Tug of War," *Washington Post,* 3 June 2002.

115. HRW, "India's Secret Army in Kashmir: New Patterns of Abuse Emerge in the Conflict" (May 1996); *NYT,* 9 January 2002.

116. "Militant Tendencies," *The Economist,* 5 June 1999; "Talking and Killing in Kashmir," *The Economist,* 3 June 2000.

117. HRW, "Kashmir: Wave of Attacks on Civilians Condemned" (21 August 2000).

118. *NYT,* 9 January 2002.

119. On 14 May 2002, Kashmiri rebels killed thirty-four people, mainly women and children, in an attack on an army camp. On 13 July 2002, twenty-five Hindus were massacred as they were watching a cricket game (*Washington Post,* 14 July 2002).

120. A disgruntled Nur Misuari, who was accused of abusing his governorship over the Autonomous Region of Muslim Mindanao, launched an uprising in the Island of Jolo in which more than one hundred people died in November 2001.

121. "South Sea Trouble," *The Economist,* 9 August 2001.

122. "No End of War in Sight," *The Economist,* 10 February 2001; BBC News, 20 March and 3 July 2000.

123. "Russia's Brutal Folly," *The Economist,* 13 November 1999; "Russia's Merciless War," *The Economist,* 11 December 1999; HRW, "Field Update on Chechnya" (22 January 2001); Francois Jean, "Chechnya: Moscow's Revenge," *Harvard International Review,* January 2000; Sharon LaFraniere, "Chechen Refugees Describe Atrocities by Russian Troops: Villagers Tortured, Killed in Assault, Reports Say," *Washington Post,* 29 June 2002.

124. Russian president Vladimir Putin believes that the Chechen forces are splintered into small groups of ten fighters ("Russia's Stalemate in Chechnya," BBC News, 31 July 2001).

125. Radio Free Europe/Radio Liberty Newsline, vol. 2, no. 8, 14 January 1998.

126. "Chechnya's Endless War," BBC News, 23 April 2001.

127. HRW, 30 November 1999; 13 January 2000; 22 January 2001; *The Independent* (London), 11 September 1999; *NYT,* 10 February 2002.

128. HRW, 5 October 2001.

129. *NYT,* 20 October 2000; International Crisis Group "Tajikistan: An Uncertain Peace" (Asia Report No. 30, 24 December 2001).

130. In 1997, two French citizens were taken hostage in east Dushanbe. One was released but the other was killed during a rescue attempt. In that same year, explosions took place in public transports. In July 1998, four United Nations workers were killed in the Karotegin Valley. In 2001, three high-ranking political figures were assassinated. In June of that year, former UTO rebels took fifteen German nationals working as humanitarian aid workers hostage along with four policemen. All were released unharmed.

131. This observation was made by Stanley T. Escudero, former U.S. ambassador to Tajikistan, who maintained that schisms within the Tajik opposition created some doubt that an agreement signed by the leaders would be adhered to by all the factions (6 June 1995 forum on Tajikistan organized by the United States Institute of Peace).

5

Ideology and Anticivilian Violence

slamist rebellions invariably produce anticivilian violence and terrorist outrages that shock the consciousness of humanity. Insurgencies that initially target government officials and security forces often turn into nihilistic wars against foreigners, intellectuals, journalists, public employees, and ordinary citizens. In Algeria, GIA Islamists massacred countless innocent villagers and public workers during the course of its insurgency. In Egypt, a faction in the Jama'a slaughtered tourists at Luxor in 1997, a crime that galvanized international attention and discredited the armed movement at home. In Kashmir, radical Islamists belonging to Jaish Muhammad and Lashqar-e Toiba repeatedly butchered Hindu pilgrims and workers, and have killed Muslims suspected of collaborating with the Indian government. In the southern Philippines, the Abu Sayyaf Group has specialized in the mass murder of Christians and beheading of foreign hostages when they fail to secure ransom money. In Chechnya, rebels placed bombs in huge apartment buildings, knowing that their actions would result in civilian carnage. In Tajikistan, armed rebels responded to clan and state repression by carrying out atrocities against villagers in pro-communist strongholds. The list of Islamist militants engaging in anticivilian violence is a long one.[1]

How could Muslim rebels that often speak in the name of the people end up killing civilians with impunity? In this chapter, I argue that patterns of anticivilian violence are often a product of antisystem ideological frames that develop under conditions of repression and within the context of exclusive mobilization structures. Antisystem frames facilitate what social psychologists call "moral disengagement," which deactivates self-sanctioning norms against brutality and makes anticivilian violence a permissible, indeed legitimate, mode of contention (Bandura 1998, 1999; Bandura et al. 1996, 2001).

This chapter highlights how antisystem frames make possible at least three mechanisms of moral disengagement: ethical justification of violence, advantageous comparison among episodes of violence, and displacement of responsibility for violence. Antisystem ideologies deny the possibility of personal or group neutrality; every individual is responsible for maintaining or overthrowing the system under which he or she lives. When individuals or groups refuse to aid in the overthrow of incumbent regimes or are seen as supportive of these regimes, they become targets of rebellious movements.

Defining Antisystem Ideological Frames

Ideological frames refer to the "conscious strategic efforts by groups of people to fashion shared understandings of the world and of themselves that legitimate and motivate collective action" (McAdam et al. 1996: 6). The concept of frames made its way into social movement studies through the works of Snow and his colleagues (Snow et al. 1986; Snow and Benford 1988; Benford and Snow 2000), who drew on Erving Goffman's (1974) frame analysis. A *frame* is an "interpretive schemata that simplifies and condenses the 'world out there' by selectively punctuating and encoding objects, situations, events, experiences, and sequences of actions within one's present or past environment" (Snow and Benford 1992: 137).

"Abortion is murder" is an example of an ideological frame used by antiabortion activists in the United States to motivate protest against abortion clinics. Such framing accentuates the perceived nefariousness of abortion and suggests the need for legal sanctions against it. A frame, therefore, is a form of discourse that draws on shared meanings, not merely to reproduce those meanings, but also to embellish them and generate new ones conducive for collective action (Hunt et al. 1994).

Frames can also be thought of as "condensed symbols" (Moss 1997) that situate contemporary actors and their experiences within historical narratives that are intelligible, meaningful, and suggestive. The symbols are "condensed" in that they express a series of ideas and convoke a number of familiar images that are mythically, if not logically, coherent. The act of framing is ideological because it *selectively* draws from shared histories, revered symbols, and "cultural repertoires" to produce change (Swindler 1986). Framing is not an objective process; it is replete with subjectivity and strategic choices.

Antisystem ideological frames portray the institutional political system and the state elite as fundamentally corrupt and deny "legitimacy to the routinized functioning of the political process" (Diani 1996: 1057). Two closely interrelated features of antisystem frames are relevant for explaining anticivilian violence. First, antisystem frames are all-encompassing. They depict social ills and individual grievances as manifestations of problems deeply rooted in the system, as opposed to products of misguided policies or ineffective leadership. Unlike reconciliatory frames, which portray adversaries as competitors with whom one can negotiate, influence, and compromise in order to reach an agreement that will lead to non-zero-sum outcomes, antisystem frames reject the possibility of reform through mutually beneficial agreements. Communist movements, for example, can be characterized as antisystem movements because they deny the possibility of reconciliation between capitalists and workers. Exploitation and class struggle are built into the system.

Second, antisystem frames are polarizing. They represent the relationship between the movement and its opponents as a conflict between two antithetical opposites—us versus them, just versus unjust, faithful versus impious. The sharp dividing lines drawn by such frames depict the opponent as a monolithic entity that is incapable of adjustment due to intrinsic characteristics that preclude reform; the opponent must be displaced.

Antisystem Frames and Mechanisms of Moral Disengagement

So how do antisystem frames contribute to violence against civilians? They do so through a gradual process of deactivating self-inhibitory moral codes against murder and mayhem. Clandestine high-risk activities, especially violence, require a great deal of justification and motivation. As Apter (1997: 2) aptly put it, "People do not commit political violence without discourse. They need to talk themselves into it."

Violent groups consciously employ what Bandura (1998: 161, 164) terms mechanisms of "moral disengagement" to legitimate and motivate violent repertoires of contention. These mechanisms include the ethical justification of violence, advantageous comparison of one's violence with the transgressions of the "oppressors," and the shifting of blame onto exogenous forces that allegedly make violence "inevitable." According to Bandura: "Self-sanctions [against cruelties] can be disengaged by reconstructing conduct as serving moral purposes, by obscuring personal agency in detrimental activities, by disregarding or misrepresenting the injurious consequences of one's actions, or by blaming and dehumanizing the victims." Bandura points to several mechanisms of moral disengagement. Three, however, suffice to explain anticivilian violence in Islamist movements.

Ethical Justification

The ethical justification of violence can be achieved in several ways. Rebels could frame their actions as a necessary evil to end real or perceived social injustices; they could claim that they are resisting foreign aggression or alien domination; and they could argue that violence is justified to reverse a historic trend that is deleterious to the moral or physical health of their people. For example, left-wing terrorists in Europe during the 1960s and 1970s perpetrated anticivilian bombings in order to overthrow an "exploitative" system. More recently, Hamas members justified their suicidal missions against Israeli civilians by arguing that their actions will liberate Palestine.[2] Governments also justify expansive violence in times of war by arguing that it is a necessary evil to prevent a greater one, such as domination by an aggressor. The United States justified the atomic attacks on Japan at the end of World War II on the basis that it "saved" more lives by ending the war swiftly.

Advantageous Comparison

Advantageous comparison is another mechanism employed by rebels to make their violence legitimate. The purveyors of violence justify their actions by framing theirs as "minor" transgressions compared to the cruelties inflicted on them by the enemy. As Bandura (1998: 171) explains, "Self-deplored acts can be made to appear righteous by contrasting them with flagrant inhumanities. The more outrageous the comparison practices, the more likely it is that one's own destructive conduct will appear trifling or even benevolent." Suicide bombers in the Israeli-occupied West Bank and Gaza, for instance, often declare in their videotaped messages to the world that their violence is intended to avenge the disproportionate killing of their brothers and sisters in the territories.[3]

Displacement of Responsibility

The displacement of blame is perhaps the most common mechanism of moral disengagement employed by rebels. Shifting the culpability onto other groups or agencies that "forced" the rebels to "react in self-defense" minimizes in the minds of rebels the deleterious effects of their violence. Violence is not a matter of choice, they say; it is an inevitable backlash against the violations of others. By insisting on the "reactive" nature of their violence, however, the perpetrators of inhumane cruelties undercut the claim that they exercise free will. Kramer (1998: 150) points out that Hizballah in Lebanon struggled to justify hostage-taking against Westerners during the 1980s but eventually did so by accusing them of being "spies" and "agents of imperialism." In doing so, Hizballah shifted blame for violence onto the victims. Similarly, supporters of suicide bombings in Israel deflect the charge that they are responsible for killing innocent people by arguing that all Israelis are soldiers or potential soldiers that could come to kill Palestinians because of Israel's system of compulsory conscription. Therefore, they are not innocent.[4]

Antisystem Frames and Anticivilian Violence

Antisystem frames facilitate all three mechanisms of moral disengagement. They do so by attributing fault to the entire system. If societal and governmental institutions were more just or righteous, they claim, violence would not be necessary. To the extent violence exists, it is a product of injustice, not the cause of it. Those who brought about or maintain such a system are the culprits, not the rebels who are seeking to rectify the injustice. Such moral displacement stems directly out of the antisystem framing of the conflict.

Second, antisystem frames distort the consequences of violence by giving it an ethical dimension. Antisystem frames portray violence as necessary for bringing about a rupture with the prevailing unjust or unholy society. By framing the struggle as an all-encompassing war against entrenched institutions and elites, the victims of violence become conceived as small sacrifices for the greater good of humanity.

Finally, antisystem frames make the advantageous comparison of violence possible by insisting that the system, with all its governors, institutions, and agents, perpetrates grave injustices through its mere functioning. Marxist rebels, for instance, often counter condemnations of extreme violence by pointing out that capitalism perpetrates violence every day by impoverishing millions of people around the globe. Wasmund's (1986: 215) analysis of the Red Army Faction in Germany is illuminating: "In the process of defining symbolic figures of the political system as the personification of everything evil and bad, terrorists repress their guilt feelings and provide themselves with a 'good conscience,' justifying their deeds. The liquidation of the political enemy thus does not become a necessity but also a legitimate act."

Violence by antisystem groups is not likely to be limited to few targets. Antisystem ideologies portray few people as neutral; anyone who is perceived as lending support to an "unjust" social order or opposing the legitimacy of total war is part of the problem and, hence, fair game. History is replete with examples of guerrilla movements and militant groups attacking more noncombatants than they do government soldiers and functionaries. Wickham-Crowley (1991: 74, 79–80) points out that the Vietnamese Viet Cong and the Venezuelan Armed Forces of National Liberation (FALN), among others, unleashed terror campaigns against ordinary civilians to impose territorial control and deter defections. In the case of Vietnam, approximately 80 percent of the Viet Cong's victims were civilians. Crenshaw (1995: 477, 483–484) notes a similar pattern in the Algerian National Liberation Front (FLN), which carried out a violent campaign against rival groups and civilians who refused to abide by its edicts during its war of liberation.

The case of left-wing terrorism in Italy is also illustrative. As Della Porta (1995b: 113–117, 133–134) points out, survivors of state repression in the first phase of left-wing violence (1969–1974) served as a reservoir for recruitment in the "77 movement," which saw the list of enemies expand to social democracy, the Communist Party, and trade unions. Anticivilian violence, however, is exemplified best in Peru's Shining Path movement. Only 17 percent of its victims over the course of twelve years were security forces. Instead, most of its targets were ordinary civilians, including preachers, nuns, foreign development workers, journalists, human rights activists, teachers, students, and, above all, peasants (McClintock 1998: 67–68).

What is interesting about all these examples is that in each instance the movement concerned was an antisystem movement that sought to oust foreign forces or overthrow incumbent regimes. None adopted reconciliatory frames; instead, each portrayed its insurgency as a total struggle for social and political transformation. Each justified the expansion of violence by claiming that it was necessary for the good of the nation, people, or humanity.

In the previous chapter, I showed how exclusive organizations contribute to prolonging conflicts. Antisystem frames are also important for explaining protracted insurgencies. It is not easy to uproot antisystem thinking once it has been planted in the movement. Ideological intransigence in early interactions may solidify into collective identities that preclude reconciliation in later interactions. Once individuals begin to cross over from the sphere of uncommitted supporters into the realm of organized activists, identity gains salience. Symbolic orientations that define participants in relation to nonparticipants create expectations among actors, consolidate boundaries between real and perceived adversaries, and set parameters to the range of strategic options available to them—some options, in an objective sense, cease to be perceived as options (Melucci 1992, 1995). That is why many failed antisystem movements persist in their violence, despite the fact that their violence serves to further alienate the larger public that may have supported them at one point or another. Their violence ceases to be entirely strategic but instead becomes "redemptive" violence or "an end in itself" (Post 1998: 35; Juergensmeyer 2000).

Linking Repression, Exclusive Organizations, and Antisystem Frames

State repression and exclusive organizations facilitate the diffusion of antisystem frames within the insurgent movement. Mass movements rarely emerge as antisystem actors bent on social transformation. Some movement organizations and groups may begin with radical ideologies that call for revolution, but the mass public often comes to embrace revolutionary goals only when other avenues of contention are deemed blocked or ineffective (Goodwin 2001b). Moral disengagement, Bandura (1998: 164) writes, is "facilitated when nonviolent options are judged to have been ineffective and utilitarian justifications portray the suffering caused by violent counterattacks as greatly outweighed by the human suffering inflicted by the foe."

Antisystem frames that deny the possibility of reform and reconciliation with the incumbent regime are likely to resonate with movement supporters in the context of repression and political exclusion. In her study of the Campesino movement in Guatemala, May (2001: 8, 98) observes that some popular organizations shifted from pluralist explanations of state behavior to an antisystem perspective due to indiscriminate repression. "The political violence, particularly as it evolved into reactionary terror and became both more intense and more random, effectively conflated material and political concerns. Physical safety became increasingly contingent upon political transformation."

Antisystem frames, moreover, are not merely cultivated and solidified by individuals; groups in the context of exclusive organizations nurture them and give them legitimacy. "The disinhibitory training is usually conducted within a communal milieu of intense interpersonal influences insulated from mainstream social life," explains Bandura (1998: 186). Exclusive organizations promote such frames to maintain group cohesiveness and ensure against defections. Antisystem frames, characterized by ideological intransigence, emphasize the purity of the movement's cause and imbue movement activists with a sense of historical righteousness; the fight is not against this or that individual or party, it is a fight for new and better social order (Sprinzak 1998).

Antisystem frames, therefore, lead to moral demarcation between the insurgents' world and the system against which they are fighting. The former is the realm of righteous sacrifice and struggle against an iniquitous order, while the latter is the realm of exploitation, corruption, and narrow self-interest. This division is essential for the solidification of exclusive organizations because it makes defection to the other side more than just a strategic decision for survival; defection is "selling out" to or reconciling oneself with an illegitimate order. As Jabri (1996: 7) explains in relation to international and civil conflicts: "The discourse of inclusion and exclusion cannot allow uncertainty or doubt, so if such are expressed, they must be represented as irrational or even treacherous. Any representation which blurs the inclusion/exclusion boundary breaks down certainties constructed in the name of war and forms a counter-discourse which deconstructs and delegitimates war and thereby fragments myths of unity, duty and conformity."

Repressive political environments and exclusive organizations encourage the diffusion of antisystem frames. These ideological frames facilitate three mechanisms of moral disengagement: ethical justification, advantageous comparison, and displacement of blame. All three mechanisms make possible violent conduct against noncombatants. Although antisystem frames may exist in all societies, their "empirical credibility" is enhanced only under conditions of political exclusion and intense repression, and they are solidified within the context of exclusive mobilization structures.

In the following sections, I analyze the ideological frames of Algerian and Egyptian Islamists with particular emphasis on how antisystem rebels justified their expansive violence against civilians. I conclude by addressing how Al-Qaida leaders motivate anticivilian violence through the use of antisystem frames.

From Marginalization to Massacres: GIA Violence in Algeria

The GIA and AIS represented different strategic and tactical orientations within the armed movement. The GIA waged a total war that sought to replace the regime with an Islamic state. In its war, the GIA spared few people from the threat of violence. It attacked policemen and soldiers, government officials, state employees, journalists, intellectuals, foreigners, and ordinary civilians. Its tactics included assassinations, armed attacks, bombings, sabotage, massacres, mutilations, and throat cutting.

In contrast, the AIS waged a limited war against the state as a way to force the military regime to release FIS leaders, rehabilitate the FIS as a legitimate political party, and reinstitute the electoral process. The AIS limited its violence to security forces, government officials, and some journalists. The AIS opposed and denounced attacks on intellectuals, foreigners, and anyone who was not directly involved in the persecution of Islamists. Similar to the GIA, the AIS relied on assassinations, armed attacks, bombings, and sabotage, but it restricted its violence to targets that would cause the fewest civilian casualties.

Islamist insurgency underwent fundamental changes between 1992 and 1997. Islamist violence in Algeria since 1992 initially took the form of clashes with security forces and assassinations of policemen and military personnel. Until 1994, the majority of victims of Islamist violence were policemen and state security forces. In 1993 violence expanded to include government officials—especially those who were members of the quasiparliamentary National Consultative Council and the National Transition Council. Violence then expanded to include representatives of opposition groups, foreigners, and, shortly after, journalists and intellectuals. However, the victims of violence since 1995 have been mainly civilians, killed randomly through bombings or deliberately through attacks in villages, markets, cafés, and fake checkpoints (see Figure 5.1). Schools and school workers remained a constant target since 1994.[5]

Violence reached stupefying levels in a series of massacres that began to take place at the end of 1996. There were at least seventy-six massacres between November 1996 and July 2001, most of which were in 1997 (forty-two massacres).[6] Massacres were concentrated in villages around Algiers, Blida and Medea (south of Algiers), Ain Defla (southwest

Figure 5.1 Targets of Islamist Militants in Algeria, 1992–1998ᵃ

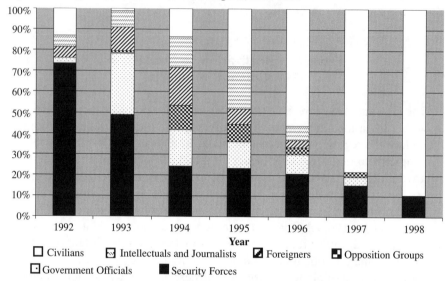

Source: The data were collected from *MEJ* chronologies and *MEI*. Only records that specify the date and place of an episode were included. Many reported incidents were not included in these numbers because they do not provide enough information to ensure their reliability.

Note: a. Measured in the number of separate attacks in each category, not in the total number of victims.

of Algiers), and Relizane (west of Algiers). They involved groups of militants armed with guns, crude bombs, knives, and axes descending on villages at night and killing their inhabitants, often by hacking them to death and cutting their throats. In many of these incidents the killers sought specific individuals and families, but in others the killing was random and unrestrained.[7]

The GIA's Antisystem Frames

When insurgency broke out in 1992, the GIA promoted antisystem frames that portrayed its jihad as a struggle against apostates (murtedeen), infidels (kufar), and tyrants (tawaghit). Furthermore, the GIA did not distinguish among actors outside of its camp; those who sustained the regime in one way or another were considered apostates, infidels, and tyrants themselves.

The AIS portrayed its jihad as a struggle against a self-interested elite who put an end to an otherwise legitimate process. They wanted a return to the system that briefly came into being and was subverted by the coup. Unlike the GIA, the AIS distinguished between those directly involved in the persecution of Islamists and neutral observers in the conflict. The AIS sought dialogue with those willing to come to a political solution, while it condemned those who wanted to eradicate the movement.

Although the coup was the impetus for armed struggle, the leaders of the GIA did not refer to the coup to justify jihad. On the contrary, GIA literature rarely mentioned the coup or did so only to deny that it motivated its insurgency. For example, in an August 1993 communiqué, Jafar al-Afghani, the third commander of the GIA, declared "the Armed Islamic Group was not born today; it was in secret preparation for years, but its entry into open jihadist military operations was precisely a year and ten months ago, that is since the Guemmar operation [less than two months prior to the coup]."[8] This claim is repeated by Zitouni (1995: 14), the sixth commander of the GIA, in *Hidayat Rab al-'Alamin*. By dating the start of the insurgency to the Guemmar attack in November 1991, the GIA explicitly rejected the argument that the military coup was the source of its violence.

The refusal of the GIA to use the coup as its justification for armed struggle is logical in light of the group's rejection of the electoral process and democracy. The militants that formed the core of the GIA always claimed that democracy is un-Islamic because sovereignty (hakimiya) belongs to God alone. The word of God cannot be subject to majority rule. For example, Layada, the first commander of the GIA, reproached the FIS in 1993 by declaring, "We warned them [the FIS] but they chose to enter into parliament, that wicked house and cursed tree; they knew that legislation is for God."[9] As indicated earlier, the GIA rejected alliances with the FIS because the latter believes in "polytheistic" (sherki) parliaments.[10]

Given this rejection of democracy, the GIA could not use the cancellation of the electoral process as its justification for armed struggle. Instead, it justified jihad on the basis that Islamic law did not reign in Algeria. As Layada put it: "The great tragedy the Muslim community is living in this era is the collapse of the Caliphate, because it is now living an abnormal and disharmonious life due to the separation between its high values, ideals and principles in which it believes and the pagan (jahili) reality imposed upon it" (quoted in al-Tawil 1998: 79).

To augment the aforementioned claim, the GIA maintained that the Algerian state is an apostate and infidel one because it refuses to apply Islamic law and represses Islamists who call for Islamic *sharia*. In a *fatwa* issued on 2 December 1992, Layada declared: "[Algerian] leaders in this age are, without exception, infidels. Their ministers, soldiers, and supporters and anyone who works under them, and helps them and all who accept them or remain silent to their deeds are also infidels outside of the creed."[11]

In an ominous communiqué issued on 13 September 1994, the day after Abassi Madani was released from prison in preparation for negotiations with the regime, the GIA declared that they fight the state "on the basis of apostasy and nothing else."[12] Zitouni maintained in *Hidayat Rab al-'Alamin* (1995: 27) that "the [GIA] considers the institutions of the [Algerian] state, from its agencies and ministers, to its courts and legislative and parliamentary assemblies, to its army, gendarme and police, to be apostate institutions."

In contrast, the AIS did not make the claim that the state has committed apostasy. In a series of open letters issued by the AIS commander in 1995, Madani Mezraq not once refers to the regime as an apostate one.[13] Likewise, letters written by Belhaj to his supporters and government officials, while replete with phrases about tyrants and tyranny, do not once mention the words *apostate* or *apostasy.*[14]

The GIA adopted two additional arguments to justify a total war against the regime. First, it argued that "jihad is an individual obligation (fard 'ayn) until judgment day."[15] As long as apostasy and infidelism rule, every Muslim is obligated to continue battle. By portraying jihad as an Islamic obligation, as opposed to one of many means to an end (as the AIS claimed), the GIA reinforced its antisystem framing of the conflict (Hafez 2000a). The war was a religious war, not a political one; jihad must continue until an Islamic state is constructed and the "word of God" reigns.

Second, the GIA claimed that the struggle in Algeria is part and parcel of a greater struggle by Muslims to bring down secular governments in all Muslim societies: "The regimes in the Muslim world in general and in Algeria in particular have been exposed to the people, and many of the false symbols and banners have fallen. Today they are extremely weak and the slightest nudge will bring them down, God willing. The phase of their destruction has begun" (Layada quoted in al-Tawil 1998: 83).

Ensuing writings by the GIA portrayed their struggle as one against "historic enemies" of Islam—"the West, Crusaders, and Jews." In a communiqué issued in August 1993, the GIA declared, "Our struggle is with infidelism and its supporters beginning with France and ending with the leader of international terrorism, 'The United States of Terrorism,' its ally Israel, and among them the apostate ruling regime in our land.''[16] The problem, in other words, was framed as a systemic problem whereby Muslims are governed by pagan states and besieged by un-Islamic forces inside and outside of Algeria. The crisis is not the fault of a few putschists that monopolize power; it is a crisis rooted in the Algerian and international system.

As part of its antisystem framing, the GIA polarized the conflict by adopting an us-versus-them, Muslims-versus-infidels, and Islam-versus-apostasy rhetoric. The GIA refused to distinguish between those who directly support the persecution of Islamists and those who sustain the state through their positions in the various branches and levels of government; all were considered apostates and tyrants because they maintained the un-Islamic system. Layada views all those who work for the state—from ministers to soldiers to all those who work under them—to be infidels. Zitouni (1995: 27) promoted a similar stance: "The [GIA] does not distinguish between those who fight us with arms or money or tongue."

In contrast, the AIS made distinctions between conciliators and eradicators, soldiers and state employees, and combatants and civilians. For example, in one letter to Zeroual, Mezraq differentiates between the president and the eradicators that have "led him astray." The AIS commander wrote: "They have deceived you, overturned the truth and distorted reality for you. . . . You standing in the ranks of the eradicators is dishonorable, and adopting their discourse is wrong and ridiculous" (in al-Tawil 1998: 298–299). In an open letter to Zeroual, FIS leader Rabeh Kebir urged the president to "resign and declare his innocence from the ruling tyranny."[17] Unlike the GIA, which lumped the president together with the entire state apparatus and denied the possibility for reconciliation with such an apparatus, the FIS and AIS recognized those within the state who were open to dialogue and reached out to them for the purpose of reconciliation.

Antisystem Justifications for Violence

The GIA repeatedly utilized antisystem frames in its communiqués to justify and motivate expansive violence against a range of "enemies." In 1993 the GIA expanded its violence to include journalists and intellectuals. A GIA communiqué issued on 12 January 1993 justified this expansion of violence by reference to the "obfuscation and distortion" of the "mercenary press" that "maligns" the holy fighters and refuses to report the truth. Another communiqué in August 1993 simply declared "he who fights us with the pen, we fight him with the sword" (quoted in al-Tawil 1998: 74–76).

In 1993 the GIA expanded its violence to foreigners. This was justified in the following terms:

> The jihadist operations commenced with prior planning and scheming, targeting all the symbols of the infidel regime from the head of state through the military, and ending with the last hypocrite working for the regime. In this equation enters *all who support the unjust, infidel system whether inside or outside [Algeria]*. . . . As we previously stated in our communiqués, the nationals of the resentful crusading countries are a target for the holy fighters because they represent part of the wicked colonialist plan, which is led by the leader of international terrorism [the United States], succored by its crusading friend [France].[18]

In 1994 the GIA expanded its threats to state employees and public schools. It justified this expansion in a communiqué issued in July 1994, which declared "the Armed Islamic Group issues its order to all customs and tax employees to leave their positions through which they support the tyrants. . . . Whoever refuses to obey this order, his judgment will be the judgment of the tyrants."[19] Antar Zouabri, the seventh commander of the GIA, ordered all workers in state oil and gas companies to cease work or face death.[20]

The GIA justified its attacks on schools in an August 1994 communiqué by declaring that "continuing with schooling is aiding the tyrants achieve stability. . . . It is known in [Islamic] law that it is not permissible to work in the institutions of apostate rulers."[21] In 1995 and 1996, the GIA expanded its threats to voters who were warned to stay away from the ballot boxes of the tyrants and apostates. The GIA promised to "spill the blood" of those who vote on election day.[22]

What all these communiqués had in common is an underlying antisystem and Manichean worldview that divided the world into Muslims and apostates, supporters and enemies of the state. Few people were viewed as neutral in the conflict; almost everyone was implicated in the struggle. Consequently, the GIA politicized individuals and groups that were not political or interested in taking sides. All the GIA had to do was warn people in advance that their actions aided the state. If the people refused to abide by the GIA's orders, they became targets. By accentuating the need for total war, the GIA gave its violence an "ethical" dimension. Attacking those who constituted the life-support for the "apostate" regime was permissible because the greater goal of salvaging the Muslim community demanded it.

Describing the Algerian ruling regime as apostate and infidel is not merely highly charged hyperbole; these terms are condensed symbols rooted in Islamic traditions and full of implied meaning. They suggest mutual negation, irreconcilability, and total war. In Islam, infidelism—nonbelief in the creator—is one of the greatest sins one can commit, especially when ruling over Muslim societies. The Quran repeatedly implores Muslims to struggle against infidels and promises great suffering toward the unbelievers.

Apostasy (turning away from Islam after upholding the creed), on the other hand, implies that reconciliation with the ruling regime is virtually impossible. In Islam, the punishment of an apostate is death; there can be no compromise with apostates. Entire wars were fought against apostates after the death of the Prophet Muhammad in what came to be known as *huroub al-ridha* or the apostasy wars. Therefore, one cannot reconcile with apostates and maintain the sanctity of Islam and the Muslim community. The GIA oft repeated mantra of "no dialogue, no cease-fire, no reconciliation, and no security and guarantee with the apostate regime" was justified with reference to the Quranic verse: "So, fight them [the unbelievers] till all opposition ends, and obedience is wholly God's."[23]

Ideology and Massacres in Algeria, 1997–2001

The violence of the GIA began to discredit the armed movement in the eyes of the Algerian public in general and Islamist supporters in particular. On the one hand, GIA violence fed into the rhetoric of eradicators who claimed that Islamism is an anti-enlightenment, antimodern movement bent on removing all traces of progress in Algeria. Communiqués that demanded an end to mixed-sex tours, forbade men and women from swimming together, made obligatory the donning of the *hijab*, ordered people to avoid state courts, and threatened to kill those who do not pray and pay the Islamic alms (zakat) to the GIA gave credence to the claims of eradicators.[24]

Just as detrimental to the Islamist movement were the attacks on the economic infrastructure of Algeria. Between 1995 and 1998 there were approximately 5,400 sabotage operations. The gas and electric company

reported 722 acts of sabotage, while the post and telephone communications infrastructures suffered 434 attacks. Roads and bridges—260 of
them—were not spared acts of sabotage.[25]

Perhaps most damaging to the Islamist movement were the GIA's
attacks on state employees. Its demand that people abandon work in
public companies could not be fulfilled in an economy where the state
is the largest employer and unemployment rates are high. Yet the GIA
went ahead with its threat to kill state employees and began to execute
them, often at fake security checkpoints where those identified as state
workers were simply shot, hacked to death, or had their throats slit.

In addition to seemingly senseless and cruel violence, the activities
of the GIA in its strongholds alienated people. In the "liberated zones,"
the GIA banned French-speaking press, satellite dishes, cigarettes,
music festivals, beauty salons, and the collection of government taxes.
They also regulated the price of meat and gasoline (Labat 1995: 270;
Qawas 1998: 181). Martinez (2000) highlights the racketeering activities of some GIA bands in areas where state control had collapsed. The
insurgents required food, supplies, contributions, and shelter. In *Hidayat
Rab al-'Alamin* (1995: 9), Zitouni claimed that the money of Muslims
should be directed to the commanders of the GIA, who are more worthy
of it, until the condition of sufficiency (al-kiffaya) has been achieved.
The GIA sometimes acquired its resources through consent but at other
times through coercion.[26]

As the conflict went on, the people who were initially sympathizers and supporters of the movement could no longer endure the material
costs of the insurgency. Many stopped giving their support, while others
turned against the movement. Some began to join the government-
sponsored armed militias to counter the violence of the insurgents.[27]
Some GIA militants, in turn, relied on more coercion—including massacres—to impose their authority in their strongholds as well as punish
those who had taken up arms against them (Dardour 1996; Kalyvas
1999; Martinez 2000). In an interview with *al-Hayat* journalist Camille
al-Tawil, a resident of Bentalha, where a gruesome massacre took place
on 22 September 1997, recalls: "We were forbidden from smoking a
cigarette, reading a newspaper, watching television, listening to radio,
or having a satellite. . . . They tried to impose their viewpoint on the
people and the straw that broke the camel's back [for the militants] was
the mass participation in the 1995 elections despite the many communiqués the GIA posted on the walls, in which it threatened to cut off the
heads of those who vote." When asked about the support the GIA

received from the locals, another Bentalha resident replied, "Do you believe that the residents supported the GIA willingly? Can you say to anyone that comes brandishing a weapon in your face and threatening to kill you that you will not give support?"[28]

There are suspicions as to the culpability of government-sponsored militias and the armed forces in some of the massacres that have taken place in Algeria since late 1996.[29] It is difficult to dismiss these charges without a series of investigations into each of the massacres. However, there can be no doubt that the GIA is responsible for much of the slaughter. Ahmed Bin Aicha, the AIS commander in the western zone, while raising questions about the identity of perpetrators of some of the massacres, stated in an interview that "what the [GIA] is doing in terms of massacres is known and apparent. But it has nothing to do with Islam. It is deviation from [the proper] understanding of Islamic law."[30] Mustapha Karatali, the commander of al-Rahman militia, which split from the GIA in December 1995, accused the latter of massacring relatives of the Larbaa militias at fake checkpoints. He explained the reason for splitting from the GIA in the following terms: "We fled [to the mountains] to die as a persecuted people, not as persecutors or perpetrators of killing the innocent."[31]

Many of these attacks have targeted specific individuals, families, and neighborhoods that have agreed to form antiterrorist militias (officially known as the Groupes de Légitime Défense; commonly referred to as "Patriots"). In some instances, entire families and hamlets were punished because some of their members and inhabitants had decided to fight alongside the government to combat militants.[32]

The ideological justifications for GIA impositions and carnage increasingly relied on sharper divisions between the armed groups and the people. These justifications were rooted in its earlier antisystem discourse that denied the possibility of neutrality in the struggle and portrayed the struggle as a holy obligation commanded by God. This was best expressed by one of the spiritual leaders of the GIA, Abu al-Mu'min al-Zoubair (known as Abu al-Munzer), in his pamphlet *al-Sayf al-Batar* (The Sharp Sword):

> The necessity of waging battle against those infidel and apostate tyrants was made clear and incumbent upon the Muslim community; it must fight them and show them hostility and loathing. . . . Every individual in this Muslim community must, as a duty, wage battle against the tyrants, and he is not permitted to turn to them or rely on them. . . .

For the entire [Muslim] community is called upon to join the ranks of the holy fighters. . . . *The issue is one of unity of God [tawhid] versus polytheism, and a clash between faith and infidelism.* . . . And whoever lags behind, or cowers, leans toward tameness, . . . or says that those leaders are not infidels . . . is an offender deserving punishment and he has fallen into great danger.[33]

Many Islamist groups that were once part of the GIA split after accusing its leadership of adopting a *kharijite* or *khawarij* (seceders) orientation that excommunicates Muslims for failing to uphold their religious obligations.[34] Two of the FIS leaders that defected to the GIA in May 1994, Abdelrazak Rejjam and Yousuf Boubras, withdrew their groups from the GIA in 1995 after accusing the latter of justifying the killing of the innocent.[35] Similarly, Anwar Haddam, the FIS-PDA leader who congratulated the unification pact of the GIA in 1994, subsequently denounced the GIA and accused it of being a khawariji movement.[36] The FIS-EBA also accused the GIA, the "monster of this age," of killing innocent people.[37] Perhaps most telling is the statement by Hassan Hattab, a former GIA commander in zone two and currently the leader of al-Jama'a al-Salafiya lil-Dawa wal-Qital. He broke with the GIA in 1996 after accusing it of "spilling the blood of the nation, looting its property and kidnapping its women."[38]

AIS's Cease-Fire Call

It is in this context that the AIS decided to bring to a halt its armed struggle against the regime. The AIS wanted to maintain support for the Islamist movement in the face of an eradicationist state policy that sought to marginalize the Islamists by giving limited political space to such groups as HAMAS and the MNI (Martinez 1997/1998). GIA violence was aiding the regime in achieving this aim by depleting the movement of its legitimacy and threatening to turn Islamist support into government support.

The first signs of a disenchanted public came during the 1995 presidential elections. Despite the call for a boycott made by the FIS and despite GIA threats to attack voters, voter turnout was high. Many observers interpreted the results of the election as a political defeat for the FIS. Just as important, HAMAS, one of the main competitors of the FIS, was allowed to compete during the presidential elections, and its leader, Nahnah, secured a sizable percentage of the votes. In 1997, other Islamist parties were allowed to compete for the parliamentary elections, and Islamist candidates won many seats.

Given that the AIS never justified its struggle against the state in religious or antisystem terms, and once it became clear that armed struggle was a futile endeavor, it made little sense to continue with the insurgency. The AIS was created to offer an alternative to total war and as a way to force the government to negotiate a settlement whereby the FIS would be rehabilitated. Once it became clear that armed struggle was not serving this aim but had an opposite effect, the AIS pursued an alternative strategy.[39]

The AIS declared a cease-fire largely to distance itself from ongoing violence and to make clear to the public, above all its supporters, that it was not behind the massacres and the senseless violence of the armed movement. The armed struggle, as the AIS claimed, had given opportunists a chance to exploit religion and distort its message. As one of the AIS leaders explained: "We do not wish for Islam, which is part of our identity, to become distorted in Algeria by the hands of Algerians." The cease-fire, he added, was intended to "lift the cover of the conspirators against religion."[40] Its cease-fire communiqué made it a point to condemn the "abominable carnage" as well as "the GIA criminals and those hiding behind them."[41]

From Moral Preaching to Moral Disengagement: Anticivilian Violence in Egypt

Islamist violence in Egypt in the 1990s featured a number of attributes that distinguished it from earlier periods. First, whereas violence in the 1970s and 1980s largely struck at "soft" targets—leftist students, Copts, and "places of sin"—violence in the 1990s was mainly aimed at the state and its institutions, as evinced by attacks on policemen, security forces, and prominent government officials.[42]

Second, Coptic Christians increasingly became targets of Islamist violence. While the number of violent incidents against Copts during the 1982–1991 period was estimated at twenty, the years 1992 and 1993 alone witnessed fifty-eight violent attacks against the Coptic community (Abulala 1998). The attacks on Copts continued well into the late 1990s.[43]

Third, violence was characterized by greater sophistication, as Islamists increasingly relied on high-tech explosives, intelligence gathering, and military training to better enable their units to inflict damage (Fatah 1995; Bakr 1996). For the first time since its inception, the Jama'a formed a clandestine armed wing with its own leadership separate from the preaching (dawa) wing.[44] The decision to form an armed wing marked a clear shift in strategy from prior periods, when the Jama'a rejected clandestine work as an un-Islamic innovation as well as a politically unsound strategy for building a mass movement (Mubarak 1995: 188).

Fourth, Islamist violence for the first time began to strike at tourists,[45] the tourism industry,[46] and financial centers—principally state and foreign banks.[47] Finally, Islamist violence was expansive. In addition to the aforementioned increase in attacks on Copts, tourists, and banks, Islamists struck at secular intellectuals and ordinary civilians suspected of collaborating with security forces. Among the notable intellectuals to come under attack were Faraj Fuda, an outspoken critic of Islamism killed in June 1992, and Najib Mahfouz, a Nobel Prize–winning novelist wounded in October 1994. There were also threats issued against intellectuals and entertainers such as Judge Said al-Ashmawi, feminist writer Nawal al-Sadawi, writer and professor Nasr Hamed Abu Zeid, and actor Adel Imam.[48] Since 1996, the Jama'a has escalated its rhetoric against the United States, Israel, Jews, and "Crusaders." It issued a series of communiqués threatening to strike at them.[49]

When rebellion broke out in 1992, antisystem frames were widespread in the Islamist movement. Islamist insurgents portrayed their struggle as a fight against secularism and infidelism, as opposed to a fight against specific state policies or officials misguided by erroneous beliefs. The insurgents wanted to uproot the social order; mere reforms were deemed insufficient. The insurgents also portrayed their struggle in polarizing terms: Islam versus jahiliya, God's sovereignty versus the sovereignty of people, and the party of God (hizb allah) versus the party of Satan (hizb al-shaytaun). The main group responsible for Islamist violence since 1992—the Jama'a—promoted these ideological frames in its struggle with the state.

It was not until the beginning of the 1980s that the Jama'a, especially its upper Egypt leaders, began to formulate an antisystem ideology as a result of their merger with the incipient Jihad group. The 1980s witnessed the consolidation of antisystem frames in the movement as the radicals produced a number of "religious studies" concerning the central questions and debates in the movement. These documents include the *Mithaq al-Amal al-Islami, Manhaj Jama'it al-Jihad al-Islami, Hatmiat al-Muwajaha, al-Jihad wa Ma'aalim al-Amal al-Thawri,* and *al-Hisaad al-Mur.*[50] Out of these documents at least six themes emerge: primacy of God's sovereignty; comprehensiveness and superiority of Islam; conspiracy against the Muslim world; irreconcilability of Islam with jahiliya; necessity for jihad; and impermissiblity of democracy.

On all these issues, the Muslim Brotherhood (MB) sought to counter the frames of radicals through a number of their own studies and documents, including *al-Ikhwan al-Muslimun, al-Hujum ala Rumouz wa Qiyadat Amal al-Islam,* and *Bayan lil-Nas.*[51]

The Primacy of God's Sovereignty

Both the Jama'a and Jihad groups believed in God's sovereignty (hakimiat allah) as opposed to human sovereignty.[52] God, the creator of the world, is the only giver of law and it is only to Him, His Prophets, and those who uphold His commandments that obedience is due. All other sovereignties—the state or the people—are subordinate to God's sovereignty. In the opening pages of the *Mithaq,* the stated goals of the Jama'a are obedience to God, the fulfillment of His commandments, and life in the path of His Prophet.

The Jama'a rejected all rulers who do not rule according to God's laws and commandments. Moreover, it did not take into account the interests of the state or its man-made institutions when deciding on a course of action; the interests of Islam supersede all other loyalties. The ultimate goal was to reestablish the Caliphate for the purpose of raising God's word on earth (*Mithaq,* 20, 87, 89–90, 96, 128). The Jihad group similarly argues that there can be no higher authority other than God. All systems that displace God's sovereignty or supplement it with another are infidel or polytheistic systems that must be rejected, indeed overthrown.

In contrast to the radicals, the MB rejected the view that the primacy of God's sovereignty precludes man-made laws. The essay *al-Hujum* (284–285) argues that "Islamic law has given Muslims the freedom to innovate on its basis." While God's words should be the foundations on which Muslim societies should rule themselves, these foundations permit Muslims the freedom through *ijtihad* (legal innovation or independent judgment) to legislate laws that are not found in the Islamic tradition. El-Hodaiby (1997: 23), an MB leader, explains: "The fixed and unchangeable tenets of the Islamic *sharia* are very few, consisting of basic principles designed to achieve justice and social and economic equality, as well as protect human rights, dignity, soul, and property. . . . There can always be access to ijtihad to deduce views that are appropriate to global, economic, and social changes." Thus, whereas the radicals saw the application of the *sharia* as an all-or-nothing process, the MB viewed the application of man-made laws based on the principles of Islam as part and parcel of applying the *sharia.*

The MB also argued that the primacy of God's sovereignty does not preclude a government based on the sovereignty of the people. In the document *Bayan lil-Nas*, the MB argued that rulers are fallible and therefore "they do not have a divine authority over people akin to God's truth." The document added, "The legitimacy of the government in an Islamic society depends on the government's ability to win the approval of the people and their choice." El-Hodaiby (1997: 22-23) expressed similar ideas: "While the government in Islam is required to abide by the principles of the Islamic *sharia,* it is still a civil government that is subject to accountability."

The Comprehensiveness and Superiority of Islam

Both the Jihad and Jama'a groups believed that Islam is a comprehensive religion that guides all aspects of life, not just matters of worship. The comprehensiveness of Islam means that there is no need to supplement it with other ideologies or borrow from other systems. The application of Islamic laws, as understood by the righteous forefathers (salaf al-salih), is all that Muslims need to lead the good life. As the Jama'a explained, today it is common to hear of "socialist Muslims" or "liberal Muslims." These Muslims do not comprehend the totality of Islam, which organizes all the needs of humanity in the one message sent by God to His Prophet. The comprehensiveness of Islam is the source of its superiority vis-à-vis secularism, socialism, and nationalism. All other systems, especially when applied in the Muslim world, erroneously impose ideas that are rooted in other religions, traditions, and beliefs, most of which are based on fallible human reasoning and self-interest that contravene Islam and perpetuate the subjugation of people to foreign and domestic rulers. The chief weakness of Muslims today is their abandonment of the path of God and his Prophet for human-centered systems (*Mithaq,* 25–26, 96; *al-Jihad,* 7, in Mustapha 1992).[53]

In contrast, the MB maintained that the belief in the comprehensiveness and superiority of Islam does not mean that there can be no room for learning from others or incorporating the beneficial contributions of other religions and civilizations. As the *Bayan lil-Nas* declared: "Pluralism in Islam requires the recognition of the other as well as the self, and mental preparation to acquire from that other all that is true, good, and within our interests."

The superiority of Islam, argued the MB, does not mean that Muslims can force others to adhere to Islam; there can be no compulsion in religion. El-Hodaiby (1997: 63) cites verse 13 of *Surat al-Hujurat* to justify tolerance toward other religions: "And we made you into nations and tribes, that you may know each other." Finally, the superiority of Islam does not mean that Muslims can transgress the rights of non-Muslims or treat them as unequal. In a 1994 communiqué, the MB endorsed the tolerant view that Christians and Jews are "people of the book" by calling for "serious constructive dialogue with everyone, especially the sons of the heavenly message with whom we are in agreement based on faith in God and the Judgment day."[54]

The Conspiracy Against the Muslim World

Both the Jama'a and Jihad groups portrayed their struggle as a fight against an international conspiracy led by the combined forces of Zionists, communists, and Crusaders who are out to destroy Islam. These forces fear the truth of Islam and unity of Muslims and, consequently, conspire to distort Islam and weaken the faith of Muslims. Secularism and nationalism are instruments of this nefarious international plot because they deny the totality of Islam and split Muslims into many states. The demise of the Caliphate is the ultimate expression of this conspiracy (*Mithaq,* 17–18).

Furthermore, existing rulers are also mere instruments of the broader conspiracy against Islam. They are either imposed by colonial powers or supported by them against their own people (*Hatmiat,* 20–22; *Manhaj,* 10–11). As the *Mithaq* (90–91) explained, "this loathsome secularism was inserted and forcefully planted in our land, thus producing these jahili and infidel regimes that exchange God's law with the law of Satan."

The MB is in complete agreement with radicals that there exists an international conspiracy by Zionists, Crusaders, and communists to destroy Islam. Like the radicals, it views secularism, nationalism, and communism, as well as Western media, as instruments of this plot to penetrate Muslim societies, draw Muslims away from their faith, and dominate them through alien concepts and systems. This belief was a constant feature of the MB's discourse since its emergence in 1928 and has been taken up by its allies in the Labor and Liberal parties since the 1980s (Abdelnasser 1994: 221–225; Ismail 1998).

However, unlike the radicals, the MB did not accuse the Egyptian government of being a willing partner in this plot or an instrument of it. More importantly, the MB used this supposed conspiracy against Islam to condemn the violence of militant Islamists because it weakens the Islamic community and permits the plotting forces to fulfill their grand design. In the August 1994 communiqué, the MB declared that violence has "granted foreign intelligence agencies an opportunity to fulfill their plans of creating confusion, striking at the unity of the nation, and exposing Islam to danger." It added, secular forces "have exploited violence to discharge the fire of their canons and bombs, aiming at Islam and its people under the pretext of fighting terrorism." Thus, whereas the jihadists used the "fact" of an international conspiracy against Islam to wage war against the secular conspirators, including indigenous rulers, the MB argued that violence against the Egyptian regime could only aid the plotters by further dividing the Muslim community.

The Irreconcilability of Islam with Jahiliya

Both the Jama'a and Jihad groups believed that there are only two systems of rule: Islam and jahiliya (pre-Islamic paganism, which was based on the belief in multiple Gods or sovereignties). Those who do not rule in accordance with God's law are infidels. Both groups based their argument on the Quran passage: "Those who do not judge by God's revelations are infidels indeed."[55]

The infidels comprise secularists, liberals, communists, socialists, nationalists, and anyone who does not call for the complete application of Islamic law. They are infidels because they seek to displace the sovereignty of God by elevating human reason and law above God's commandments. As the document *al-Jihad* (13, in Mustapha 1992) explained, "the ruling order in Egypt is a jahili, infidel order as are all systems that have taken secularism as a paradigm and discarded the rule of Islam."

The comprehensiveness and superiority of Islam mean there can be no compromise with such ideologies, nor is the mere application of some of God's laws while ignoring others permissible. In the *Mithaq* (108), the Jama'a averred that Muslims "cannot take part in jahili institutions for the sake of advancing [their] goal. For in doing so [Muslims] aid the jahiliya to fulfill its objectives." In another document in which they attack the MB for working with secular rulers, the Jama'a declared "the struggle between Islam—as an idea and system—and secularism is a decisive one; it does not end until one of them is eliminated or submerged within the other."[56] In the *Manhaj* (2), Aboud Zumur argued that the goal should be "Islamic revolution to overturn the jahili orders in our lands; we reject all of the partial solutions that tend toward gradualism in applying [the *sharia*] or the mere application of the Islamic punishments [hudud]."

In contrast to the radicals, the MB rejected the notion of contemporary jahiliya. It argued that the Egyptian polity is inherently Islamic because the constitution upholds Islam as the state religion and Islamic law to be the principal source of legislation. In addition, the people in Egypt generally adhere to Islam and abide by its commandments. As the essay *al-Hujum* (285) explained, "the most important feature of the Egyptian constitution is that it declares in article 2 that Islam is the religion of the state, Arabic is its official language, and the pillars of the Islamic *sharia* are the principal source of legislation." Thus, despite the government's refusal to apply Islamic law in all areas of public policy, the state is not jahili and its rulers are not infidels. In the August 1994 communiqué, the MB stated that it "distinguishes between the general system of the state—the constitution and laws on which it is based—and the actions of some individuals, prominent officials, and agencies that belong to the ruling regime, and which contravene the [laws] of the state itself." The MB leadership continued to stress that they are willing to support any ruler who is serious about applying the Islamic *sharia*.[57]

The Necessity for Jihad

Both the Jama'a and Jihad groups believed that jihad is an Islamic obligation against infidel regimes who do not rule according to God's laws. Similar to the GIA in Algeria, the Jama'a (*Mithaq*, 150, 157) based its argument on the Quran passage: "So, fight them [the unbelievers] till all opposition ends, and obedience is wholly God's."[58]

Moreover, the Jama'a viewed its fight against secularism as a war not dissimilar to the apostate wars that were fought after the death of the Prophet in the first century of Islam (*Hatmiat al-Muwajaha*, 57). This historical paradigm must be emulated, the Jama'a suggested, because it was only through fighting apostates that Islam consolidated itself and became a world religion. Furthermore, jihad is an indispensable component of comprehensive Islamic activism, which begins with the dawa, progresses to forbidding vice, and culminates with holy war. This three-pronged strategy is the only appropriate one because it comes from the Quran (*Mithaq*, 80–81, 101, 141–159; *Hatmiat,* 5, 16, 23).

As for the Jihad group, the name of its organization speaks to its view on the issue.[59] It too argued that jihad was necessary to counter foreign aggression and depose jahili rulers who do not rule with what

God brought down to humanity. Moreover, jihad is continuous until judgment day and is an obligation on every Muslim until enough Muslims have stepped forward to wage battle against infidel rulers and aggressors (*Manhaj,* 13–14, 17, 25).

Both the Jihad and Jama'a groups also believed that jihad is necessary to ward off the international conspiracy against Islam. The Jihad group, in its document *al-Jihad* (22–23, in Mustapha 1992), argued that "The struggle between Islam and the West has a special priority within the broader struggle between Islam and the jahiliya. . . . The complete consolidation of Islam will not occur until the Western jahiliya is redeemed." Similarly, the Jama'a argued that jihad is necessary to liberate the land of Muslims in Palestine, Spain, and the Balkans as well as to initiate new conquests "to preach Islam to kings and emperors through the Quran and the sword" (*Mithaq,* 157). In this conception, jihad is an aggressive doctrine, not a defensive concept.

Like the radicals, the MB believes that jihad is an important component of Islam and it is the obligation of Muslims to uphold it when circumstances demand it. The MB argued that the precept of "commanding the good and prohibiting the forbidden" applies to it as much as it applies to self-proclaimed jihadists. However, in both instances the MB takes issue with the radicals as to the appropriateness of jihad in the Egyptian context, as well as to the means by which to forbid vice.

Given that the MB rejected the claim that contemporary Egyptian society is jahili, it also rejected that Egypt is a house of war (dar al-harb) and that jihad is necessary to raise God's word within it. Jihad is applicable against foreign invaders, as well as to liberate occupied Muslim lands. In Egypt, however, the state upholds Islam as the state religion and the *sharia* as its principal source of legislation. Therefore, jihad is not necessary.

Muslims are instructed in the Quran not to create disorder (fitna). Yet the violence of the militants does precisely that and in the process harms the interests of the Islamic nation by turning Muslims against Muslims. The violence of the radicals distorts the image of Islam and creates conditions harmful to Islamic preaching. The MB repeatedly made reference to two Quranic verses: "Call them to the path of your Lord with wisdom and words of good advice" and "Remind them, you are surely a reminder. You are not a warden over them."[60] The violence of the radicals, argued the MB, "only leads to more turmoil and shakes the stability of the nation and its security," making it vulnerable to foreign conspiracies.[61] In a 1994 communiqué, the MB condemns the violence of the radicals, calling it a "clear conspiracy to tear the one nation."[62]

The Impermissiblity of Democracy

Both the Jama'a and Jihad groups rejected democracy as a secular innovation that is thoroughly un-Islamic and, more importantly, cannot be Islamized. They based their argument on the Quranic passage "authority belongs to God alone."[63] Democracy, as the radicals saw it, is akin to polytheism (shirk), for it elevates the will of the people above the will of God.

In *al-Hisaad al-Mur,* the Jihad group argued that democracy gives the right to legislate to someone other than God, which is equivalent to deifying the people. The majority in a democratic system can make permissible something that God has forbidden, which means their authority is higher than God's will. The only way to reaffirm God's sovereignty is by making His laws the sole source of legislation.

In addition, the Jihad group rejected democracy because it is based on absolute freedom and equality. Absolute freedom, it argued, is not permissible when it means that Muslims have a choice between accepting and rejecting their faith. As for equality, there can be no equivalence between Muslims, Christians, and Jews. Non-Muslims have to pay monetary tribute (jizya) to Muslims and are not allowed to convert Muslims to other faiths, whereas it is the obligation of Muslims to preach to non-Muslims. Nor can there be equality between men and women; both have different rights and obligations that distinguish them from each other (*al-Hisaad,* quoted in Mubarak 1995: 345).

Similarly, the Jama'a cited the following Quranic passage to reject the equality imposed on Muslims by democracy: "Is one who is a believer like one who is a transgressor? No, they are not alike."[64] They also rejected democracy because it treats equally *hizb allah* (the party that upholds Islamic law) and *hizb al-shaytaun* (any party that does not call for Islamic law); both have an equal chance to come to power and legislate.

In contrast, the MB believes that democracy and pluralism are not only permissible but also desirable because they are part and parcel of the Islamic notion of consultation (shura). As the *Bayan lil-Nas* claimed, "The *shura* has a specific meaning in the Islamic viewpoint. In its essence, it corresponds to the democratic order, which puts the reins of power in the hands of the majority without injuring the rights of minorities who disagree and hold another opinion or position." In the document *al-Ikhwan al-Muslimun* (26), it argued that the shura "is an extension of the authority of the nation with which it specifies the responsibilities of the rulers to the nation and the manner with which it evaluates and corrects them." El-Hodaiby (1997: 23) averred: "The *ummah,* or nation, is the source of authority in Islam, and Quranic verses require that Muslims conduct their affairs by *shura,* or mutual consultation. It is the nation that appoints its leaders. Power cannot be taken by the edge of the sword, but only through proper free choice."

The MB also confirmed that it accepts the alternation of power based on regularly scheduled elections. In *al-Ikwan al-Muslimun* (38–39), the organization maintained "that adhering to party pluralism in an Islamic society entails accepting the alternation of power between the groups and political parties through election cycles." In *al-Hujum* (in Aamer 1995: 296), Habib declared that "it is the people who are the source of authority and they alone have the right to choose its deputies and rulers . . . through a free and fair ballot box."

Antisystem Frames in the Six Themes

The six themes highlighted the antisystem frames of the jihadist wing of the Islamist movement during the 1980s. First, their objective was to uproot the secular social order and the state system in which it is grounded. There could be no compromise on this issue because the comprehensiveness of Islam, as they saw it, precludes reconciliation with secularism; the two are antithetical.

Second, rather than seek specific reforms, the radicals sought a greater unity based on Islamic allegiance and a caliphate system of rule. Third, the Jama'a repeatedly referred to the rulers of Egypt as infidels, apostates, and tyrants. As with the GIA in Algeria, this choice of terminology is suggestive; apostates and infidels must be fought. Compromise with them is impermissible.

Fourth, the discursive mode of the jihadists was that of binary oppositions: Islam versus jahiliya; God's sovereignty versus the sovereignty of the people; and the party of God versus the party of Satan. There was no room in their discourse for middle positions or ambiguities. They made no distinctions between secular rulers of Muslim countries and foreign powers; all were part and parcel of a foreign conspiracy to displace Islam. Nor did they make a distinction between the ruling elite and its institutions, on the one hand, and the parties, police-men, soldiers, or government officials of the state, on the other; all were implicated in the secular order. Thus, there were only two forces: the forces of Islam and the forces of jahiliya.

Antisystem Justification for Violence During the 1990s

The Jama'a used antisystem frames to justify is violence against a wide range of targets. Talat Fouad Qasim was explicit about the antisystem goals of the insurgents: "What is occurring now [in 1993] with regards to the struggle with the regime has as its aim the bleeding of the system before the all-encompassing confrontation, . . . not, as some claim, mere protest activities. We are not a limited protest or opposition move-ment; we are an alternative group to the regime" (quoted in Mubarak 1995: 414).

During a court trial in 1993, imprisoned Jama'a leaders justified their attacks on tourists as a reaction to government torture, arrests, and expulsions from schools and mosques.[65] In a communiqué issued on 2 February 1994, the Jama'a threatened tourists with "bloodshed" because they help the "regime which fights Islam, tortures its sons, abuses its women, and executes its young."[66] In two other commu-niqués, the Jama'a claimed responsibility for the bombing of a tourist train and a bank in revenge for the death sentences issued by a military court against three of its activists.[67]

What is noteworthy about all these communiqués is that the Jama'a viewed the killing of tourists and the bombing of banks as means to strike at the state. It made no distinction between a military court, a government official, a tourist, and a bank. They are all part of one sys-tem because they sustain the system. Striking at one is striking at the system.

This logic was made explicit by Talat Fouad Qasim during an inter-view with Hisham Mubarak in 1993. When asked why the Jama'a attacks tourists, Talat's response was "striking at such an important source of income will be a major blow against the state. It does not cost us much to strike at this sector" (in Mubarak 1997: 321). Omar Abdel Rahman denied that tourists per se were targets. It was the tourist infra-structure that the Jama'a sought to dismantle. However, in a telling side remark he states, "How can we cry for a tourist and not cry for the hun-dreds of thousands of the oppressed."[68] This advantageous comparison of one's violence can be found throughout the literature of the group.

The Jama'a also justified its attacks on state officials, policemen, and banks by displacing responsibility for violence. When asked why the Jama'a kills local policemen with no power or responsibility within the state, Abdel Rahman replied: "A policeman under orders is not free from responsibility. When he meets God almighty [will he] say to Him I am just an employee? . . . The police is a complete and unified apparatus; the transgressor [the Egyptian state] could not act without having the support of a police force behind it."[69]

In another telling communiqué, the Jama'a claimed responsibility for killing a secret agent, as well as blowing up a tourist train and a bank in revenge for the massacre of Palestinians in Hebron by an Israeli settler. The communiqué declared that these attacks are our "duty to the jihadist brothers in Muslim Palestine."[70] Thus, the Jama'a viewed attacks on government agents and the economic infrastructure in Egypt as a way to avenge the killing of Muslims abroad. In other words, it did not distinguish between foreign enemies and the Egyptian state; striking at the latter is equivalent to striking at the former because they are part of one system or alliance against Islam and Muslims. This logic manifested itself in one of the massacres against tourists in Egypt. In April 1996, the Jama'a claimed responsibility for the killing of eighteen Greek tourists in central Cairo in revenge for Israeli bombings in Lebanon.[71]

Even random bombings and killings of individuals for the sake of creating confusion and instability in an "iniquitous" social order made strategic sense for rebels bent on the fundamental restructuring of the polity. As two Egyptian political experts noted, the attacks on Copts and random bombings in the center of Cairo were not aimed at the victims; they were intended to expose the inability of the ruling regime to maintain order and to shake its legitimacy by raising doubt as to its ability to carry the central task of any state: the protection of its citizenry (Fatah 1995: 41 and 65; H. Ibrahim 1996: 303).

The Jama'a in the mid and late 1990s continued to insist that there was an international conspiracy of Zionists, Jews, and Crusaders against Islam. In one communiqué it declared war on Jews—vowing to "kill them all"—and the "new crusading system" in response to the killing of the leader of the Palestinian Islamic Jihad group.[72] In two other communiqués the Jama'a condemned the "New Terrorist Order" imposed by the United States and declared U.S. interests to be legitimate targets because of the "war" waged by the United States on Iraq, Somalia, Libya, and Palestine.[73]

Similar to the GIA in Algeria, the antisystem discourse of the Jama'a contributed to the expansive violence of the 1990s. Such frames polarized the social conflict and treated few actors as neutral. Antisystem frames also facilitated the moral disengagement of Jama'a militants as they increasingly exercised their violence against tourists, Copts, and ordinary policemen who could hardly do anything to aid or hinder the cause of Islamists. All three mechanisms of moral disengagement—ethical justification, advantageous comparison, and displacement of responsibility—were facilitated by Jama'a antisystem frames.

Sanctioning Mayhem:
The Antisystem Frames of Al-Qaida

On 11 September 2001 terrorists belonging to the Al-Qaida network hijacked four U.S. airliners and proceeded to crash two of them into the World Trade Center in New York and one into the Pentagon in Washington, D.C., resulting in over 3,000 deaths. This attack was not the first anticivilian carnage perpetrated by the Al-Qaida network. On 7 August 1998, it struck at U.S. embassies in Tanzania and Kenya, killing 223 people and injuring more than 4,700 people. Most of the victims in this simultaneous attack were not Americans; most, in fact, were Africans and many were Muslims.

Osama bin Laden, the founder and leader of the Al-Qaida organization, has never taken direct responsibility for these atrocities. However, he did condone them as "blessed terror" against the United States. Bin Laden's war against the West and the United States in particular stems from his professed dissatisfaction with Western support for dictatorial Arab regimes and the presence of U.S. forces in Saudi Arabia.[74] Bin Laden and his terrorists have also taken up the cause of Palestine, Iraq, Kashmir, Bosnia, Uzbekistan, and Chechnya, blaming their misfortunes on the West.

Al-Qaida is the quintessential exclusive organization that combines hierarchy and bureaucracy with a loosely structured network of radical Islamist groups from around the Muslim world. Many of its members have been recruited from the pool of Afghan fighters that came to fight Soviet forces during the 1980s. Others came to it as Islamist dissidents fleeing repression in their own countries. Still others joined as "freelance" adventurers seeking financial and moral support for their violent plans to strike at the United States. In any case, Al-Qaida constitutes a radical organization of the most dedicated militants in the Muslim world (Bodansky 1999; Rashid 2000; Jacquard 2002).

Many of its recruits are unmarried young men. Although some of the leadership of Al-Qaida come from affluent families and accomplished educational backgrounds, few of its cadres have completed secondary schools and mainly have studied only the Quran. Each recruit was given a code name and underwent a "regimented, demanding basic training that infantry soldiers get in much of the world, but with steady infusions of Islamic fervor." Its training camps were run like a university, with course curriculums, scheduled classes, training manuals, and required reading lists. Recruits had to complete basic courses on the use of the Kalashnikovs, mortars, grenades, secure communications, map reading, and celestial navigation. A select few went on to take advanced courses in espionage and explosives. Everyone had to complete Quranic studies. Despite some variation across the camps, "Islamic Groups developed a uniform training program that assimilated recruits with different cultures and skills." The mission statement of the camps was emblazoned on the walls of some its houses under the statement "Goals and Objectives of Jihad." It entailed the following aims: (1) establishing the rule of God on earth; (2) attaining martyrdom in the cause of God; (3) purifying the ranks of Islam from the elements of depravity.

Trainers and recruits had to abide by a budget and completed expense forms, maintained records on the accomplishments of "students," and kept inventories of resources. Training camps also had rules akin to what one would find in university dormitories, including "clean beds and tents once a week," "no political discussions," and, of course, "go to bed early."[75] Yet despite the apparent hierarchy and bureaucracy that prevailed in the camps, the organization was a loosely knit one, with groups and "sleeper" cells all over the world with nominal allegiance to and financial support from the Al-Qaida network.[76]

Al-Qaida leaders have justified anti-Western violence in a number of communiqués and videotaped messages to the world. In all those statements one can discern the antisystem frames that revolve around a master narrative of a "clash of civilizations" between the Muslim world, on the one hand, and an alliance of Christian "Crusaders" and Jewish "Zionists" on the other. This alliance is bent on the destruction of the holy Muslim community and the subjugation of its people. As bin Laden declared during an interview with al-Jazeera Television in October 2001, the "battle is not between Al-Qaida and the U.S. This is a battle of Muslims against the global crusaders." Like the radical movements in Algeria and Egypt, Al-Qaida leadership deploys ideological frames to facilitate three mechanisms of moral disengagement—ethical justification, advantageous comparison, and displacement of responsibility—to motivate violence against the West.

Ethical Justification of Violence

On 23 February 1998, Osama bin Laden, with the support of other radical Islamist leaders from around the Muslim world, issued the first communiqué of the "World Islamic Front for Combating Jews and Crusaders." In this communiqué, bin Laden declares that it is the individual duty of every Muslim to "kill Americans and their allies—civilian and military" whenever and wherever they may find them. Such a statement was not the first to be made by bin Laden.[77] However, its unequivocal tone and actual rhetoric amounted to a declaration of war on the West. What is perhaps most important is that bin Laden did not make a distinction between military and civilians, nor did he distinguish between those directly supportive of the "Crusader-Zionist" aggression and those who are allied with them.[78] Both were equally culpable and, therefore, fair game. On what basis did bin Laden justify such expansive violence?

The Al-Qaida network believes that existing governments in the Muslim world are corrupt and un-Islamic because they do not rule according to God's laws. These governments, moreover, rely excessively on the West for political sustenance. Indeed, bin Laden and his deputies have maintained that but for Western support, these leaders would fall easily to the armed struggle waged by indigenous Islamic movements.

The West supports these leaders, argues bin Laden (in an October 2001 interview), because it is "against the establishment of any Islamic government." Such a unified Islamic government would resist U.S. domination, refuse to allow it to plunder its wealth, and would pose a real challenge to Israel and eventually destroy it. The 23 February 1998 communiqué of the World Islamic Front declares that "crusader armies are spreading in [the Arabian Peninsula] like locusts, eating its riches and wiping out its plantations." These forces are "dictating to its rulers, humiliating its people, and terrorizing its neighbors." America's endeavor is "to fragment all the states in the region such as Iraq, Saudi Arabia, Egypt, and Sudan" to guarantee "Israel's survival."

Thus, according to bin Laden, the terror against the forces of the West is an ethical struggle to protect the Muslim community and end its suffering at the hands of unbelievers. Ours is a "blessed terror to rebuff suppression" and roll back the "crusader campaign against Islam," bin Laden declared in a taped message that aired on 26 December 2001.

What is interesting, but by no means unique, is his antisystem framing of the conflict. Although bin Laden's grievances were initially focused on the presence of Western forces in Saudi Arabia, his claims quickly expanded to include the plight of Muslims from Africa to Europe to Central and Southeast Asia. In his October 2001 interview with al-Jazeera, bin Laden states, "We are being attacked in Palestine, Iraq, Lebanon, Sudan, Somalia, Kashmir, the Philippines, and everywhere." In other communiqués, he speaks of the suffering of Muslims in Bosnia and Chechnya.

His focus, moreover, goes back in time and is not limited to contemporary events. In his videotaped message aired on 7 October 2001, bin Laden speaks of "eighty years of humiliation." In doing so, he attempts to link disparate events in time and space to accentuate the perceived danger posed by Western forces and gives those events a conspiratorial coherence that they otherwise lack when viewed independently of each other. Surely, so his logic goes, in the face of such an omnipotent and ubiquitous danger, extraordinary measures against aggressors, their agents, and civilian populations are warranted and legitimate.

Bin Laden's symbols justify violence in another way. By constantly referring to the West and the United States as crusaders and infidels, and by referring to Muslim leaders that "serve" the West as apostates and sinners, he makes violence against them a religious imperative and a holy deed. Ethical justification for violence, in other words, becomes bound to God's word as if God has ordered it himself. Indeed, bin Laden's February 1998 communiqué states, "We call upon every Muslim, who believes in Allah and asks for forgiveness, to abide by *Allah's order* by killing Americans and stealing their money anywhere, anytime, and whenever possible [emphasis added]." Bin Laden's statements are replete with religious verses that command Muslims to battle the infidels.

By insisting on the use of the term *Crusaders,* bin Laden attempts to associate contemporary Western states with historic enemies that have inflicted great suffering on Muslim peoples. This frame serves a dual purpose. First, it turns the conflict into a religious battle between irreconcilable opposites and heightens the threat posed by Western states, thus making extreme violence in defense of faith permissible. As bin Laden put it in his videotaped message that aired on 7 October, the struggle "has divided the world into the camp of faith and unbelief." In another taped statement aired on 3 November, he declared "this is a matter of religion and creed."

Second, if the description of Crusaders is accepted, it makes it binding that Muslims must rise up to defend themselves against aggressors, for in Islam it is a religious duty to fight in defense of one's religion and lands. In an open letter to the Muslims of Pakistan, issued on 24 September 2001, bin Laden attempts to rally the people by reciting the words of the Prophet: "Whoever does not participate in a battle or does not support a fighter for Allah . . . God will punish before the Day of Judgment."

Advantageous Comparison and Displacement of Responsibility

Another of Al-Qaida's means to motivate and justify horrific attacks on civilians has been to belittle the consequences of its violence by comparing it to the present and historic "crimes" committed by the United States and Israel against Muslims around the globe. In an interview with CNN in March 1997, bin Laden justifies his war on America by claiming that the United States "has committed acts that are extremely unjust, hideous and criminal whether directly or through its support of the Israeli occupation."[79]

In the 23 February 1998 communiqué, the leaders of Al-Qaida begin by citing the "continuing aggression against the Iraqi people" that has resulted in "great devastation." The World Islamic Front for Combating Jews and Crusaders 12 August 1998 communiqué justifies the mass murder of civilians by pointing out that the "two embassies that the Islamic Army for the Liberation of the Holy Places blew up had supervised the killing of at least 13,000 Somali civilians in the treacherous attack led by the United States against this Muslim country."

In the October 2001 interview, bin Laden was asked point blank "how about the killing of innocent civilians?" Bin Laden warded off the implied contradiction between his Islamic beliefs and the killing of civilians by answering the question with a series of his own: "Who said that our children and civilians are not innocent and that shedding their blood is justified? . . . When we kill their innocents, the entire world from East to West screams at us, and America rallies its allies, agents, and the sons of its agents. . . . Who has been getting killed in our countries for decades? More than 1 million children died in Iraq and others are still dying."

Recently, the Abu Sayyaf Group, one of the groups that declares allegiance to Al-Qaida in the Philippines, employed this method of moral disengagement to justify its hostage-taking. In a videotaped message released in March 2002, two U.S. missionaries taken hostage in 2001 declare under gunpoint that the actions of the group were in response to U.S. support for Israel and sanctions against Iraq and Libya.[80]

In addition to advantageous comparison of violence, the most common means of justifying inhumane conduct against civilians deployed by Al-Qaida has been to displace blame and shift it onto others, principally the victims of violence themselves. In a 12 August 1998 communiqué (issued five days after the bombing of American embassies in Kenya and Tanzania), the Islamic Army for the Liberation of the Holy Places, which is supported by Al-Qaida, declared: "Given the American Crusader and Jewish Israeli occupation of the places of al-Aqsa mosque, given what the Jews are doing in Palestine by killing our children and women; . . . given that more than a million Iraqis have died; given the imprisonment of Islamic preachers in America and in the countries controlled by the United States, and given the theft of Muslim fortunes through oil development, we are *compelled* to wage jihad throughout the world and at all times [emphasis added]."

In the October 2001 interview with al-Jazeera Television, bin Laden declares that the "brave men" who conducted the 11 September attacks did it "as a matter of self-defense, in defense of our brothers and sons in Palestine, and to liberate our sacred religious sites. If inciting people to do that is terrorism, and if killing those who kill our sons is terrorism, then let history bear witness that we are terrorists." He added, "Just as they're killing us, we have to kill them so that there is a balance of terror." When reminded that the Prophet Muhammad forbade the killing of innocents, bin Laden responded, "This is not absolute. There is a saying [by the Prophet], 'If the infidels killed women and children on purpose, we shouldn't shy away from treating them in the same way to stop them from doing it again. . . . If they kill our women and our innocent people, we will kill their women and their innocent people until they stop.'"

Both the portrayal of one's violence as a "minor" response to the enemy's enormous violations of human rights and the displacement of blame for the violence are intended to shift the focus away from one's crimes as well as make the victimizer appear to be the victim. This moral inversion elevates the Al-Qaida militant to the status of legitimate defender of rights while it simultaneously deprives his Western victims of innocence and imbues them with culpability. Moreover, by framing violence as an "inevitable" manifestation of cruelties and oppression inflicted by the West, Al-Qaida terrorists are able to relinquish free will and parry the condemnations of their critics.

Conclusion

Militant Islamists have deployed several ideological frames to justify and motivate collective violence against civilians. Violent militants must talk themselves into carrying out inhumane conduct by deactivating self-inhibitory norms against violent behavior. They do this through at least three mechanisms of moral disengagement: ethical justification of violence, advantageous comparison of one's own violence in relation to the violence of others, and displacement of responsibility for violence by shifting it onto its victims.

Antisystem frames that polarize social actors, heighten the threat posed by "oppressors," and portray the struggle as a total war against corrupt and irredeemable enemies facilitate all three mechanisms of moral disengagement. In the case of Muslim rebellions, insurgents and terrorists employed a master frame that spoke of a nefarious plot by Crusaders and Zionists and their subservient apostate agents to destroy Islam and subjugate Muslims in their lands. In the case of Algeria and Egypt, those who advanced antisystem frames that portrayed their enemies as infidels, apostates, and tyrants perpetrated horrific violence against civilians, while those who rejected such framing of the conflict either abstained from violence or limited it to government officials and security forces.

Al-Qaida, of course, has been an antisystem movement par excellence. The communiqués and videotaped messages of its leaders reflect the extent to which they have sought to deactivate moral codes against killing civilians. They have done so by accentuating the alleged threat posed by the West and refusing to recognize the possibility of neutrality in the epic conflict between Islam and the "unbelievers."

Antisystem frames alone cannot explain recurring anticivilian violence. These radical ideological frames exist in almost every Muslim society. Yet not all those societies experience anticivilian violence on the scale witnessed in Algeria and Egypt. These frames gain broad support and are acted upon in a context of mass mobilization and under conditions of indiscriminate political repression.

Moreover, antisystem frames are generally nurtured by exclusive organizations that wish to draw sharp dividing lines between insiders and transgressors. Ideas alone, virulent as they may be, are not enough to unleash mass violence. Even the most fanatical and determined militants cannot engage in recurring patterns of anticivilian violence without some level of organizational support and resources. What made the extremists in the Al-Qaida network capable of striking repeatedly at U.S. civilian targets was that they had the financial backing of the wealthy Osama bin Laden. They also had the material support of the Taliban government in Afghanistan, as well as the organizational skills of experienced leaders and rebels from around the Muslim world. Antisystem ideological frames, however, are indispensable for mass civilian violence even if they are not sufficient to produce it. Perhaps the most convincing proof for this proposition is the fact that Islamists go to great lengths to articulate justifications for violence and counter the condemnations of their critics.

Notes

1. Islamic movements are not alone in perpetrating anticivilian violence. Militant Christians, Jews, Buddhists, and Sikhs have also been inspired by their religious beliefs to engage in anticivilian violence. For an excellent analysis and comparative perspective on religious violence that targets civilians, see Juergensmeyer (2000).

2. See, for example, the last testament of Muhammed Hiz'a al-Ghoul, the twenty-two-year-old suicide bomber who killed nineteen Israelis in a bus on 18 June 2002. In it he wrote: "How beautiful it is for the splinters of my bones to blow up the enemy, not because we love to kill, but to live as others live. . . . We do not sing the song of death but recite the hymns of life. . . . We die so that future generations can live."

3. See, for example, the story of Darin Abu Eisheh, who videotaped a message before carrying out an attack in the West Bank. She justified her pending action by comparing it to the violence inflicted by indiscriminate Israeli suppression of the Palestinian uprising ("Portrait of an Angry Young Arab Woman," *NYT,* 1 March 2002).

4. Sohail Hashmi, "Not What the Prophet Would Want," *Washington Post,* 9 June 2002.

5. Between 1992 and 1995, approximately 950 schools were sabotaged. See *al-Sharq al-Awsat,* 26 July 1995.

6. I define a massacre as the killing of fifteen or more people in one episode of violence.

7. For the dates and places of these massacres, refer to the quarterly chronology sections of the *MEJ*. For a description of some of the massacres, see AI, November 1997; *The Guardian,* 20 and 21 October 1997; *The Times,* 22 and 23 October 1997; and *Daily Telegraph,* 23 October 1997.

8. *al-Hayat,* 27 August 1993.

9. *al-Wasat,* 19 September 1994. See similar remarks by Layada in Willis (1996: 282) and al-Tawil (1998: 81).

10. The argument of the radicals is that Islam is a monotheistic religion that believes in the unity (tawhid) and sovereignty of God. By participating in parliaments that are elected by the people, the FIS is abiding by the sovereignty

of the people, which is tantamount to accepting two Gods. Hence, the accusation of polytheism.

11. *al-Wasat,* 19 September 1994.

12. *al-Hayat,* 15 September 1994. See similar statements by GIA leaders in *al-Ansar,* 28 October 1993 and 24 August 1995, and in *al-Hayat,* 6 August 1994, 25 July 1995, and 23 November 1996.

13. The letters are quoted at length in al-Tawil (1998: 298–307). The July 1994 communiqué announcing the unification of the AIS also does not mention the word *apostasy.*

14. These letters are published by the FIS in a booklet entitled *Ghayet al-Murad fi Qadhayya al-Jihad* (The Desired Objectives in the Cause of Jihad), authored by Belhaj and published in 1994.

15. These claims were made in the unification communiqué of May 1994 (see the full text in al-Tawil 1998: 152–154). Jihad as "fard 'ayn" can be contrasted with jihad as "fard kiffaya," which means that if enough Muslims wage holy war, the rest of the Islamic nation is not obligated to fight.

16. *al-Hayat,* 27 August 1993. See similar remarks in a GIA communiqué in *al-Ansar,* 28 October 1993.

17. *al-Hayat,* 26 August 1994.

18. *al-Ansar,* 28 October 1993 (emphasis added).

19. *al-Hayat,* 25 July 1994.

20. *al-Hayat,* 14 February 1996.

21. *al-Hayat,* 6 August 1994.

22. *al-Hayat,* 23 November 1996.

23. Sura VIII, al-Anfal, verse 39: "wa qatiluhum hata la takuna fitnatun wa-yakuna al-din kulluhu li-llah."

24. For these communiqués, see *al-Hayat,* 25 July 1994 and 3 November 1996.

25. *al-Hayat,* 4 September 1999.

26. See some of the testimonies of Algerians in *The Observer,* 26 October 1997, and *Le Monde,* 10 February 1998.

27. By 1997 there were an estimated 150,000 militiamen around the country, including in Islamist strongholds (Martinez 1997/1998).

28. *al-Hayat,* 31 May 2002.

29. See, for instance, AI, *Algeria: Civilian Population Caught in a Spiral of Violence,* MDE 28/23/97 (November 1997), and *Le Monde,* 10 November 1997. Both raise questions about the inaction of security forces stationed near besieged towns. Also see an interview with former Algerian prime minister Abdelhamid al-Ibrahimi in *al-Wasat,* 15 March 1999. He claims that government-sponsored militias are behind the massacres. Yous (2000) implicates the authorities in the Bentalha massacre of 1997, and Souaïdia's (2001) book, *The Dirty War,* is often cited as evidence of state complicity in the massacres. I have addressed some of these claims in an earlier publication (see Hafez 2000a).

30. Interview with *al-Hayat,* 3 February 2000.

31. Interview with *al-Hayat,* 8 February 2000, 8.

32. See Scott Peterson, "Algeria's Real War: Ending the Cycle of Violence," *Christian Science Monitor,* 24 June 1997; AI, *Algeria: Civilian Population*

Caught in a Spiral of Violence (November 1997*); Le Monde,* 11 November 1997; *Le Monde Diplomatique,* March 1999; Wadhah Sharara, "al-Siyasa that al-Anf al-Jama'ai (al-Jazairi) wal-Rasmi," *al-Hayat,* 9 April 1999.

33. Passage taken from the booklet *al-Sayf al-Batar fi al-Rad ala min Ta'ana fi al-Mujahedin al-Akhyar wa Aqama bayna Adhhur al-Kufar* (60 pages, n.p., 1996, emphasis added). In *Hidayat Rab al-'Alamin,* Zitouni (1995: 46) claims that it is "a duty of Muslims to rise against the ruler, remove and disobey him if he commits apostasy." In another passage, Zitouni (1995: 47) maintains that since the GIA offers an alternative authority, the people should not enter into the guardianship of infidels and apostates; they have a duty to listen and obey the amir of the GIA.

34. See their communiqués in *al-Hayat,* 3 February 1996, 3 and 23 March 1996, 23 July 1996, and 17 September 1998. The khawarij is a sect that emerged in early Islamic history. They are known for their religious intransigence and extreme interpretations of Islamic texts.

35. See their communiqué in *al-Hayat,* 5 July 1995.

36. *al-Sharq al-Awsat,* 19 December 1995. This claim is repeated by an unnamed AIS chief in an interview with *al-Hayat,* 28 December 1999.

37. *al-Hayat,* 7 May 1998.

38. AFPI, 17 October 1997. Hattab's group consisted of 1,200 to 1,500 militants operating mainly in east Algeria—Tizi Ouzo, al-Bouwira and Boumerdes. The militants were divided into several militias—al-Farouk, al-Mahjiroun, al-Ansar, al-Nur, etc. The group became a serious competitor of both the GIA and AIS by 1999 and refused to abide by the cease-fire called in 1997. By 2000, Hattab was reported to have entered into negotiations with the military to end the violence (*al-Hayat,* 16 January 2000). However, he issued a communiqué dated 15 January 2000 denying secret negotiations and affirming that there will be "no dialogue, no cease-fire, and no reconciliation with the apostates" (*al-Hayat,* 23 January 2000). Hattab's radical credentials give credence to his charges against the GIA.

39. In response to the question "what has changed since 1992 to make the FIS cease fighting?" Rabeh Kebir stated that in every conflict a time comes when the opposing sides realize that they cannot eliminate each other and must talk to resolve their differences. This was his justification for the cease-fire. See interview with Ahmed Mansour, host of the "Bila Hudoud" (Without Borders) television program aired by al-Jazeera out of Qatar on 26 January 2000.

40. See interview with the unnamed AIS leader in *al-Hayat,* 28 December 1999, 14.

41. AFPI, 24 September 1997.

42. Between 1992 and 1995, 754 security forces and policemen were killed and injured (Ahmed 1995: 299–305). The number of security casualties decreased significantly in the years 1996 and 1997 (*NYT,* 15 March 1997). Al-Din (1998: 506) puts the number of policemen killed and injured in 1996 at sixty-nine. The Jama'a repeatedly claimed responsibility for killing policemen and security forces (see *al-Hayat,* 22 January 1994, 24 February 1994, 19 June 1994, 23 August 1997, and 16 October 1997). Some of the prominent government officials that were subject to assassinations and assassination attempts are

Atif Sidqi (prime minister); Hasan al-Alfi (minister of the interior); Safwat al-Sharif (minister of information); and President Mubarak in Addis Ababa, Ethiopia, in 1995 (Fatah 1995: 40).

43. The Jama'a did not regularly claim responsibility for attacks on Copts but did not deny them or condemn them until two gruesome massacres took place in February and March 1997. The first was in Abu Qurqas on 12 February, when nine Coptic Christians were gunned down during prayer services. The second was on 13 March in Naj Dawud, where thirteen Copts were killed (*NYT,* 15 March 1997). See communiqués denying responsibility in *al-Hayat,* 16 February 1997 and 16 March 1997. The denials of the Jama'a were not consistent. In one communiqué it denied all responsibility; in another it said misguided youth within the Jama'a, lacking proper leadership due to the arrest of their leaders, were behind the attacks.

44. The decision to form an armed wing was made in late 1990, after a series of mosque stormings by security forces and the assassination of Ala Muhyi al-Din, the official spokesman of the Jama'a in September of that year (Mubarak 1995: 399–400). In the late 1980s and first two years of the 1990s the Jama'a, under the pretext of fighting Soviet forces in Afghanistan, sent some of its leaders and activists to set up training camps in Pakistan and Afghanistan to instruct militants in guerrilla and clandestine warfare. Some observers claim that the regime encouraged Islamists to volunteer in Afghanistan because it thought it was ridding itself of potential troublemakers (*al-Hayat,* 25 September 1999).

45. Islamists repeatedly issued communiqués warning Western tourists to stay away from Egypt. See the August 1992 communiqué in *MECS* (1992: 370) and the February 1994 communiqué in *al-Hayat,* 3 February 1994. The Jama'a also repeatedly claimed responsibility for attacking tourists. See its communiqués in *al-Hayat,* 1 October 1994 and 21 April 1996.

46. The Jama'a repeatedly issued communiqués declaring responsibility for attacking tourist sites and trains. See *al-Hayat,* 24 February 1994, 10 March 1994, 18 January 1995, and 10 November 1995.

47. The Jama'a repeatedly issued communiqués claiming responsibility for bombing banks and Exchange Bureaus. See *al-Hayat,* 10 and 25 February 1994, 21 March 1994.

48. See *al-Hala al-Diniya fi Misr* (1995: 191; 1998: 241).

49. See its communiqués in *al-Hayat,* 21 January 1996, 1 May 1996, 13 February 1997, 26 June 1997.

50. See *Mithaq* (1984); *Manhaj* (1986); and *Hatmiat* (1987). *Al-Jihad wa Ma'aalim al-Amal al-Thawri* (The Jihad and the Signposts of Revolutionary Activism, 1988) and *al-Hisaad al-Mur* (The Bitter Harvest) both were produced by the Jihad group and are quoted in Mustapha (1992) and Mubarak (1995) respectively.

51. See *al-Ikhwan* (1994). *Al-Hujum ala Rumouz wa Qiyadat Amal al-Islam Ouslub Khusoum al-Islam fi Kuli Asr* (The Attack on the Representatives and Leaders of Islamic Activism Is the Method of Islam's Opponents in Every Era) by Muhammad Sayid Habib, former representative of the MB in parliament, is published in its entirety in Aamer 1995: 283–303. *Bayan lil-Nas* (A

Message to the People) is published in *al-Shaab,* 2 May 1995. Also see the communiqué issued in August 1994 by Muhammad Sayid Habib (published in *al-Hayat,* 7 August 1994) and the four-page article by El-Hodaiby (1997).

52. The notion of God's sovereignty, as advanced by contemporary Islamists, is largely derived from the works of Abu ala al-Mawdudi and Sayyid Qutb. See Robert Worth, "The Deep Intellectual Roots of Islamic Terror," *NYT,* 13 October 2001.

53. In a content analysis of sixteen documents—eight by each of the Jama'a and Jihad groups—Bakr (1996: 187) finds the theme of the comprehensiveness of Islam repeated 65 times by the Jihad group and 92 times by the Jama'a while the theme of the superiority of Islam is repeated 195 times by the Jihad group and 165 times by the Jama'a.

54. *al-Hayat,* 23 August 1994.

55. Surat al-Maida, verse 44: "wa man lam yahkimu bima anzala Allah faoulaika huma al-kafirun."

56. The document is entitled *Nahnu wal-Ikhwan* (The Brotherhood and Us) and quoted in Mubarak (1995: 222).

57. These comments were made by both Ma'moun El-Hodaiby (interview with *al-Hayat,* 15 April 1995) and Mustapha Mashhur (interview with *al-Hayat,* 24 January 1996).

58. Surat al-Anfal, verse 39: "wa-qatiluhum hata la-takuna fitnatun wa-yakuna al-din kulouhu lil-lah."

59. The Jihad group's position is best articulated in *al-Faridha al-Ghaiba* (The Hidden Obligation), authored by their executed leader Abdel Salam Faraj. The latter argued that jihad against infidels and apostates is an appointed obligation (fard 'ayn) for every Muslim until judgment day. In one passage, he argued that "the Islamic state will not arise except through battle. . . . It is a continuous struggle that does not end until one of two things happen: death or the eradication of jahiliya and the establishment of the *hakimiya*" (in Janinah 1988: 224).

60. Surat al-Nahl, verse 125: "id'uou ila sabil rabika bil-hikma wal-maw'aidha al-hasana"; Surat al-Ghashiya, verses 21 and 22: "fa-thakir inama anta muthakir, lasta 'alayhim bi-musayter."

61. See their communiqué dated 18 December 1992 in Moro (1994: 199–200). See similar communiqués in *al-Sha'ab,* 2 and 23 April 1993.

62. *al-Hayat,* 23 May 1994.

63. Surat Yusuf, verse 40: "ina al-hukmu ila lil-lah."

64. Surat al-Sajdah, verse 18: "afaman kan mu'minan kaman kan fasiqan la yastawun."

65. *al-Hayat,* 10 March 1993.

66. *MECS* (1994: 262).

67. *al-Hayat,* 24 and 25 February 1994.

68. Interview with *al-Hayat,* 18 March 1993.

69. Ibid.

70. *al-Hayat,* 10 March 1994.

71. *al-Hayat,* 21 April 1996. In March 1995 the Jama'a claimed responsibility for attacks on Egyptian targets in response to U.S. aggression in Iraq, Palestine, Lebanon, and Libya (*al-Hayat,* 5 March 1995).

72. *al-Hayat,* 1 November 1995.

73. *al-Hayat,* 1 May 1996, 21 January 1996.

74. Neil MacFarquhar, "Bin Laden's Wildfire Threatens Saudi Rulers," *NYT,* 6 November 2001.

75. All previous quotations and information come from two reports by David Rohde and C. J. Chivers, "Al Qaeda's Grocery Lists and Manuals of Killing," *NYT,* 17 March 2002; and "Afghan Camps Turn Out Holy War Guerrillas and Terrorists," *NYT,* 18 March 2002. These reports draw on primary documents uncovered in abandoned Al-Qaida training camps after the defeat of the Taliban in Afghanistan in 2001–2002.

76. Stephen Engelberg, "One Man and a Global Web of Violence," *NYT,* 14 January 2001; Don Van Natta Jr., "Running Terrorism as a Business," *NYT,* 11 November 2001; and Pierre Conesa, "Al-Qaida, the Sect," *Le Monde Diplomatique,* January 2002.

77. On 23 August 1996, bin Laden issued a "Declaration of Jihad on the Americans Occupying the Lands of the Two Sacred Sites." In it, he states that "Muslims have realized they are the main target of the aggression of the coalition of Jews and Crusaders."

78. On 28 May 1998, bin Laden, in an interview with an ABC News reporter, confirmed that "we do not differentiate between those dressed in military uniforms and civilians—they are all targets."

79. Quoted in *Washington Post,* 23 August 1998.

80. *al-Hayat,* 8 March 2002.

6

Conclusion: Patterns of Rebellion

S ince the tragic events of 11 September 2001, many Westerners—privately and publicly—are looking at Islamic movements with a mixture of fear and hostility. Simmering debates about the true nature of Islamic fundamentalism and its potential threat to Western states have resurfaced and spilled over into public discourse. Terrorism, of course, has been an important catalyst for resurgent misgivings toward Islamists and the Muslim world in general. Images of ordinary Muslims celebrating attacks on America and proclaiming support for radical Islamists have riveted Western fears around the "threat of Islam."

Such fears are understandable given the magnitude of the carnage that took place on that fateful day. In the long run, however, Western responses to Islamist violence must be measured and well thought out. Misconstruing the underlying causes of Islamist rage or overreacting to Islamist violence may only intensify militancy, not temperate it. In this book I put forward a framework by which to analyze Islamist militancy. This framework not only explains rebellious behavior; it also implies policy prescriptions for diminishing militancy and violence in the Muslim world. Before discussing the theoretical and policy implications of the political process approach to Islamist strategies, it is important to summarize the argument presented in this book as well as review its empirical foundations.

Theoretical Claims and Empirical Findings

Muslims rebel because they encounter an ill-fated combination of political and institutional exclusion, on the one hand, and reactive and indiscriminate

repression on the other. When states do not provide their Islamist opposition movements opportunities for institutional participation, and employ
repression indiscriminately against these movements after a period of prior
mobilization, Islamists will most probably rebel. When they do so, Islamists will organize themselves in exclusive, loosely structured organizations
that demand strict ideological and behavioral adherence from their members. These organizations draw a sharp dividing line between insiders and
outsiders, and they produce "spirals of encapsulation" that gradually isolate
Islamist rebels from their broader environment. These rebels will also rely
on antisystem ideologies that portray the conflict as a "total war" against
irremediable enemies and deny the possibility of neutrality in such a war.
Such framing of the conflict is intended to solidify the division between
insiders and outsiders, as well as to justify and motivate collective violence.

The combination of exclusive mobilization structures and antisystem ideological frames is conducive to protracted conflict and expansive anticivilian violence. Movements that consist of exclusive, loosely
knit groups speak with many voices and are less likely to coalesce
around common solutions to end violence. They are more likely to compete with and sabotage each other than they are to unite and agree on
ways to promote reconciliation. Violence against civilians is one way to
undermine peace efforts and ensure that the conflicting parties are
irreparably polarized. Such violence is made possible by antisystem
frames that facilitate the deactivation of moral codes against killing and
injuring noncombatants.

In Algeria, Islamists rebelled after the military canceled elections,
banned the most prominent Islamist party—the FIS—and arrested thousands of its supporters en masse. Thereafter, the state engaged in a brutal campaign of repression that involved extrajudicial killings, disappearances, and torture. Repression came after two years of Islamist
mobilization and organization of supporters for electoral participation.
Once violence broke out, inclusive movement organizations splintered
into numerous exclusive groups with no clear hierarchy or command
structure. Some of the prominent groups in the armed movement competed violently with each other and intentionally subverted attempts at
reconciliation with the Algerian regime. They did so by increasingly
engaging in anticivilian violence, including bombings in public places,
execution of state employees, and massacres of villagers. Those who perpetrated such carnage justified their actions by portraying their victims as
"apostates" and "supporters of tyrants." They did not distinguish between
those who repressed them directly and those who "maintained the ruling
order" through pursuing their everyday lives.

In Egypt, insurgency broke out during a period of political de-liberalization and after the state made the crucial decision to dismantle with brute force loosely structured networks of radical Islamists in upper Egypt. After acquiescing to militant organizing on the periphery of Egyptian society during the 1980s, the authorities sought to crush the Jama'a al-Islamiyya in the early 1990s. The repression violated basic principles of human rights and, consequently, gave legitimacy to violent Islamist responses. Even the peaceful Muslim Brotherhood movement encountered greater restrictions on its conduct in the 1990s, despite its unequivocal denunciation of militant violence. Similar to the Algerian military, the Egyptian government provided few avenues for non-militant forms of contention; it effectively channeled the opposition toward rebellion.

The Egyptian insurgents were organized in exclusive groups that operated independently of each other. These groups set strict criteria for inclusion and became highly secretive. Although competition for leadership of the movement was not as fierce as in Algeria, there were struggles over the direction of the armed struggle. Those who favored reconciliation with the regime and an end to violence were subverted by those who wanted to continue the rebellion until it concluded with either victory for Islamists or "martyrdom in the path of God."

Anticivilian violence was part of the Egyptian Islamists' tactical repertoire during the 1980s. However, during the 1990s anticivilian violence reached unprecedented levels and culminated in the massacre of tourists in Luxor. The violence was motivated by antisystem ideologies that did not distinguish between soldiers and ordinary policemen or between indigenous government officials and foreign tourists. All were portrayed as part and parcel of one system that contributed to the repression of Muslims.

The exclusion-repression-rebellion nexus is not unique to Algeria and Egypt. Islamist rebellions in Kashmir, the southern Philippines, Chechnya, and Tajikistan followed a similar pattern, despite the variation in their historic circumstances and differences in the substance of rebel grievances. In all these societies, Islamists rebelled because institutional channels for participation were blocked *and* movement militants and their supporters were threatened by predatory state practices that did not discriminate among their targets.

In Kashmir, nationalists and Islamists were historically undermined and politically thwarted by India's central government through disenfranchisement and electoral manipulation. When those same nationalists and Islamists protested and took up arms to reverse their fortunes, they encountered indiscriminate repression that worsened the situation and gave rebels legitimacy and fertile ground in which to grow.

In the southern Philippines, rebellion broke out when martial law was declared and after a series of massacres against Muslim populations by Christian gangs. The failure of the Philippine authorities to protect Muslim communities gave impetus to the rise of rebel groups who were viewed as saviors.

In Chechnya, Russia sought to oust violently a breakaway government after it had existed for three years. It did so through indiscriminate bombardment of civilian cities and terror in filtration centers. Its actions brought back historic memories of "genocide" against the Chechen people during the Soviet years and turned the increasingly unpopular President Dudayev into a national hero.

In Tajikistan, rebellion and civil war broke out when neo-communist forces refused to cede any control of the government to the combined opposition of nationalists, Islamists, and democrats. Not only was the opposition ousted from power through mass repression, their organizations and parties were subsequently banned and suppressed. Indiscriminate repression against anyone suspected of supporting the opposition—often driven by regional and clan-based associations—produced hundreds of thousands of refugees, from whom the ranks of the rebels were recruited.

Islamist rebellions in Kashmir, the southern Philippines, Chechnya, and Tajikistan also produced protracted conflicts and patterns of anti-civilian violence similar to what we witnessed in Algeria and Egypt. Dominant rebel organizations in those societies gave way to tens, if not hundreds, of newcomers with more radical ideologies and extreme tactical repertoires.

In Kashmir, the Jammu and Kashmir Liberation Front (JKLF) was made irrelevant in the mid-1990s by Hizb-ul Mujahedin, Lashkar-e Toiba, and Jaish Muhammad. Terrorist acts and anticivilian violence by these groups not only prolong the conflict, they also could precipitate a major nuclear conflagration between India and Pakistan.

In the southern Philippines, the once dominant Moro National Liberation Front (MNLF) has been forced into the background by the Moro Islamic Liberation Front (MILF) and Abu Sayyaf Group. The latter is particularly vicious in its violence against civilians. The combined intransigence and militancy of these groups have turned the rebellion in the Philippines into a permanent revolution.

In Chechnya, hundreds of armed groups have come into existence during the war with Russia. The anarchy created by Russia's devastating attacks made possible—politically and logistically—the influx of transnational fundamentalists from all over the Muslim world in support of the rebels' cause. Today, some of these groups continue to engage in daring attacks against Russian civilians and military forces.

In Tajikistan, the United Tajik Opposition has concluded a peace deal with the state regime and set up a reconciliatory political arrangement that could serve as a model for other beleaguered states in the Muslim world. However, despite the qualitative progress, not all of the rebel commanders have adhered to this agreement. Consequently, Tajikistan continues to witness residual violence.

"It is the vicious combination of repression and lack of institutional regulation which is the main explanation for 90 percent of political violence in the contemporary Arab world," writes François Burgat (1997: 38). It is not clear how Burgat arrived at this statistic, but its validity is self-evident in light of the preceding discussion. In answer to the question of why Muslims rebel, we may say with a high degree of confidence that Muslims rebel because they are denied access to conventional means of political participation and because their organizations and members feel threatened by indiscriminate repressive policies.

Theoretical Propositions

In the introductory chapter of this book, I challenged the prevailing academic and journalistic wisdom that Muslims rebel because of economic deprivation due to failed modernization and psychological alienation coming from excessive Westernization. Cases such as Jordan, Tunisia, and Morocco present "anomalies" that cannot be explained by the theory of relative deprivation, which explicitly or implicitly shapes the thinking of many experts on Islamist movements.

My alternative view to the prevailing theory draws on the conceptual and empirical insights of social movement theorists within the political process approach. Specifically, it builds on the emerging synthesis of three theoretical traditions that investigate the *political environment* in which social movements develop; *mobilization structures* through which movements acquire and allocate resources; and *ideological frames* with which movement actors justify and motivate collective struggles. These approaches have been applied and tested in countless studies that cover nearly every type of social movement in every region of the globe. What is unique about this book is the way this synthesis is formulated and applied to explain the causes and dynamics of Muslim rebellions.

My ambition has been to explain as many instances of Muslim rebellions as possible using this framework. Time and resource restrictions have forced me to focus this study on two countries—Algeria and Egypt—and to settle for a more general comparison with other rebellions without the depth necessary to make my claims entirely convincing to a rigorous reader. Nagging doubts as to the complete validity of this approach will remain. All I can do, however, is formulate testable propositions based on what I presented in this book. I will leave it for other researchers to confirm or remove those doubts.

Proposition 1. If, in early state-movement interactions, the ruling regime provides Islamists access to the institutionalized political system, Islamists will avoid violent strategies and accommodate the state regime. If, however, the ruling regime denies Islamists meaningful access to the system, they are likely to opt for nonaccommodative strategies. Institutional exclusion contributes to the outbreak of rebellion; however, it is not sufficient to cause rebellion. The timing and targeting of state repression matter as well.

Proposition 2. If state repression is preemptive—applied before the Islamist opposition has had a chance to acquire material and organizational resources, develop mass organizations, and engage in popular mobilization—mass rebellion is less likely to occur, irrespective of how economically deprived or politically aggrieved the opposition. If, however, repression is reactive, Islamists are likely to resort to violence and rebellion to defend their organizations and cadres.

Proposition 3. If state repression is selective—targeting only leaders and core activists—mass Islamist rebellion is less likely to occur. If, however, repression is indiscriminate, it will likely expand Islamist violence and induce mass rebellion.

Proposition 4. If the political system denies the Islamist movement substantive access to state institutions and violently represses that movement, Islamists are likely to adopt exclusive, loosely structured organizations and promote antisystem ideological frames.

Proposition 5. If rebellious Islamist movements splinter into exclusive, loosely structured organizations that adopt antisystem frames, their rebellions are likely to turn into protracted conflicts and produce patterns of anticivilian violence.

The five propositions are intended to explain *patterns*, not instances, of rebellious conduct, terrorism, or extra-institutional militancy. They assume an iterative dynamic of action-reaction-learning-adapting on the part of state authorities and Islamist movements. Thus, a systematic comparative study of Islamist strategies using the five propositions must make clear that it is addressing movement strategies over a period of time.

Policy Prescriptions

The attacks of 11 September 2001 have brought to the forefront the debate on how best to deal with Islamist movements and their potential for violence. This study bears directly on this debate. Currently, there appear to be at least three approaches to addressing Islamist violence. The first approach either explicitly or implicitly draws on the theory of relative deprivation. It argues that the best way to deal with Islamist violence—indeed conflict in general—is to promote economic development and equality. For example, in a United Nations General Assembly session after the 11 September terrorist attacks on the United States, South Africa's president Thabo Mbeki attributed violence to "socioeconomic deprivation of billions of people across the globe, coexisting with islands of enormous wealth and prosperity within and among countries."[1] Similarly, Philippine's president Gloria Arroyo urged Western states combating terrorism to turn their energies to combating poverty because, as she put it, "terror has its sustenance when you have poverty."[2]

Promoting economic development to alleviate poverty and misery in the Muslim world is a noble cause in itself and should be pursued irrespective of whether it diminishes Islamist violence or not. However, by itself economic development does not address the root cause of why Muslims rebel. As the introductory chapter has shown, many economically deprived societies such as Jordan and Morocco have not had to deal with high levels of Islamist violence. Conversely, an economically developing country like Iran experienced a revolution in the 1970s. Economic deprivation may feed the grievances of ordinary Muslims, but it is not the underlying cause of their rebellions. Muslims rebel because other avenues of political contestation are blocked and their states repress them indiscriminately.

Moreover, promoting economic development and eliminating poverty are long-term processes that could take decades and, sadly, may not succeed. Therefore, if we are interested in containing violence in the near future, we must look for more efficient means to do so. It is wrong to think that poor societies are doomed to suffer political violence until poverty is eliminated. As I will show below, there are steps that governments can take on the political front to encourage conventional means of political participation. We need not wait until the crisis of poverty is resolved for violence to diminish.

The second approach to deal with Islamist militancy focuses strictly on repressive measures and geostrategic considerations to make the "containment" of terrorism effective.[3] Underlying this approach is the view most clearly expressed by former British prime minister Margaret Thatcher: "Islamic extremism today, like Bolshevism in the past, is an armed doctrine. It is an aggressive ideology promoted by fanatical, well-armed devotees. And, like Communism, it requires an all-embracing long-term strategy to defeat it."[4] Thatcher's view is not unique. Many Western policymakers and advisers have been motivated by fear of Islamism and view repression as the lesser of two evils.[5] Some even go so far as to point out that "repression is working" and is a viable strategy for dealing with the "Islamist threat" (Kramer 1997: 170).[6]

The evidence and conclusions of this study naturally lead us to reject the second option as a viable long-term strategy to combat the underlying causes of Muslim extremism. Contrary to the aforementioned conclusion drawn by Kramer, repression does not always work and may actually expand, not lessen, Islamist violence. Repression did work in Syria, Tunisia, and Iraq. However, in Algeria, Egypt, Kashmir, the southern Philippines, and Chechnya, repression has resulted in higher rates of violence and protracted conflicts. More recently, in the Israeli-occupied territories sustained repression of the second Palestinian uprising that began in September 2000 did not succeed in deterring Islamist suicide bombers and expansion of violence in general.[7] To be sure, Israel's security measures may have saved many Israeli lives, but the point is that the sole reliance on repression as a state strategy to deal with radicalism and rebellions may actually expand, not curtail, the violence.[8]

Repression may prevent Islamists from coming to power and may even force them to disband and run, but it is not a viable solution to ending Islamist violence in the Muslim world or around the globe. Many repressed Islamists reemerge in newly constituted organizations with more radical ideologies and tactical repertoires. Many of the groups and individuals that constituted the Al-Qaida terrorist network, including the GIA and the Egyptian Jihad group, have been products of exclusionary and repressive political environments.[9]

The sole reliance on repression must also be rejected on moral grounds. Human rights and democratic principles are ends in themselves. They must not be subordinated to the politics of expediency. In almost every instance of repression in the Muslim world, governments have inflicted untold suffering on Islamists and their supporters through mass arrests, torture, extrajudicial killings, and disappearances. Encouraging those governments to carry out more repression is ethically wrong.

The third approach to dealing with actual and potential Islamist militancy blends the previous two but adds the element of political reform to promote moderation in Muslim societies. This perspective maintains that states that provide a modicum of political access, even if mere formal inclusion, fare much better than those that opt for exclusion and repression. It calls on Western and Muslim governments to distinguish between moderates (advocates of peaceful participation through institutional channels and civic associations) and radicals (proponents of violent insurgency) in order to apply differential policies that encourage the former and marginalize the latter.[10]

Although the line between moderates and radicals may be fluid and not always distinguishable, Western and Muslim governments could force Islamists to choose sides by establishing enforceable rules and parameters of acceptable political conduct within inclusive, preferably democratic, state institutions. As indicated in Chapter 2, Jordan has applied this strategy toward Islamists with success. It permits the Muslim Brotherhood there to organize legally and express itself through governmental institutions while simultaneously prohibiting extrainstitutional mobilization on an extended basis. Gerges (1999: 238) eloquently represents the third option in relation to U.S. foreign policy: "The United States must impress upon the ruling elites of its allies the need to broaden their social base by integrating the new classes into the political mainstream: Exclusive politics is a recipe for disaster, but inclusive politics is the key to survival. All groups that are willing to participate in democratic politics should be actively encouraged to do so."

While Gerges is correct to stress the deleterious effects of exclusive politics on Islamist conduct, he overstates the advantages of inclusion when he does not add that open access must be accompanied by rules and conditions that prohibit violent mobilization as a supplementary strategy to institutional participation. As the case of Pakistan illustrates (in Chapter 2), including Islamists while simultaneously acquiescing to violent militancy can embolden the radicals and increase violence. Political inclusion of Islamists is the most propitious approach for promoting the long-term moderation of Islamism only if it is part of a broader strategy of political institutionalization.

The Politics of Institutionalization

Political institutionalization requires opposition groups to abide by conventional means of conflict resolution and shuns strategies that threaten their legality and legitimacy. It requires them to become more like political parties and interest groups, and less like social protest movements or revolutionary groups (Kriesi et al. 1995; Kriesi 1996). Institutional inclusion and a policy of targeted repression will facilitate political institutionalization of Islamist movements.

Institutional access will encourage Islamists to promote inclusive organizations because electoral politics demands mass appeal to attract voters, a large base of supporters to run election campaigns, and substantial sums of money through membership contributions. Exclusive organizations most often cannot deliver these requirements under political openness. Institutional access will also encourage Islamists to advance reconciliatory ideological frames that discourage the wholesale rejection of the system. Radical frames will not resonate with the mass public in the context of freedom and political inclusion.

To the extent that radical tactics and mass mobilization by Islamists threaten to unleash repression that could jeopardize their political access and legal status, Islamists will seek alternative ways to press their demands. In Algeria, the crackdown of June 1991 threatened to unleash all-out repression against the FIS. The latter responded by ousting some of the radicals from its organization, avoiding major demonstrations until the state of siege was lifted later that year, and moderating its rhetoric to make sure it remained a legitimate party. The promise of institutional participation through elections was a moderating force on the FIS.

Over time, inclusive organizations and reconciliatory frames will result in declining commitments on the part of activists and ideological moderation on the part of Islamist parties. Given that inclusive organizations do not demand high levels of commitment and activity from their members—only general support, dues, and minimum participation when called on—they are more likely to create some distance between supporters and leaders (Lichbach 1995: 262). This gap between leaders and members, in turn, "*may* create a certain class of individuals who come to value the maintenance of that organization over the realization of movement goals" (McAdam 1982: 55). This was the chief complaint of Lenin and revolutionary communists against German Social Democrats prior to World War I. Revolutionaries averred that political participation in parliaments led to institutional co-optation. Kalyvas (1996: 241–242) noted a similar dilemma within Christian Democratic parties in Europe during the opening decades of the twentieth century. They had to strike a balance between sectarianism, which solidified internal unity, and declericalization of confessional parties, which threatened the loss of Catholic electoral support.

The politics of institutionalization may explain why many communist and green parties in Western Europe were willing to make "historical compromises" and abandoned revolutionary strategies, even if some of them did not completely abandon revolutionary rhetoric. The civil rights movement in America underwent a similar process of institutional channeling in the 1970s (Jenkins and Eckert 1986). While institutional co-optation and goal displacement are not inevitable, "the long list of movements that have failed to negotiate these obstacles attests to the difficulties inherent in the effort" (McAdam 1982: 56).

In an inclusive organization that seeks to bring people together around a common denominator, the identity of individual members is not likely to be defined by their membership in the group. In this case, "spirals of encapsulation" are not as likely as they would be in exclusive organizations. While the salience of a shared identity in exclusive organizations often results in commitment to the struggle, the low prominence of a single identity in inclusive organizations is likely to result in declining participation in movement affairs as state-movement interactions mature. As Zald and Ash Garner (1987: 126) explain: "The inclusive [movement organization's] membership declines and rises faster than that of the exclusive's because competing values and attitudes are more readily mobilized in the inclusive organization. While members of both organizations may have similar goals, the members of inclusive organizations are more likely to be subjected to conflicts in the face of threats or in the face of competing social movements that appeal to other values. Their allegiances to other groups and values lead them to rather switch than fight."

Declining participation, in turn, is likely to force inclusive organizations to rely more and more on their institutional resources to effect reforms over time. The Egyptian Muslim Brotherhood, which developed into an inclusive organization and promoted reconciliatory frames during the 1980s, refused to support militancy and accommodated the regime further when it began to encounter repression in the 1990s.

The politics of institutionalization is facilitated by a policy of targeted repression that distinguishes between violent militants who will not adhere to democratic principles of participation and those who seek to represent the legitimate grievances and demands of devout Muslims through participatory channels. Selective repression is critically important for institutionalization because it delineates the parameters of acceptable conduct while simultaneously offering an alternative to nonmilitant strategies. A strategy of all sticks and no carrots will delegitimate the moderates while leaving few options for committed activists determined to effect change; a strategy of all carrots and no sticks might entice opposition forces to press their demands through extra-institutional channels if they deem the repercussions to be negligible.

In conclusion, governments in the Muslim world, and the Western states that take them as their allies, have a choice to make. They may choose to exclude Islamists from the political system and repress them violently as Algeria and Egypt chose to do, or they may seek accommodation with those who will work through established rules of conflict resolution and political contestation. The first option may work, but it is risky and morally objectionable. The second option can bear fruit in the form of political institutionalization, but it requires astute leadership that must exercise a delicate balance between institutional inclusion of moderates and targeted repression of radicals.

In his masterly study of the origins of Christian Democracy in Europe, Kalyvas (1996: 259–260) remarks:

> Looking today at the benign Christian Democratic parties, one can easily forget the aliberal and often intolerant nature of the Catholic movement from which they emerged. Catholic mobilization occurred as a counter-revolutionary reaction against Liberalism. . . . Intransigent Catholics, who rejected the notion that any spheres of life lay beyond the reach of religious regulation, were instrumental in creating and running the Catholic movement. . . . Yet political Catholicism mediated by confessional parties proved to be a factor of mass incorporation and democratic consolidation.

Whether the future holds for political Islam what it held for political Catholicism will be largely determined by the present policies of governments toward Islamist movements and the political dynamics these policies unleash.

Notes

1. "Leaders Seek to Discern Root Causes of Violence," *NYT,* 11 November 2001.

2. "The Philippine Wars," *NYT,* 15 February 2002.

3. See, for example, Henry Kissenger's advice in "Where Do We Go from Here," *NYT*, 6 November 2001, and Posen (2001/2002).

4. Margaret Thatcher, "Advice to a Superpower," *NYT,* 11 February 2002.

5. See Judith Miller, "The Challenge of Radical Islam," *Foreign Affairs,* Spring 1993: 43–56; Peter Rodman, "Co-opt or Confront Fundamentalist Islam?" *Middle East Quarterly,* vol. 1, no. 4 (December 1994): 61–64; Daniel Pipes, "There Are No Moderates: Dealing with Fundamentalist Islam," *The National Interest,* no. 41 (Fall 1995): 48–57; Elaine Sciolino, "The Red Menace Is Gone, but Here Is Islam," *NYT,* 21 January 1996.

6. For a critique of this perspective, see Leon Hadar, "What Green Peril?" *Foreign Affairs,* vol. 72, no. 2 (Spring 1993). Also see Halliday (1995), Esposito (1999), and Gerges (1999).

7. According to the Israeli Ministry of Foreign Affairs (www.mfa.gov. il/mfa/), in 2000 there was only one suicide bombing; in 2001, there were twenty-seven attacks; and from January to June 2002, there were twenty-nine suicide missions. The Israeli death toll also increased as the uprising intensified. According to the *NYT* (27 June 2002), in 2000 approximately 50 Israelis were killed; in 2001, about 160 Israelis were killed; and from January to June 2002, approximately 300 Israelis were killed.

8. This point was recently made by Gal Luft, former lieutenant colonel in the Israeli Defense Forces, in an article entitled "The Palestinian H-Bomb: Terror's Winning Strategy," *Foreign Affairs,* July/August 2002.

9. Susan Sachs, "An Investigation in Egypt Illustrates Al Qaeda's Web," *NYT*, 21 November 2001; Doug Struck et al., "Borderless Network of Terror," *The Washington Post*, 23 September 2001; Ahmed Rashid, "They're Only Sleeping: Why Militant Islamicists in Central Asia Aren't Going to Go Away," *New Yorker*, January 2002; Andrew Higgins and Alan Cullison, "Saga of Dr. Zawahri Illuminates Roots of al Qaeda Terror," *Wall Street Journal,* 2 July 2002.

10. Fareed Zakaria, "Why Do They Hate Us?" *Newsweek,* 15 October 2001; Graham E. Fuller, "The Future of Political Islam," *Foreign Affairs,* March/April 2002; Pauline Jones Luong and Erika Weinthal, "New Friends, New Fears in Central Asia," *Foreign Affairs,* March/April 2002; Ahmed Rashid, "To Boost Military Campaign, U.S. Blinks at Repression in Central Asia," *Wall Street Journal,* 13 May 2002.

Abbreviations and Acronyms

ACR	*African Contemporary Record*
AFPI	Agence France Presse International
AI	Amnesty International
AIS	Armée Islamique du Salut (Islamic Salvation Army)
ASG	Abu Sayyaf Group
EOHR	Egyptian Organization for Human Rights
FFS	Front des Forces Socialistes (Socialist Forces Front)
FIDA	Front Islamique du Djihad Armé (Islamic Front for Armed Jihad)
FIS	Front Islamique du Salut (Islamic Salvation Front)
FIS-EBA	FIS Executive Bureau Abroad
FIS-PDA	FIS Parliamentary Delegation Abroad
FIS-PNEB	FIS Provisional National Executive Bureau
FLN	Front de Libération Nationale (National Liberation Front)
GIA	Groupe Islamique Armé (Armed Islamic Group)
GSPC	Groupe Salafiste pour la Prédication et le Combat (Salafist Group for Preaching and Combat)
HAMAS	Harakat al-Mujtama al-Islami (Islamic Society Movement)
HATM	Harakat al-Islah wal-Tajdid bil-Maghrib (Movement of Reform and Renewal in Morocco)
HCE	Haut Comite d'Etat (High State Committee)
HRW	Human Rights Watch
IHT	*International Herald Tribune*
IRP	Islamic Renaissance (or Rebirth) Party

JI	Jama'at-i Islami
JKLF	Jammu and Kashmir Liberation Front
JMB	Jordanian Muslim Brotherhood
MB	Muslim Brotherhood
MECS	*Middle East Contemporary Survey*
MEI	Mouvement pour l'Etat Islamique (Islamic State Movement)
MEI	*Middle East International*
MEJ	*Middle East Journal*
MIA	Movement Islamique Armé (Armed Islamic Movement)
MILF	Moro Islamic Liberation Front
MIM	Muslim (later Mindanao) Independence Movement
MNI	Mouvement de la Nahda Islamique (Islamic Renaissance Movement)
MNLF	Moro National Liberation Front
MSP	Mouvement de la Société pour la Paix (Society of Peace Movement)
MTI	Mouvement de la Tendance Islamique (Islamic Tendency Movement)
MUF	Muslim United Front
NYT	*New York Times*
UTO	United Tajik Opposition

Bibliography

Aamer, Aisam (1995). *al-Islam al-Siyasi wa Dhahiret al-Anf wal-Irhab* (Cairo: Khulud lil-Nashrwal-Tawzia).

Abdelmajid, Wahid (1989). "Amaliyet al-Intiqal ila al-Ta'adudiya fi al-Jazair," *al-Manar,* vol. 53.

Abdelnasser, Walid Mahmoud (1994). *The Islamic Movement in Egypt: Perceptions of International Relations, 1967–1981* (London: Kegan Paul).

Abdo, Geneive (2000). *No God but God: Egypt and the Triumph of Islam* (New York: Oxford University Press).

Abdullah, Thina Fouad (1997). *Aliyat al-Taghier al-Dimuqrati fi al-Watan al-Arabi* (Beirut: Markaz al-Dirasat al-Wihda al-Arabiya).

Abed-Kotob, Sana (1995). "The Accommodationists Speak: Goals and Strategies of the Muslim Brotherhood of Egypt," *International Journal of Middle East Studies,* vol. 27: 321–339.

Abulala, Muhammed Hussein (1998). *Al-Anf al Dini fi Misr: Dirasat fi 'alm al-Ijtima'a al-Siyasi* (Cairo: al-Mahrousa).

Ahmad, Mumtaz (1991). "Islamic Fundamentalism in South Asia: The Jama'at-i-Islami and the Tablighi Jama'at of South Asia" in Martin E. Marty and R. Scott Appleby, eds., *Fundamentalisms Observed* (Chicago: University of Chicago Press).

Ahmed, Abdel Aati Muhammad (1995). a*l-Harakat al-Islamiya fi Misr wa Qadhiyet al-Tahawal al-Dimuqrati* (Cairo: Markaz al-Ahram lil-Tarjama wal-Nashr).

Ahmed, Muhammad Sayid (1984). *Mustaqbal al-Nizam al-Hizbi fi Misr* (Cairo: Dar al-Mustaqbal al-Arabi).

Ahmed, Samina (2001/2002). "The United States and Terrorism in Southwest Asia: September 11 and Beyond," *International Security*, vol. 26, no. 3 (Winter): 79–93.

Al-Ahnaf, M., B. Botiveau, and F. Frégosi (1991). *L'Algérie par ses islamistes* (Paris: Karthala).

Akiner, Shirin, and Catherine Barnes (2001). "The Tajik Civil War: Causes and Dynamics" in Kamoludin Abdullaev and Catherine Barnes, eds., *Politics of*

Compromise: The Tajikistan Peace Process (*Accord: International Review of Peace Initiatives* [March]).

Ali, Haider Ibrahim (1996). *Al-Tiyarat al-Islamiyya wa Qadhiyat al-Dimuqratiyya* (Beirut: Markaz Dirasat al-Wihda al-Arabiyya).

Almond, Gabriel A., Emmanuel Sivan, and R. Scott Appleby (1995a). "Explaining Fundamentalisms" in Martin E. Marty and R. Scott Appleby, eds., *Fundamentalisms Comprehended* (Chicago: University of Chicago Press).

——— (1995b). "Politics, Ethnicity, and Fundamentalism" in Martin E. Marty and R. Scott Appleby, eds., *Fundamentalisms Comprehended* (Chicago: University of Chicago Press).

Aly, Abd al-Monein Said, and Manfred W. Wenner (1982). "Modern Islamic Reform Movements: The Muslim Brotherhood in Contemporary Egypt," *The Middle East Journal*, vol. 36, no. 3 (Summer).

al-Amar, Mon'am (1996). "al-Jazair wal-Tadidiyya al-Muklifa" in *al-Azma al-Jazairyya: al-Khalifiyyat al-Siyasiya wal-Ijtimaiyya wal-Iqtisadiyya wal-Thaqafiyya* (Beirut: Markaz Dirasat al-wihda al-Arabiyya).

Amoud, Muhammad Saad Abu (1991). "al-Buna al-Tanzimi li-Jama'at al-Islam al-Siyasi fi al-Watan al-Arabi wa Athruoh fi al-Solouk al-Siyasiya lihathihi al-Jama'at (Misr Kahala lil-Dirasa)," *al-Mustaqbal al-Arabi*, no. 143 (January).

Amuzegar, Jahangir (1992). "The Iranian Economy Before and After the Revolution," *The Middle East Journal*, vol. 46, no. 3.

Anderson, John (1997). *The International Politics of Central Asia* (Manchester, UK: Manchester University Press).

Anderson, Lisa (1997). "Fulfilling Prophecies: State Policy and Islamist Radicalism" in John L. Esposito, ed., *Political Islam: Revolution, Radicalism, or Reform?* (Boulder, Colo.: Lynne Rienner).

Ansari, Hamied N. (1984a). "The Islamic Militants in Egyptian Politics," *International Journal of Middle East Studies*, vol. 16: 123–144.

——— (1984b). "Sectarian Conflict in Egypt and the Political Expediency of Religion," *The Middle East Journal*, vol. 38, no. 3 (Summer): 397–418.

——— (1986). *Egypt, The Stalled Society* (Albany: State University of New York Press).

Apter, David E. (1992). "Democracy and Emancipatory Movements: Notes for a Theory of Inversionary Discourse," *Development and Change*, vol. 23, no. 3: 139–173.

——— (1997). "Political Violence in Analytical Perspective" in David E. Apter, ed., *The Legitimization of Violence* (New York: UN Research Institute for Social Development).

Apter, David E., and Tony Saich (1994). *Revolutionary Discourse in Mao's Republic* (Cambridge, Mass.: Harvard University Press).

Arjomand, Said Amir (1988). *The Turban for the Crown: The Islamic Revolution in Iran* (New York: Oxford University Press).

——— (1995). "Unity and Diversity in Islamic Fundamentalism" in Martin E. Marty and R. Scott Appleby, eds., *Fundamentalisms Comprehended* (Chicago: University of Chicago Press).

———, ed. (1984). *From Nationalism to Revolutionary Islam* (Albany: State University of New York Press).

Asadullaev, Iskander (2001). "The Tajikistan Government" in Kamoludin Abdullaev and Catherine Barnes, eds., *Politics of Compromise: The Tajikistan Peace Process* (*Accord: International Review of Peace Initiatives* [March]).

Asfahani, Nabiha (1981). "Mafhum al-Hizb al-Wahed fi al-Jazair bayna al-Nazariya wal-Tatbiq," *al-Siyasa al-Dawliya*, vol. 14 (February).

Atkin, Muriel (1997). "Thwarted Democratization in Tajikistan" in Karen Dawisha and Bruce Parrott, eds., *Conflict, Cleavage, and Change in Central Asia and the Caucasus* (Cambridge: Cambridge University Press).

Auda, Gehad (1994). "The 'Normalization' of the Islamic Movement in Egypt from the 1970s to the Early 1990s" in Martin E. Marty and R. Scott Appleby, eds., *Accounting for Fundamentalisms* (Chicago: University of Chicago Press).

Auda, Huda Ragheb, and Hasanin Tawfiq Ibrahim (1995). *al-Ikhwan al-Muslimun wal-Siyasa fi Misr: Dirasa fi al-Tahalufat al-Intikhabiya wal-Mumarasat al-Barlamaniya lil-Ikhwan al-Muslimin fi Dhal al-Ta'adudiya al-Siyasiya al-Muqayada, 1984–1990* (Cairo: Markaz al-Mahrous lil-Bihouth wal-Tadrib wal-Nashr).

Ayadat, Zaid (1997). "The Islamic Movement and Political Participation" in Jillian Schwedler, ed., *Islamic Movements in Jordan* (Amman: al-Urdun al-Jadid Research Center).

Ayubi, Nazih (1991a). *Political Islam: Religion and Politics in the Arab World* (London: Routledge).

——— (1991b). *The State and Public Policies in Egypt Since Sadat* (Political Studies of the Middle East, no. 29, Reading, UK: Ithaca Press).

Ayyashi, Ahmeda (1993). *al-Haraka al-Islamiyya fi al-Jazair: al-Joudhour, al-Rumouz, al-Masar* (Casablanca: Uyun al-Magalat).

Baker, Raymond William (1990). *Sadat and After: Struggles for Egypt's Political Soul* (Cambridge, Mass.: Harvard University Press).

Bakr, Hasan (1996). *al-Anf al-Siyasi fi Misr, 1977–1993* (Cairo: Markez al-Mahrousa lil-Bihouth wal-Tadrib wal-Nashr).

Bandura, Albert (1998). "Mechanisms of Moral Disengagement" in Walter Reich, ed., *Origins of Terrorism: Psychologies, Ideologies, Theologies, States of Mind* (Washington, D.C.: Woodrow Wilson Center Press).

——— (1999). "Moral Disengagement in the Perpetration of Inhumanities," *Personality and Social Psychology Review*, vol. 3: 193–209.

Bandura, Albert, C. Barabarenelli, G. V. Caprara, and C. Pastorelli (1996). "Mechanisms of Moral Disengagement in the Exercise of Moral Agency," *Journal of Personality and Social Psychology*, vol. 71: 364–374.

Bandura, Albert, G. V. Caprara, C. Barabarenelli, C. Pastorelli, and C. Regalia (2001). "Sociocognitive Self-Regulatory Mechanism Governing Transgressive Behavior," *Journal of Personality and Social Psychology*, vol. 80: 125–135.

Barraclough, Steven (1998). "Al-Azhar: Between the Government and the Islamists," *The Middle East Journal*, vol. 52, no. 2 (Spring).

Batatu, Hanna (1982). "Syria's Muslim Brethren," *Middle East Report* (November-December).

Bayat, Asef (1997). *Street Politics: Poor People's Movements in Iran* (New York: Columbia University Press).

————— (2002). "Activism and Social Development in the Middle East," *International Journal of Middle East Studies,* vol. 34, no. 1 (February): 1–28.

Bekkar, Rabia (1997). "Taking Up Space in Tlemcen: The Islamist Occupation of Urban Algeria" in Joel Beinin and Joe Stork, eds., *Political Islam* (Berkeley and Los Angeles: University of California Press).

Belhaj, Abu Abdel Fatah Ali (1994). *Ghayat al-Murad fi Qadhaya al-Jihad: Four Letters* (Algeria: al-Jabha al-Islamiya lil-Inqaz).

Benamrouche, Amar (1995). "État conflits sociaux et mouvement syndical en Algérie (1962–1995)," *Monde arabe Maghreb Machrek,* no. 148 (April–June).

Benford, Robert D., and David A. Snow (2000). "Framing Processes and Social Movements: An Overview and Assessment," *Annual Review of Sociology,* vol. 26: 611–639.

Bennoune, Mahfoud (1988). *The Making of Contemporary Algeria, 1830–1987* (Cambridge: Cambridge University Press).

Berejikian, Jeffery (1992). "Revolutionary Collective Action and the Agent-Structure Problem," *American Political Science Review,* vol. 86, no. 3 (September): 647–657.

Bianchi, Robert (1989). *Unruly Corporatism: Associational Life in Twentieth-Century Egypt* (New York: Oxford University Press).

Bodansky, Youssef (1999). *Bin Laden: The Man Who Declared War on America* (Roseville, Calif.: Prima Publishing).

Bouhouche, Ammar (1998). "The Essence of Reforms in Algeria" in Azzedine Layachi, ed., *Economic Crisis and Political Change in North Africa* (Westport, Conn.: Praeger).

Boulby, Marion (1988). "The Islamic Challenge: Tunisia Since Independence," *Third World Quarterly,* vol. 10, no. 2.

————— (1999). *The Muslim Brotherhood and the Kings of Jordan, 1945–1993* (Atlanta: Scholars Press).

Brenninkmeijer, Olivier A. J. (1997). "International Concern for Tajikistan: UN and OSCE Efforts to Promote Peace-Building and Democratisation" in Mohammad Reza Djalili, Frederic Grare, and Shirin Akiner, eds., *Tajikistan: The Trials of Independence* (New York: St. Martin's Press).

Brockett, Charles D. (1991). "The Structure of Political Opportunities and Peasant Mobilization in Central America," *Comparative Politics,* vol. 23: 253–274.

————— (1995). "A Protest-Cycle Resolution of the Repression/Popular-Protest Paradox" in Mark Traugott, ed., *Repertoires and Cycles of Collective Action* (Durham, N.C.: Duke University Press).

Brown, Bess A. (1997). "The Civil War in Tajikistan, 1992–1993" in Mohammad Reza Djalili, Frederic Grare, and Shirin Akiner, eds., *Tajikistan: The Trials of Independence* (New York: St. Martin's Press).

Burgat, François (1997). "Ballot Boxes, Militaries, and Islamic Movements" in Martin Kramer, ed., *The Islamism Debate* (Tel Aviv: The Moshe Dayan Center for Middle Eastern and African Studies).

Burgat, François, and William Dowell (1997). *The Islamic Movement in North Africa* (Austin: University of Texas Center for Middle Eastern Studies).

Burke, Edmund, III, and Ira M. Lapidus (1988). *Islam, Politics and Social Movements* (Berkeley and Los Angeles: University of California Press).

Campagna, Joel (1996). "From Accommodation to Confrontation: The Muslim Brotherhood in the Mubarak Years," *Journal of International Affairs,* vol. 50, no. 1 (Summer).

Cassandra (1995). "The Impending Crisis in Egypt," *The Middle East Journal,* vol. 49, no. 1 (Winter).

Chalk, Peter (2002). "Militant Islamic Extremism in the Southern Philippines" in Jason F. Isaacson and Colin Rubenstein, eds., *Islam in Asia: Changing Political Realities* (New Brunswick, N.J.: Transaction Publishers).

Charef, Abed (1994). *Algérie: Le Grand Dérapage* (Paris: Éditions de l'Aube).

Chellaney, Brahma (2001/2002). "Fighting Terrorism in Southern Asia: The Lessons of History," *International Security,* vol. 26, no. 3 (Winter): 94–116.

Choueiri, Youssef M. (1997). *Islamic Fundamentalism* (London: Pinter Press).

Cleary, M. R. (2000). "Democracy and Indigenous Rebellion in Latin America," *Comparative Political Studies,* vol. 33, no. 9: 1123–1150.

Cohen, Jean L. (1985). "Strategy or Identity: New Theoretical Paradigms and Contemporary Social Movements," *Social Research,* vol. 52, no. 4 (Winter): 663–716.

Cooper, Mark N. (1982). "The Demilitarization of the Egyptian Cabinet," *International Journal of Middle East Studies,* vol. 14, no. 2 (May): 203–225.

Costain, Anne W. (1992). *Inviting Women's Rebellion: A Political Process Interpretation of the Women's Movement* (Baltimore: Johns Hopkins University Press).

Crecelius, Daniel (1966). "Al-Azhar in the Revolution," *The Middle East Journal,* vol. 20, no. 1 (Winter).

Crenshaw, Martha (1978). *Revolutionary Terrorism: The FLN in Algeria, 1954–1962* (Stanford, Calif.: Hoover Institution Press).

——— (1981). "The Causes of Terrorism," *Comparative Politics,* vol. 13, no. 4: 379–399.

——— (1992). "Decisions to Use Terrorism: Psychological Constraints on Instrumental Reasoning" in Bert Klandermans and Donatella della Porta, eds., *Social Movements and Violence: Participation in Underground Organizations* (*International Social Movement Research,* vol. 4).

——— (1995). "The Effectiveness of Terrorism in the Algerian War" in Martha Crenshaw, ed., *Terrorism in Context* (University Park: Penn State University Press).

Dalin, Alexander F., and George W. Breslauer (1970). *Political Terror in Communist Systems* (Stanford, Calif.: Stanford University Press).

Dardour, Abdel Baaset (1996). *al-Unf al-Siyasi fi al-Jazair wa Azmet al-Tahawul al-Dimuqrati* (Cairo: Dar al-Ameen).

al-Darif, Muhammad (1994). *al-Islam al-Siyasi fi al-Jazair* (Casablanca: Manshurat al-Majalla al-Maghribiyya li-Ilm al-Ijtima'a Asiyasi).

Davies, James C. (1962). "Toward a Theory of Revolution," *American Sociological Review,* vol. 27 (February).

——— (1969). "The J-Curve of Rising and Declining Satisfaction as a Cause of Some Great Revolutions and a Contained Rebellion" in Hugh Davis Graham and Ted Robert Gurr, eds., *Violence in America* (New York: Signet).

Davis, Anthony (1995). "The Conflict in Kashmir," *Jane's Intelligence Review,* vol. 7, no. 1.

———— (1998). "Islamic Guerrillas Threaten the Fragile Peace on Mindanao," *Jane's Intelligence Review,* vol. 10, no. 5.

Davis, Eric (1984). "Ideology, Social Class and Islamic Radicalism in Modern Egypt" in Said Amir Arjomand, ed., *From Nationalism to Revolutionary Islam* (Albany: State University of New York Press).

Davis, S., and J. Hodson (1982). *Witnesses to Political Violence in Guatemala: The Suppression of a Rural Development Movement* (Oxfam America).

Dekmejian, R. Hrair (1995). *Islam in Revolution: Fundamentalism in the Arab World,* 2d ed. (Syracuse, N.Y.: Syracuse University Press).

Della Porta, Donatella (1988). "Recruitment Processes in Clandestine Political Organizations: Italian Left-Wing Terrorism," *International Social Movement Research,* vol. 1: 155–169.

———— (1992). "Introduction: On Individual Motivations in Underground Political Organizations" in Bert Klandermans and Donatella della Porta, eds., *Social Movements and Violence: Participation in Underground Organizations* (*International Social Movement Research,* vol. 4).

———— (1995a). *Social Movements, Political Violence, and the State: A Comparative Analysis of Italy and Germany* (Cambridge: Cambridge University Press).

———— (1995b). "Left-Wing Terrorism in Italy" in Martha Crenshaw, ed., *Terrorism in Context* (University Park: Penn State University Press).

———— (1996). "Social Movements and the State: Thoughts on the Policing of Protest" in Doug McAdam, John D. McCarthy, and Mayer N. Zald, eds., *Comparative Perspectives on Social Movements* (Cambridge: Cambridge University Press).

Della Porta, Donatella, and Dieter Rucht (1995). "Left-Libertarian Movements in Context: A Comparison of Italy and West Germany, 1965–1990" in Jenkins and Klandermans, eds., *The Politics of Social Protest* (Minneapolis: University of Minnesota Press).

DeNardo, James (1985). *Power in Numbers: The Political Strategy of Protest and Rebellion* (Princeton, N.J.: Princeton University Press).

Denoeux, Guilain (1993). *Urban Unrest in the Middle East: A Comparative Study of Informal Networks in Egypt, Iran, and Lebanon* (Albany: State University of New York Press).

Desmond, Edward W. (1995). "The Insurgency in Kashmir, 1989–1991," *Contemporary South Asia,* vol. 4, no. 1 (March).

Diani, Mario (1996). "Linking Mobilization Frames and Political Opportunities: Insights from Regional Populism in Italy," *American Sociological Review,* vol. 61 (December): 1053–1069.

al-Din, Nabil Sharaf (1998). *Umara wa Muwatinun: Rasd li-Dhahirt al-Islam al-Haraki fi Misr Khilal Aqd al-Tisinat* (Cairo: Madbouli).

Dix, Robert (1984). "Why Revolutions Succeed and Fail," *Polity,* vol. 16, no. 3 (Spring): 423–446.

Dudoignon, Stephane A. (1997). "Political Parties and Forces in Tajikistan, 1989–1993" in Mohammad Reza Djalili, Frederic Grare, and Shirin Akiner, eds., *Tajikistan: The Trials of Independence* (New York: St. Martin's Press).

Dunlop, John B. (1998). *Russia Confronts Chechnya: Roots of a Separatist Conflict* (Cambridge: Cambridge University Press).

Eckstein, Harry (1965). "On the Etiology of Internal Wars," *History and Theory,* vol. 4, no. 2: 133–163.

Eickelman, Dale F., and James Piscatori (1996). *Muslim Politics* (Princeton, N.J.: Princeton University Press).

Eisinger, P. K. (1973). "The Conditions of Protest Behavior in American Cities," *American Political Science Review,* vol. 67: 11–28.

Entelis, John P. (1986). *Algeria: The Revolution Institutionalized* (Boulder, Colo.: Westview Press).

———— (1992). "Introduction: State and Society in Transition" in John P. Entelis and Phillip C. Naylor, eds., *State and Society in Algeria* (Boulder, Colo.: Westview Press).

———— (1994). "Islam, Democracy and the State: The Reemergence of Authoritarian Politics in Algeria" in John Ruedy, *Islamism and Secularism in North Africa* (London: Macmillan).

———— (1996). "Civil Society and the Authoritarian Temptation in Algerian Politics: Islamic Democracy vs. the Centralized State" in A. R. Norton, ed., *Civil Society in the Middle East,* Vol. 2 (Leiden, Netherlands: E. J. Brill).

———— (1997). "Political Islam in the Maghreb: The Nonviolent Dimension" in John P. Entelis, ed., *Islam, Democracy and the State in North Africa* (Bloomington and Indianapolis: Indiana University Press).

Esposito, John L. (1997). *Political Islam: Revolution, Radicalism, or Reform?* (Boulder, Colo.: Lynne Rienner).

———— (1999). *The Islamic Threat: Myth or Reality?* New York: Oxford University Press.

————, ed. (1983). *Voices of Resurgent Islam* (New York: Oxford University Press).

Esposito, John L., and John O. Voll (1996). *Islam and Democracy* (New York: Oxford University Press).

Étienne, Bruno (1984). *L' Islamisme radical* (Paris: Hachette).

Fahmy, Ninette S. (1998). "The Performance of the Muslim Brotherhood in the Egyptian Syndicates: An Alternative Formula for Reform?" *The Middle East Journal,* vol. 52, no. 4 (Autumn).

Faksh, Mahmud A. (1997). *The Future of Islam in the Middle East: Fundamentalism in Egypt, Algeria, and Saudi Arabia* (Westport, Conn.: Praeger).

Fandy, Mamoun (1994). "Egypt's Islamic Group: Regional Revenge?" *The Middle East Journal,* vol. 48, no. 4 (Autumn).

Farhi, Farideh (1990). *States and Urban-Based Revolutions: Iran and Nicaragua* (Urbana: University of Illinois Press).

Fatah, Nabil Abdel (1995). *al-Wajeh wal-Qina'a: al-Haraka al-Islamiya wal-Anf wal-Tatbi'a* (Cairo: Shishat lil-Dirasat wal-Nashr wal-Tawzi'a).

———— (1997). *al-Nus wal-Rasaas: al-Islam al-Siyasi wal-Aqbat wa-Azmat al-Dawla al-Haditha fi Misr* (Beirut: Dar al-Nihar lil-Nashr).

Fawzi, Mahmoud (1993). *Aboud al-Zumur: Kayfa Ightalna al-Sadat* (Cairo: Dar al-Nashr al-Hatiya).

Feierabend, Ivo K., and Rosalind L. Feierabend (1972). "Systematic Conditions of Political Aggression: An Application of Frustration-Aggression Theory" in Ivo K. Feierabend, Rosalind L. Feierabend, and Ted Robert Gurr, eds., *Anger, Violence and Politics* (Englewood Cliffs, N.J.: Prentice-Hall).

Francisco, Ronald A. (1995). "The Relationship Between Coercion and Protest: An Empirical Evaluation in Three Coercive States," *Journal of Conflict Resolution*, vol. 39, no. 2: 263–282.

——— (1996). "Coercion and Protest: An Empirical Test in Two Democratic States," *American Journal of Political Science*, vol. 40: 1179–1204.

Gall, Carlotta, and Thomas de Waal (1998). *Chechnya: Calamity in the Caucasus* (New York: New York University Press).

Gamson, William A. (1975). *The Strategy of Social Protest* (Homewood, Ill.: Dorsey Press).

Gamson, William A., Bruce Fireman, and Steven Rytina (1982). *Encounters with Unjust Authority* (Homewood, Ill.: Dorsey Press).

Ganguly, Sumit (1990/1991). "Avoiding War in Kashmir," *Foreign Affairs* (Winter).

——— (1997). *The Crisis in Kashmir: Portents of War, Hopes of Peace* (Cambridge: Cambridge University Press).

Gartner, Scott S., and Patrick M. Regan (1996). "Threat and Repression: The Non-Linear Relationship Between Government and Opposition Violence," *Journal of Peace Research*, vol. 33: 273–288.

George, Alexander L. (1979). "Case Studies and Theory Development: The Method of Structured, Focused Comparison" in Paul Gordon Lauren, ed., *Diplomatic History: New Approaches* (New York: Free Press).

George, T.J.S. (1980). *Revolt in Mindanao: The Rise of Islam in Philippine Politics* (New York: Oxford University Press).

Gerges, Fawaz A. (1999). *America and Political Islam: Clash of Cultures or Clash of Interests* (Cambridge: Cambridge University Press).

——— (2000). "The End of the Islamist Insurgency in Egypt? Costs and Prospects," *The Middle East Journal,* vol. 54, no. 4 (Autumn).

Gerlach, Luther P., and Virginia H. Hine (1970). *People, Power, Change: Movements of Social Transformation* (Indianapolis: Bobbs-Merrill).

Ghanim, Ibrahim al-Biyoumi (1992). *al-Haraka al-Islamiyya fi al-Jazair wa Azmat al-Dimuqratiyya* (Paris: Umat).

Gharaibeh, Ibrahim (1997a). "The Political Performance and the Organization of the Muslim Brotherhood" in Jillian Schwedler, ed., *Islamic Movements in Jordan* (Amman: al-Urdun al-Jadid Research Center).

——— (1997b) *Jama'at al-Ikhwan al-Muslimin fi al-Urdun, 1946–1996* (Amman: al-Urdun al-Jadid Research Center).

al-Ghinam, Muhammad Abul Fateh (1996). *Muwajehit al-Irhab fi al-Tashri'a al-Misri: Dirasa Muqarana* (Cairo: Dar al-Nahda al-'Arabiya).

Ginkel, John, and Alastair Smith (1999). "So You Say You Want a Revolution: A Game Theoretic Explanation of Revolution in Repressive Regimes," *Journal of Conflict Resolution,* vol. 43, no. 3 (June): 291–316.

Goffman, Erving (1974). *Frame Analysis: An Essay on the Organization of Experience* (New York: Harper & Row).

Goldstein, Robert J. (1983). *Political Repression in Nineteenth Century Europe* (London: Croom Helm).

Goldstone, Jack A. (1991). *Revolution and Rebellion in the Early Modern World* (Berkeley and Los Angeles: University of California Press).

Goldstone, Jack A., and Charles Tilly (2001). "Threat (and Opportunity): Popular Action and State Response in the Dynamics of Contentious Action" in Ronald R. Aminzade et al., eds., *Silence and Voice in the Study of Contentious Politics* (Cambridge: Cambridge University Press).

Goodwin, Jeff (1997). "State-Centered Approaches to Social Revolutions: Strengths and Limitations" in John Foran, ed., *Theorizing Revolutions* (New York: Routledge).

———— (2001a). "The Limits of Repression: A Qualitative Comparative Analysis of Counterinsurgency." Working paper presented at the conference on "Mobilization and Repression: What We Know and Where Should We Go from Here?" University of Maryland, 21–24 June 2001.

———— (2001b). *No Other Way Out: States and Revolutionary Movements, 1945–1991* (New York: Cambridge University Press).

Goodwin, Jeff, and Theda Skocpol (1989). "Explaining Revolutions in the Contemporary Third World," *Politics and Society,* vol. 17, no. 4: 489–509.

Gordon, C., and A. Arian (2001). "Threat and Decision Making," *The Journal of Conflict Resolution,* vol. 45, no. 2: 196–215.

Gorvin, Ian (1997). "The Human Rights Situation in Tajikistan (1992–1993)" in Mohammad Reza Djalili, Frederic Grare, and Shirin Akiner, eds., *Tajikistan: The Trials of Independence* (New York: St. Martin's Press).

Gretsky, Sergei (1995). "Civil War in Tajikistan: Causes, Developments and Prospects for Peace" in Roald Z. Sagdeev and Susan Eisenhower, eds., *Central Asia: Conflict, Resolution, and Change* (Washington, D.C.: Eisenhower Institute).

Guazzone, Laura (1995). "Islamism and Islamists in the Contemporary Arab World" in Laura Guazzone, ed., *The Islamist Dilemma: The Political Role of Islamist Movements in the Contemporary Arab World* (Reading, UK: Ithaca Press).

Gupta, Dipak K., Harinder Singh, and Tom Sprague (1993). "Government Coercion of Dissidents: Deterrence or Provocation?" *Journal of Conflict Resolution,* vol. 37, no. 2 (June): 301–339.

Gurr, Ted Robert (1968a). "Urban Disorder: Perspectives from the Comparative Study of Civil Strife" in Louis H. Massotti and Don Bowen, eds., *Riots and Rebellion: Civil Violence in the Urban Community* (Beverly Hills, Calif.: Sage).

———— (1968b). "A Causal Model of Civil Strife: A Comparative Analysis Using New Indices," *American Political Science Review,* vol. 27: 1104–1124.

———— (1968c). "Psychological Factors in Civil Violence," *World Politics,* vol. 20: 245–278.

———— (1970). *Why Men Rebel* (Princeton, N.J.: Princeton University Press).

———— (1973). "The Revolution–Social Change Nexus," *Comparative Politics,* vol. 5: 359–392.

———— (1986). "Persisting Patterns of Repression and Rebellion: Foundations for a General Theory of Political Coercion" in Margaret P. Karns, ed., *Persisting*

Patterns and Emergent Structures in a Waning Century (New York: Praeger).

—— (2000). *People Versus States: Minorities at Risk in the New Century* (Washington, D.C.: United States Institute of Peace).

Gurr, Ted Robert, and Raymond D. Duvall (1973). "Civil Conflict in the 1960s: A Reciprocal Theoretical System with Parameter Estimates," *Comparative Political Studies,* vol. 6, no. 2: 135–169.

Gurr, Ted Robert, and Jack A. Goldstone (1991). "Comparisons and Policy Implications" in Jack A. Goldstone, Ted Robert Gurr, and Farrokh Moshiri, eds., *Revolutions in the Late Twentieth Century* (Boulder, Colo.: Westview Press).

Hafez, Mohammed M. (2000a). "Armed Islamist Movements and Political Violence in Algeria," *The Middle East Journal,* vol. 54, no. 4 (Autumn).

—— (2000b). "Islamism Between Accommodation and Insurgency: A Political Process Explanation of Islamist Strategies in Algeria and Egypt." Ph.D. diss., London School of Economics and Political Science, University of London.

Halliday, Fred (1995). *Islam and the Myth of Confrontation: Religion and Politics in the Middle East* (London: I. B. Tauris).

Hamdi, Mohamed Elhachmi (1998). *The Politicisation of Islam: A Case Study of Tunisia* (Boulder, Colo.: Westview Press).

Hammad, Waleed (1997). "Islamists and Charitable Work" in Jillian Schwedler, ed., *Islamic Movements in Jordan* (Amman: al-Urdun al-Jadid Research Center).

Hamouda, Adel (1987). *al-Hijra ila al-Unf* (Cairo: Dar Sina lil-Nashr).

—— (1989). *Qanabil wa Masahif* (Cairo: Dar Sina lil-Nashr).

Hardin, Russell (1982). *Collective Action* (Baltimore, Md.: Johns Hopkins University Press).

Hasan, Amar Ali (1994). "Ada al-Tahaluf al-Islami fi Majlis al-Shaab Khilal al-Fasl al-Tashri 'i al-Khames" in Muhammed Sifa al-Din Kharboush, ed., *al-Tatawur al-Siyasi fi Misr, 1982–1992* (Cairo: Center for Political Research and Studies).

Hatmiat al-Muwajaha [The Inevitability of Confrontation] (1987). Anonymous document, al-Jama'a al-Islamiyya, 29 pp.

Hefner, Robert W. (1997). "Islamization and Democratization in Indonesia" in Robert W. Hefner and Patricia Horvatich, eds., *Islam in an Era of Nation-States: Politics and Religious Renewal in Muslim Southeast Asia* (Honolulu: University of Hawaii Press).

Hendriks, Bertus (1987). "Egypt's New Political Map," *Middle East Report* (July–August).

Hermassi, Muhammed Abdelbaqi (1987). *al-Mujtama wal-Dawla fi al-Maghrib al-Arabi* (Beirut: Markaz Dirasat al-Wihda al-Arabiya).

—— (1995). "al-Islam al-Ihtijaji fi Tunis" in *al-Haraka al-Islamiya al-Mu'asira fi al-Watan al-Arabi,* 3d ed. (Beirut: Markaz Dirasat al-Wihda al-Arabiya).

Hibbs, Douglas A., Jr. (1973). *Mass Political Violence: A Cross-national Causal Analysis* (New York: Wiley).

Hilal, Ali al-Din (1986). *al-Tatawur al-Dimuqrati fi Misr: Qadhaya wa-Muna-qashat* (Cairo: Maktibet Nahdhet al-Sharq).

———— (1997). *Tatawur al-Nizam al-Siyasi fi Misr, 1803–1997* (Cairo: Markez al-Bihouth wal-Dirasat fi Misr).

al-Hilali, Ahmed Nabil (1991). "al-Tazib al-Jama'ai fi Misr wa Kayfa Nuwaji-huh" in Muhammed al-Sayid Said, ed., *Huquq al-Insan fi Misr* (Cairo: Dar al-Mustaqbal al-Arabi).

Hinnebusch, Raymond A., Jr. (1985). *Egyptian Politics Under Sadat: The Post-Populist Development of an Authoritarian-Modernizing State* (Cambridge: Cambridge University Press).

el-Hodaiby, Muhammad M. (1997). "Upholding Islam: The Goals of Egypt's Muslim Brotherhood," *Harvard International Review,* vol. 19, no. 2 (Spring): 20–63.

Hoffman, Valerie (1995). "Muslim Fundamentalists: Psychosocial Profiles" in Martin E. Marty and R. Scott Appleby, eds., *Fundamentalisms Compre-hended* (Chicago: University of Chicago Press).

Horne, Alistair (1977). *A Savage War of Peace, Algeria 1954–1962* (New York: Viking Press).

Hourani, Hani (1997). "The Future of the Islamic Movement in Jordan" in Jil-lian Schwedler, ed., *Islamic Movements in Jordan* (Amman: al-Urdun al-Jadid Research Center).

Hudson, Michael C. (1995). "Arab Regimes and Democratization: Responses to the Challenge of Political Islam" in Laura Guazzone, ed., *The Islamist Dilemma: The Political Role of Islamist Movements in the Contemporary Arab World* (Reading, UK: Ithaca Press).

Hunt, Scott A., Robert D. Benford, and David A. Snow (1994). "Identity Fields: Framing Processes and the Social Construction of Movement Identities" in Enrique Laraña, Hank Johnston, and Joseph R. Gusfield, eds., *New Social Movements: From Ideology to Identity* (Philadelphia: Temple University Press).

Hunter, Shireen T. (1995). "The Rise of Islamist Movements and the Western Response: Clash of Civilizations or Clash of Interests?" in Laura Guaz-zone, ed., *The Islamist Dilemma: The Political Role of Islamist Movements in the Contemporary Arab World* (Reading, UK: Ithaca Press).

————, ed. (1988). *The Politics of Islamic Revivalism: Diversity and Unity* (Bloomington: Indiana University Press).

Huntington, Samuel P. (1968). *Political Order in Changing Societies* (New Haven: Yale University Press).

Hussain, Mir Zohair (1994). "Islam in Pakistan Under Bhutto and Zia-ul-Haq" in Hussin Mutalib and Taj ul-Islam Hashmi, eds., *Islam, Muslims and the Modern State: Case Studies of Muslims in Thirteen Countries* (London: Macmillan).

Ibrahim, Hasanein Tawfiq (1995). "al-Anf al-Siyasi fi Misr" in Navin Abdel Mun'am Mus'ad, ed., *Dhahiret al-Anf al-Siyasi min Mandhour Muqarin* (Cairo: Markaz al-Bihouth wal-Dirasat al-Siyasiya).

———— (1996). "al-Ihtijaj al-Jama'ai wal Anf al-Siyasi" in Mustapha Kamel al-Sayid and Kamal al-Manoufa, eds., *Haqiqet al-Tadudiya al-Siyasiya fi*

Misr: Dirasat fi al-Tahawul al-Raismali wal-Musharaka al-Siyasiya (Cairo: Markaz al-Bihouth al-Arabiya, Maktibet al-Madbouli).

——— (1998). *al-Nizam al-Siyasi wal-Ikhwan al-Muslimun fi Misr: Min al-Tasamuh ila al-Muwajiha, 1981–1996* (Cairo: Dar al-Tali'a lil-Tiba'a wal-Nashr).

Ibrahim, Saad Eddin (1980). "Anatomy of Egypt's Militant Islamic Groups: Methodological Note and Preliminary Findings," *International Journal of Middle East Studies,* vol. 12: 423–453.

——— (1981). "An Islamic Alternative in Egypt: The Muslim Brotherhood and Sadat," *Arab Studies Quarterly,* vol. 4.

——— (1988). "Egypt's Islamic Activism in the 1980s," *Third World Quarterly,* vol. 10, no. 2 (April).

——— (1996). *Egypt, Islam and Democracy: Twelve Critical Essays* (Cairo: American University of Cairo Press).

Al-Ikhwan al-Muslimun: Moujez an al-Shura fi al-Islam wa Ta'adud al-Ahzab fi al-Mujtam'a al-Muslim [The Muslim Brothers: A Summary Account Concerning Consultation in Islam and Party Pluralism in a Muslim Society] (March 1994). Anonymous document (Cairo: Dar al-Tawzi'a wal-Nashr).

Ismail, Salwa (1998). "Confronting the Other: Identity, Culture, Politics, and Conservative Islamism in Egypt," *International Journal of Middle East Studies,* vol. 30: 199–225.

Jabri, Vivienne (1996). *Discourses on Violence: Conflict Analysis Reconsidered* (Manchester, UK: Manchester University Press).

Jacquard, Roland (2002). *In the Name of Osama Bin Laden: Global Terrorism and the Bin Laden Brotherhood* (Durham, N.C.: Duke University Press).

Janinah, Nimat Allah (1988). *Tanzim al-Jihad: al-Badil al-Islami fi Misr* (Cairo: Dar al-Huriya).

al-Jasour, Nazim Abdelwahed (1995). "al-Mawqif al-Faransi min al-Islam Asiyasi fi al-Jazair: Ab'aadih al-Iqlimiyya wal-Dawliyya," *al-Mustaqbal al-Arabi,* no. 202 (December): 43–59.

Jenkins, J. Craig (1983). "Resource Mobilization Theory and the Study of Social Movements," *Annual Review of Sociology,* vol. 9: 527–553.

Jenkins, J. Craig, and Craig M. Eckert (1986). "Channeling Black Insurgency," *American Sociological Review,* vol. 51, no. 6: 812–829.

Jenkins, J. Craig, and Charles Perrow (1977). "Insurgency of the Powerless: Farm Worker Movements (1946–1972)," *American Sociological Review,* vol. 42: 249–268.

Juergensmeyer, Mark (2000). *Terror in the Mind of God: The Global Rise of Religious Violence* (Berkeley and Los Angeles: University of California Press).

Kalyvas, Stathis N. (1996). *The Rise of Christian Democracy in Europe* (Ithaca, N.Y.: Cornell University Press).

——— (1999). "Wanton and Senseless? The Logic of Massacres in Algeria," *Rationality and Society,* vol. 11, no. 3: 243–285.

al-Kanani, Abdel Halim (1991). *Hadith al-Dawa: Kitabat al-Ustadh al-Murshed bi-Majalat al-Dawa: Dirasa wa T'aliq* (Tanta, Egypt: Dar al-Bashir lil-Thaqafa wal-Ulum al-Islamiyya).

Kaplan, Lawrence, ed. (1992). *Fundamentalism in Comparative Perspective* (Amherst: University of Massachusetts Press).

Katzenstein, Mary F., and Carol. M. Mueller, eds. (1987). *The Women's Movements of the United States and Western Europe: Consciousness, Political Opportunity and Public Policy* (Philadelphia: Temple University Press).

Kazemi, Farhad (1980). *Poverty and Revolution in Iran: The Migrant Poor, Urban Marginality and Politics* (New York: New York University Press).

Keddie, Nikki (1981). *Roots of Revolution: An Interpretive History of Modern Iran* (New Haven: Yale University Press).

Kepel, Gilles (1984). *Muslim Extremism in Egypt: The Prophet and Pharaoh* (Berkeley and Los Angeles: University of California Press).

——— (1994). *The Revenge of God: The Resurgence of Islam, Christianity and Judaism in the Modern World* (Cambridge, Mass.: Polity Press).

Kharfallah, al-Tahir bin (1996). "al-Huriyyat al-Umoumiyya wa Huquq al-Insan fi al-Jazair min Khilal Destour 1976 wa 1989: Dirasa Muqarana" in *al-Azma al-Jazairyya: al-Khalifiyyat Asiyasiya wal-Ijtimaiyya wal-Iqtisadiyya wal-Thaqafiyya* (Beirut: Markaz Dirasat al-wihda al-Arabiyya).

——— (1997). "Mu'ana al-Sahafa al-Mustaqila fi al-Jazair," *Shuoun al-Awsat*, vol. 59 (January–February): 81–95.

Khawaja, Marwan (1993). "Repression and Popular Collective Action: Evidence from the West Bank," *Sociological Forum*, vol. 8, no. 1: 47–71.

Khelladi, Aïssa (1992). *Les Islamistes Algériens face au pouvoir* (Algiers: Alfa).

Kienle, Eberhard (1998). "More Than a Response to Islamism: The Political Deliberalization of Egypt in the 1990s," *The Middle East Journal*, vol. 52, no. 2 (Spring): 219–235.

Kiernan, Ben (1996). *The Pol Pot Regime: Race, Power, and Genocide in Cambodia Under the Khmer Rouge, 1975–1979* (New Haven: Yale University Press).

Kitschelt, Herbert (1986). "Political Opportunity Structures and Political Protest: Anti-Nuclear Movements in Four Democracies," *British Journal of Political Science,* vol. 16: 57–85.

——— (1990). "The Medium Is the Message: Democracy and Oligarchy in Belgian Ecology Parties," in Wolfgang Rüdig, ed., *Green Politics* (Edinburgh: Edinburgh University Press).

Klandermans, Bert (1984). "Mobilization and Participation: Social-Psychological Expansions of Resource Mobilization Theory," *American Sociological Review,* vol. 49: 583–600.

Knezys, Stasys, and Romanas Sedlickas (1999). *The War in Chechnya* (College Station: Texas A&M University Press).

Koopmans, Ruud (1993). "The Dynamics of Protest Waves: West Germany, 1965–1989," *American Sociological Review,* vol. 58 (October): 637–658.

Korany, Bahgat (1998). "Resticted Democratization from Above: Egypt," in Bahgat Korany, Rex Brynen, and Paul Noble, eds., *Political Liberalization and Democratization in the Arab World, Volume 2: Comparative Experiences* (Boulder, Colo.: Lynne Rienner).

Korany, Bahgat, and Saad Amrani (1998). "Explosive Civil Society and Democratization from Below: Algeria" in Bahgat Korany, Rex Brynen, and

Paul Noble, eds., *Political Liberalization and Democratization in the Arab World, Volume 2: Comparative Experiences* (Boulder, Colo.: Lynne Rienner).

Krämer, Gudrun (1994). "The Integration of the Integrists: A Comparative Study of Egypt, Jordan and Tunisia" in Ghassan Salamé, ed., *Democracy Without Democrats? The Renewal of Politics in the Muslim World* (London: I. B. Tauris).

———— (1995). "Cross-Links and Double Talk? Islamist Movements in the Political Process" in Laura Guazzone, ed., *The Islamist Dilemma: The Political Role of Islamist Movements in the Contemporary Arab World* (Reading, UK: Ithaca Press).

Kramer, Martin (1996). *Arab Awakening and Islamic Revival: The Politics of Ideas in the Middle East* (New Brunswick, N.J.: Transaction).

———— (1997). "The Mismeasure of Political Islam" in Martin Kramer, ed., *The Islamism Debate* (Tel Aviv: Moshe Dayan Center for Middle Eastern and African Studies).

———— (1998). "The Moral Logic of Hizballah" in Walter Reich, ed., *Origins of Terrorism: Psychologies, Ideologies, Theologies, States of Mind* (Washington, D.C.: Woodrow Wilson Center Press).

Kriesi, Hanspeter (1989). "The Political Opportunity Structure of the Dutch Peace Movement," *West European Politics,* vol. 12: 295–312.

———— (1996). "The Organizational Structure of New Social Movements in a Political Context" in Doug McAdam, John D. McCarthy, and Mayer N. Zald, eds., *Comparative Perspectives on Social Movements* (Cambridge: Cambridge University Press).

Kriesi, Hanspeter, Ruud Koopmans, Jan Willem Duyvendak, and Marco G. Giugni (1992). "New Social Movements and Political Opportunities in Western Europe," *European Journal of Political Research,* vol. 22: 219–244.

———— (1995). *New Social Movements in Western Europe* (London: University College London Press).

Kurzman, Charles (1996). "Structural Opportunity and Perceived Opportunity in Social Movement Theory: The Iranian Revolution of 1979," *American Sociological Review,* vol. 61 (February): 153–170.

Labat, Séverine (1994). "Islamism and Islamists: The Emergence of New Types of Politico-Religious Muslims" in John Ruedy, *Islamism and Secularism in North Africa* (London: Macmillan).

———— (1995). *Les Islamistes Algériens: Entre les urnes et le maquis* (Paris: Seuil).

Lamchichi, Abderrahim (1992). *L'Islamisme en Algérie* (Paris: L'Harmattan).

Lapidus, Ira M. (1988). *A History of Islamic Societies* (Cambridge: Cambridge University Press).

———— (1992). "The Golden Age: The Political Concepts of Islam," *The Annals of The American Academy of Political and Social Sciences,* vol. 524 (November).

Laqueur, Walter (1987). *The Age of Terrorism* (Boston: Little, Brown).

Laremont, Ricardo Rene (2000). *Islam and the Politics of Resistance in Algeria, 1783–1992* (Lawrenceville, N.J.: Africa World Press).

Lawrence, Bruce B. (1998). *Shattering the Myth: Islam Beyond Violence* (Princeton, N.J.: Princeton University Press).

Lazreg, Marina (1994). *The Eloquence of Silence: Algerian Women in Question* (New York: Routledge).

Lee, Chris, Sandra Maline, and Will H. Moore (2000). "Coercion and Protest: An Empirical Test Revisited" in Christian Davenport, ed., *Paths to State Repression: Human Rights Violations and Contentious Politics* (Lanham, Md.: Rowman and Littlefield).

Lia, Brynjar (1998). *The Society of the Muslim Brothers in Egypt: The Rise of an Islamic Movement, 1928–1942* (Reading, UK: Ithaca Press).

Lichbach, Mark (1987). "Deterrence or Escalation? The Puzzle of Aggregate Studies of Repression and Dissent," *Journal of Conflict Resolution,* vol. 31: 266–297.

——— (1995). *The Rebel's Dilemma* (Ann Arbor: University of Michigan Press).

Lichbach, Mark, and Ted R. Gurr (1981). "The Conflict Process: A Formal Model," *Journal of Conflict Resolution,* vol. 25 (March): 3–29.

Lieven, Anatol (1998). *Chechnya: Tombstone of Russian Power* (New Haven: Yale University Press).

Liong, Liem Soei (1988). "Indonesian Muslims and the State: Accommodation or Revolt?" *Third World Quarterly,* vol. 10, no. 2 (April).

Lofland, John (1966). *Doomsday Cult* (Englewood Cliffs, N.J.: Prentice-Hall).

——— (1996). *Social Movement Organizations: Guide to Research on Insurgent Realities* (New York: Aldine de Gruyter).

Mahaba, Ahmed (1998). "Azmit al-Jazair bayn al-Tadwil wal-Wafaq al-Watani," *al-Siyasa al-Dawliya,* vol. 131 (January).

Majul, Cesar Adib (1985). *The Contemporary Muslim Movement in the Philippines* (Berkeley, Calif.: Mizan Press).

——— (1988). "The Moro Struggle in the Philippines," *Third World Quarterly,* vol. 10, no. 2: 897–922.

Makram-Ebeid, Mona (1989). "Political Opposition in Egypt: Democratic Myth or Reality?" *The Middle East Journal,* vol. 43, no. 3 (Summer): 423–436.

Manhaj Jama'it al-Jihad al-Islami [The Method of the Islamic Jihad Group] (1986). Document authored by Aboud Zumur, 27 pp.

Martinez, Luis (1997/1998). "Les Enjeux des négociations entre l'AIS et l'armée," *Politique Étrangère,* vol. 62, no. 4 (Winter).

——— (2000). *The Algerian Civil War, 1990–1998* (New York: Columbia University Press).

Mason, T., and D. Krane (1989). "The Political Economy of Death Squads: Towards a Theory of the Impact of State-Sanctioned Terror," *International Studies Quarterly,* vol. 33: 175–198.

May, Rachel (2001). *Terror in the Countryside: Campesino Responses to Political Violence in Guatemala, 1954–1985* (Athens: Ohio University Press).

Mayer, Ann Elizabeth (1993). "The Fundamentalist Impact on Law, Politics, and Constitutions in Iran, Pakistan, and the Sudan" in Martin E. Marty and R. Scott Appleby, eds., *Fundamentalism and the State* (Chicago: University of Chicago Press).

McAdam, Doug (1982). *Political Process and the Development of Black Insurgency, 1930–1970* (Chicago: University of Chicago Press.)

———— (1988). "Micromobilization Contexts and Recruitment to Activism" in Bert Klandermans, Hanspeter Kriesi, and Sidney Tattow, eds., *From Structure to Action: Comparing Social Movement Research Across Cultures* (Greenwich, Conn.: JAI Press).

———— (1996). "The Framing Function of Movement Tactics: Strategic Dramaturgy in the American Civil Rights Movement" in Doug McAdam, John D. McCarthy, and Mayer N. Zald, eds., *Comparative Perspectives on Social Movements* (Cambridge: Cambridge University Press).

McAdam, Doug, John D. McCarthy, and Mayer N. Zald (1988). "Social Movements" in Neil J. Smelser, ed., *Handbook of Sociology* (Newbury Park, Calif.: Sage).

————, eds. (1996). *Comparative Perspectives on Social Movements: Political Opportunities, Mobilizing Structures, and Cultural Framings* (Cambridge: Cambridge University Press).

McAdam, Doug, and Ronnelle Paulsen (1993). "Specifying the Relationship Between Social Ties and Activism," *American Journal of Sociology,* vol. 99, no. 3 (November): 640–667.

McAdam, Doug, Sidney Tarrow, and Charles Tilly (1997). "Toward an Integrated Perspective on Social Movements and Revolution" in Mark Irving Lichbach and Alan S. Zuckerman, eds., *Comparative Politics: Rationality, Culture and Structure* (Cambridge: Cambridge University Press).

———— (2001). *Dynamics of Contention* (Cambridge: Cambridge University Press).

McAmis, Robert D. (1974). "Muslim Filipinos, 1970–1972" in Peter G. Gowing and Robert D. McAmis, eds., *The Muslim Filipinos: Their History, Society, and Contemporary Problems* (Manila: Solidaridad Publishing House).

McCarthy, John D., David W. Britt, and Mark Wolfson (1991). "The Institutional Channeling of Social Movements by the State in the United States" in Louis Kriesberg, ed., *Research in Social Movements, Conflicts, and Change* (Greenwich, Conn.: JAI Press).

McCarthy, John D., and Mayer N. Zald (1973). *The Trend of Social Movements in America: Professionalization and Resource Mobilization* (Morristown, NJ: General Learning Press).

———— (1977). "Resource Mobilization and Social Movements: A Partial Theory," *American Journal of Sociology,* vol. 82, no. 6: 1212–1241.

McClintock, Cynthia (1998). *Revolutionary Movements in Latin America: El Salvador's FMLN and Peru's Shinning Path* (Washington, D.C.: United States Institute of Peace Press).

McKenna, Thomas M. (1997). "Appreciating Islam in the Muslim Philippines: Authority, Experience, and Identity in Cotabato" in Robert W. Hefner and Patricia Horvatich, eds., *Islam in an Era of Nation-States: Politics and Religious Renewal in Muslim Southeast Asia* (Honolulu: University of Hawaii Press).

———— (1998). *Muslim Rulers and Rebels: Everyday Politics and Armed Separatism in the Southern Philippines* (Berkeley and Los Angeles: University of California Press).

Mehri, Abdelhamid (1997). "al-Azma al-Jazairiyya: al-Waq'a wal-Ifaq," *al-Mustaqbal al-Arabi,* vol. 226 (December).

Melucci, Alberto (1992). "Liberation or Meaning? Social Movements, Culture and Democracy," *Development and Change,* vol. 23, no. 2: 43–77.

——— (1995). "The Process of Collective Identity" in Hank Johnston and Bert Klandermans, eds., *Social Movements and Culture* (London: University College of London).

Meyer, David S. (1993). "Peace Protest and Policy: Explaining the Rise and Decline of Antinuclear Movements in Postwar America," *Policy Studies Journal,* vol. 21: 29–51.

Milton-Edwards, Beverly (1996). "Climate of Change in Jordan's Islamist Movement" in Abdel Salam Sidahmed and Anoushiravan Ehteshami, eds., *Islamic Fundamentalism* (Boulder, Colo.: Westview Press).

Mitchell, Richard P. (1969). *The Society of Muslim Brothers* (New York: Oxford University Press).

Mithaq al-Amal al-Islami [The Manifesto of Islamic Activism] (February 1984). Document authored by Najih Ibrahim, Asem Abdel Majid, and Aisam al-Din Daraballa, 254 pp.

Moaddel, Mansoor (1993). *Class, Politics, and Ideology in the Iranian Revolution* (New York: Columbia University Press).

Moore, Will H. (1998). "Repression and Dissent: Substitution, Context, and Timing," *American Journal of Political Science*, vol. 42, no. 3: 851–873.

Moro, Muhammad (1990). *Tanzim al-Jihad: Afkaroh, Juzuroh, Siyasatih* (Cairo: al-Sharika al-Arabiya al-Dawliya lil-Nashr wal-Ilam).

——— (1994). *al-Haraka al-Islamiya fi Misr, 1928–1993: Ruiya min Qurb* (Cairo: Dar al-Misriya lil-Nashr wal-Tawzia).

Mortimer, Robert (1991). "Islam and Multiparty Politics in Algeria," *The Middle East Journal,* vol. 45, no. 4 (Autumn).

——— (1996). "Islamists, Soldiers, and Democrats: The Second Algerian War," *The Middle East Journal,* vol. 50, no. 1 (Winter).

——— (1997). "Algeria: The Dialectic of Elections and Violence," *Current History* (May): 231–235.

Moss, David (1997). "Politics, Violence, Writing: The Rituals of 'Armed Struggle' in Italy" in David E. Apter, ed., *The Legitimization of Violence* (New York: United Nations Research Institute for Social Development).

Moussalli, Ahmad S., ed. (1998). *Islamic Fundamentalism: Myths and Realities* (Reading, UK: Ithaca Press).

Mubarak, Hisham (1995). *al-Irhabiyun Qadimun: Dirasa Muqarana bayn Mouqif al-Ikhwan al-Muslimin wa Jama'at al-Jihad min Qadhiet al-Anf, 1928–1994* (Cairo: Markaz al-Mahrousa lil-Nashr al-Khidmat al-Sahafiya).

——— (1997). "What Does the Gama'a Islamiyya Want? Talat Fuad Qasim, Interview with Hisham Mubarak" in Joel Beinin and Joe Stork, eds., *Political Islam* (Berkeley and Los Angeles: University of California Press).

Muller, Edward N. (1985). "Income Inequality, Regime Repression, and Political Violence," *American Sociological Review*, vol. 50: 47–61.

Muller, Edward N., and Mitchell Seligson (1987). "Inequality and Insurgency," *American Political Science Review*, vol. 81: 425–451.

Muller, Edward N., and Erich Weede (1990). "Cross-National Variation in Political Violence: A Rational Action Approach," *Journal of Conflict Resolution,* vol. 34, no. 4: 624–651.

Munson, Henry, Jr. (1986). "The Social Base of Islamic Militancy in Morocco," *The Middle East Journal,* vol. 40, no. 2 (Spring).

——— (1993). *Religion and Power in Morocco* (New Haven: Yale University Press).

Mus'ad, Nevien Abdelmunim (1995). "al-Anf al-Siyasi lil-Harakat al-Ijtimaiya al-Diniya (Dirasa lil-Jabha al-Islamiya lil-Inqadh bil-Jazair)" in Nevien Abdelmunim Mus'ad, ed., *Dhahiret al-Anf al-Siyasi fi Manzour Muqarin* (Cairo: Center for Political Research and Studies).

Mustapha, Hala (1992). *al-Islam al-Siyasi fi Misr: Min Haraket al-Islam ila Jama'at al-Anf* (Cairo: Markaz al-Dirasat al-Siyasiya wal-Istratijiya).

——— (1995). "Muashirat wa Nataij Intikhabat 1995" in Hala Mustapha, ed., *al-Intikhabat al-Barlamaniya fi Misr, 1995* (Cairo: Markaz al-Dirasat al-Siyasiya wal-Istratijiya).

——— (1996). *al-Dawla wal-Harakat al-Islamiya al-Muaridha: Bayn al-Muhadana wal-Muwajaha fi Ahdi al-Sadat wa Mubarak* (Cairo: Markaz Mahrous lil-Nishr wal-Khidmat al-Sahafiya).

Nasr, S.V.R. (1994). *The Vanguard of the Islamic Revolution: The Jama'at-i Islami of Pakistan* (London: I. B. Tauris).

——— (1996). *Mawdudi and the Making of Islamic Revivalism* (New York: Oxford University Press).

——— (1997). "Islamic Opposition in the Political Process: Lessons from Pakistan" in John L. Esposito, ed., *Political Islam: Revolution, Radicalism, or Reform?* (Boulder, Colo.: Lynne Rienner).

Neuhouser, Kevin (1989). "The Radicalization of the Brazilian Catholic Church in Comparative Perspective," *American Sociological Review,* vol. 54 (April): 233–244.

Niyazi, Aziz (1994). "Tajikistan" in Mohiaddin Mebahi, ed., *Central Asia and the Caucasus After the Soviet Union: Domestic and International Dynamics* (Gainesville: University Press of Florida).

Oberschall, Anthony (1973). *Social Conflict and Social Movements* (Englewood Cliffs, N.J.: Prentice-Hall).

——— (1978). "Theories of Social Conflict," *Annual Review of Sociology,* vol. 4: 291–315.

——— (1993). *Social Movements: Ideologies, Interests, and Identities* (New Brunswick, N.J.: Transaction Publishers).

O'Kane, Joseph P. (1972). "Islam in the New Egyptian Constitution," *The Middle East Journal,* vol. 26, no. 2: 137–148.

Olimova, Saodat (1999). "Political Islam and Conflict in Tajikistan" in Lena Jonson and Murad Esenov, eds., *Political Islam and Conflicts in Russia and Central Asia* (Stockholm: Sweden Institute for International Affairs, October).

Olimova, Saodat, and Muzaffar Olimov (2001). "The Islamic Renaissance Party" in Kamoludin Abdullaev and Catherine Barnes, eds., *Politics of Compromise: The Tajikistan Peace Process* (*Accord: International Review of Peace Initiatives* [March]).

Oliver, Pamela (1980). "Rewards and Punishment as Selective Incentives for Collective Action," *American Journal of Sociology,* vol. 85: 1356–1375.

Olivier, Johan L. (1990). "Causes of Ethnic Collective Action in Pretoria-Witwatersrand Triangle, 1970–1984," *South African Sociological Review,* vol. 2: 89–108.

——— (1991). "State Repression and Collective Action in South Africa, 1970–1984," *South African Journal of Sociology,* vol. 22: 109–117.

Olson, Mancur (1965). *The Logic of Collective Action* (Cambridge, Mass.: Harvard University Press).

O'Neil, Bard E. (1990). *Insurgency and Terrorism: Inside Modern Revolutionary Warfare* (Dulles, Va.: Brassey's).

Opp, Karl-Dieter (1988). "Community Integration and Incentives for Political Protest," *International Social Movements Research,* vol. 1: 83–101.

Opp, Karl-Dieter, and Wolfgang Roehl (1990). "Repression, Micromobilization, and Political Protest," *Social Forces,* vol. 69: 521–547.

Opp, Karl-Dieter, Peter Voss, and Christine Gern (1995). *Origins of Spontaneous Revolution: East Germany 1989* (Ann Arbor: University of Michigan Press).

Owen, R. (1994). "Socio-economic Change and Political Mobilization: The Case of Egypt" in Ghassan Salamé, ed., *Democracy Without Democrats? The Renewal of Politics in the Muslim World* (London: I. B. Tauris).

Palmer, David Scott (1995). "The Revolutionary Terrorism of Peru's Shining Path" in Martha Crenshaw, ed., *Terrorism in Context* (University Park: Penn State University Press).

Parsa, Misagh (2000). *States, Ideologies, and Social Revolutions: A Comparative Analysis of Iran, Nicaragua and the Philippines* (Cambridge: Cambridge University Press).

Pfaff, Steven (1996). "Collective Identity and Informal Groups in Revolutionary Mobilization: East Germany in 1989," *Social Forces,* vol. 75: 91–118.

Piscatori, James P., ed. (1983). *Islam in the Political Process* (Cambridge: Cambridge University Press).

Piven, F. F., and R. A. Cloward (1977). *Poor People's Movements: Why They Succeed, How They Fail* (New York: Vintage).

Politkovskaya, Anna (2001). *Dirty War: A Russian Reporter in Chechnya* (London: Harvill).

Posen, Barry R. (2001/2002). "The Struggle Against Terrorism: Grand Strategy, Strategy, and Tactics," *International Security,* vol. 26, no. 3 (Winter): 39–55.

Post, J. M. (1987). "Group and Organizational Dynamics of Political Terrorism: Implications for Counterterrorist Policy" in Paul Wilkinson and Alasdair M. Stewart, eds., *Contemporary Research on Terrorism* (Aberdeen: Aberdeen University Press).

——— (1998). "Terrorist Psycho-logic: Terrorist Behavior as a Product of Psychological Forces" in Walter Reich, ed., *Origins of Terrorism: Psychologies, Ideologies, Theologies, States of Mind* (Washington, D.C.: Woodrow Wilson Center Press).

Puri, Balraj (1993). *Kashmir: Towards Insurgency* (Delhi: Orient Longman).

Qandil, Amani (1992). *Tahdidat al-Dimuqratiya fi al-Aalam al-Arabi* (Cairo: Markaz al-Dirasat al-Tanmiya al-Siyasiya wal-Dawliya).

——— (1995a). *Amaliet al-Tahawal al-Dimuqrati fi Misr, 1981–1993* (Markaz Ibn Khaldun, Dar al-Amin lil-Nashr wal-Tawzi'a).

——— (1995b). "Taqyim Ada al-Islamiyin fi al-Naqabat al-Mihniya" in Navin Abdel Mun'am Mus'ad, ed., *Dhahiret al-Anf al-Siyasi min Mandhour Muqarin* (Cairo: Markaz lil-Abhath wal-Dirasat al-Siyasiya).

——— (1996). "al-Jama'at al-Mihniya wal-Musharaka al-Siyasiya" in Mustapha Kamel al-Sayid and Kamal al-Manoufa, eds., *Haqiqet al-Tadudiya al-Siyasiya fi Misr: Dirasat fi al-Tahawul al-Raismali wal-Musharaka al-Siyasiya* (Cairo: Markaz al-Bihouth al-Arabiya, Maktibet al-Madbouli).

Qawas, Muhammed (1998). *Ghazwit "al-Inqaz": M'araket al-Islam al-Siyasi fi al-Jazair* (Beirut: Dar al-Jadid).

Quandt, William B. (1998). *Between Ballots and Bullets: Algeria's Transition from Authoritarianism* (Washington, D.C.: Brookings Institution Press).

Radhi, Muhsin (1990/1991). *al-Ikhwan al-Muslimun that Qibet al-Barlaman, Volumes 1 and 2* (Cairo: Dar al-Nashr wal-Tawzia).

Rakhila, Amer (1993). *al-Tatawur al-Siyasi wal-Tanzimi li-Hizb Jabhat al-Tahrir al-Watani, 1960–1980* (Algiers: Diwan al-Matbouat al-Jamiya).

Ramadan, Abdel Azim (1993). "Fundamentalist Influence in Egypt: The Strategies of the Muslim Brotherhood and the Takfir Groups" in Martin E. Marty and R. Scott Appleby, eds., *Fundamentalisms and the State: Remaking Polities, Economies, and Militancy* (Chicago: University of Chicago Press).

——— (1995). *Jama'at al-Takfir fi Misr: al-Usul al-Tarikhiya wal-Fikriya* (Cairo: al-Haya al-Misriya al-Almiya lil-Kitab).

Rashid, Ahmed (2000). *Taliban: Militant Islam, Oil and Fundamentalism in Central Asia* (New Haven: Yale University Press).

——— (2002). *Jihad: The Rise of Militant Islam in Central Asia* (New Haven: Yale University Press).

Rashid, Samih (1997). "al-Ta'adidiya al-Hizbiyya fi al-Jazair," *Shuoun al-Awsat,* vol. 65 (September): 57–77.

al-Rasi, George (1997). *al-Islam al-Jazairi: min al-Amir Abd al-Kader ila Umara al- Jama'at* (Beirut: Dar al-Jadid).

Rasler, Karen (1996). "Concessions, Repression, and Political Protest in the Iranian Revolution," *American Sociological Review,* vol. 61 (February): 132–152.

Richards, Alan, and John Waterbury (1998). *A Political Economy of the Middle East* (Boulder, Colo.: Westview Press).

Roberts, Hugh (1988). "Radical Islamism and the Dilemma of Algerian Nationalism: The Embattled Arians of Algiers," *Third World Quarterly,* vol. 10, no. 2 (April).

——— (1991). "A Trial of Strength: Algerian Islamism" in James P. Piscatori, *Islamic Fundamentalism and the Gulf Crisis* (Chicago: American Academy of Arts and Sciences).

——— (1992). "The Algerian State and the Challenge of Democracy," *Government and Opposition,* vol. 27, no. 4 (Autumn).

——— (1994a). "From Radical Mission to Equivocal Ambition: The Expansion and Manipulation of Algerian Islamism, 1979–1992" in Martin E. Marty and R. Scott Appleby, eds., *Accounting for Fundamentalism: The Dynamic Character of Movements* (Chicago: University of Chicago Press).

—— (1994b). "Doctrinaire Economics and Political Opportunism in the Strategy of Algerian Islamism" in John Ruedy, ed., *Islamism and Secularism in North Africa* (London: Macmillan).

—— (1994c). "Algeria Between Eradicators and Conciliators," *Middle East Report* (July–August).

—— (1995). "Algeria's Ruinous Impasse and the Honourable Way Out," *International Affairs,* vol. 71, no. 2: 247–267.

—— (1996). "The Zeroual Memorandum: The Algerian State and the Problem of Liberal Reform," *The Journal of Algerian Studies,* vol. 1: 1–19.

—— (1998). "Algeria's Contested Elections," *Middle East Report* (Winter).

Robinson, Glenn E. (1997). "Can Islamists Be Democrats? The Case of Jordan," *The Middle East Journal,* vol. 51, no. 3 (Summer).

Roff, William R., ed. (1987). *Islam and the Political Economy of Meaning* (London: Croom Helm).

Rouadjia, Ahmed (1993). *al-Ikhwan wal-Jami'a: Istitl'a lil-Haraka al-Islamiya fi al-Jazair,* translated by Khalil Ahmed Khalil (Beirut: Dar al-Muntakhab al-Arabi).

—— (1995). "Discourse and Strategy of the Algerian Islamist Movement (1986–1992)" in Laura Guazzone, ed., *The Islamist Dilemma: The Political Role of Islamist Movements in the Contemporary Arab World* (Reading, UK: Ithaca Press).

Roy, Olivier (1994). *The Failure of Political Islam* (Cambridge, Mass.: Harvard University Press).

Rubin, Barry (1990). *Islamic Fundamentalism in Egyptian Politics* (London: Macmillan).

Rucht, Dieter (1996). "The Impact of National Context on Social Movement Structures: A Cross-Movement and Cross-National Comparison" in Doug McAdam, John D. McCarthy, and Mayer N. Zald, eds., *Comparative Perspectives on Social Movements* (Cambridge: Cambridge University Press).

Ruedy, John (1992). *Modern Algeria: The Origins and Development of a Nation* (Bloomington: Indiana University Press).

Ryan, Jeffrey J. (1994). "The Impact of Democratization on Revolutionary Movements," *Comparative Politics,* vol. 27, no. 1 (October): 27–44.

El-Said, Sabah (1995). *Between Pragmatism and Ideology: The Muslim Brotherhood in Jordan, 1989–1994* (Washington, D.C.: Institute for Near East Policy).

Salama, Muatez Muhammed (1994). "Ada al-Siyasi lil-Hizb al-Watani al-Dimuqrati (1979–1992)" in Muhammed Sifa al-Din Kharboush, ed., *al-Tatawur al-Siyasi fi Misr, 1982–1992* (Cairo: Center for Political Research and Studies).

Sambanis, Nicholas (2001). "Do Ethnic and Non-Ethnic Civil Wars Have the Same Causes? A Theoretical and Empirical Inquiry," *Journal of Conflict Resolution,* vol. 45, no. 3: 259–282.

Schofield, Victoria (2000). *Kashmir in Conflict: India, Pakistan and the Unfinished War* (London: I. B. Tauris).

Scott, James C. (1985). *Weapons of the Weak: Everyday Forms of Peasant Resistance* (New Haven: Yale University Press).

Seely, Robert (2001). *Russo-Chechen Conflict, 1800–2000: A Deadly Embrace* (London: Frank Cass).

Shabad, Goldie, and Francisco José Ramo (1995). "Political Violence in a Democratic State: Basque Terrorism in Spain" in Martha Crenshaw, ed., *Terrorism in Context* (University Park: Penn State University Press).

Shadid, Mohamed K. (1988). "The Muslim Brotherhood Movement in the West Bank and Gaza," *Third World Quarterly,* vol. 10, no. 10.

Shahin, Emad Eldin (1997). *Political Ascent: Contemporary Islamic Movements in North Africa* (Boulder, Colo.: Westview Press).

al-Shawkabi, Amru (1995). "al-Maraka al-Intikhabiya: Dhawahir Jadida" in Hala Mustapha, ed., *al-Intikhabat al-Barlamaniya fi Misr, 1995* (Cairo: Markaz al-Dirasat al-Siyasiya wal-Istratijiya).

al-Sheikh, Yousuf Muhammad (1993). *Ajnihat al-Inqadh: Qusat Jabihat al-Inqadh al-Jazairiyya: min al-Wilada ila al-Itiqal* (Beirut: Muasisat al-Aarif lil-Matbouat).

Shoman, Muhammad (1996). "Azmet al-Musharaka min Khilal al-Ahzab al-Misriya" in Mustapha Kamel al-Sayid and Kamal al-Manoufa, eds., *Haqiqet al-Tadudiya al-Siyasiya fi Misr: Dirasat fi al-Tahawul al-Raismali wal-Musharaka al-Siyasiya* (Cairo: Markaz al-Bihouth al-Arabiya, Maktibet al-Madbouli).

al-Shourbaji, Manar (1994). "al-Qadhaya al-Dasturiya wal Qanuniya fi Fatret Riaset Mubarak al-Thaniya" in Muhammed Sifa al-Din Kharboush, ed., *al-Tatawur al-Siyasi fi Misr, 1982–1992* (Cairo: Center for Political Research and Studies).

Singerman, Diane (1995). *Avenues of Participation: Family, Politics, and Networks in Urban Quarters of Cairo* (Princeton, N.J.: Princeton University Press).

Singh, Tavleen (1995). *Kashmir: A Tragedy of Errors* (New Delhi: Penguin).

Sivan, Emmanuel (1985). *Radical Islam: Medieval Theology and Modern Politics* (New Haven: Yale University Press).

Sivan, Emmanuel, and Menachem Friedman, eds. (1990). *Religious Radicalism and Politics in the Middle East* (Albany: State University of New York Press).

Skocpol, Theda (1979). *States and Social Revolutions* (Cambridge: Cambridge University Press).

Smith, Christian (1991). *The Emergence of Liberation Theology: Radical Religion and Social Movement Theory* (Chicago: University of Chicago Press).

Snow, D. A., L. A. Zurcher, and S. Ekland-Olson (1980). "Social Networks and Social Movements," *American Sociological Review,* vol. 45: 787–801.

Snow, David A., and Robert D. Benford (1988). "Ideology, Frame Resonance, and Participant Mobilization," *International Social Movement Research,* vol. 1: 197–218.

——— (1992). "Master Frames and Cycles of Protest," in Aldon D. Morris and Carol McClurg Mueller, eds., *Frontiers in Social Movement Theory* (New Haven: Yale University Press).

Snow, David A., E. Burke Rochford Jr., Steve K. Worden, and Robert D. Benford (1986). "Frame Alignment Processes, Micro-Mobilization and Movement Participation," *American Sociological Review,* vol. 51: 464–481.

Snyder, David (1976). "Theoretical and Methodological Problems in the Analysis of Governmental Coercion and Collective Violence," *Journal of Political and Military Sociology,* vol. 4: 277–293.

Snyder, David, and William Kelly (1979). "Strategies for Investigating Violence and Social Change" in Mayer N. Zald and J. D. McCarthy, eds., *The Dynamics of Social Movements: Resources Mobilization, Social Control, and Tactics* (Cambridge, Mass.: Winthrop).

Snyder, David, and Charles Tilly (1972). "Hardship and Collective Violence in France, 1830 to 1960," *American Sociological Review,* vol. 37, no. 5 (October): 520–532.

Sonbol, Amira el-Azhary (1988). "Egypt" in Shireen T. Hunter, ed., *The Politics of Islamic Revivalism* (Bloomington: Indiana University Press).

Souaïdia, Habib (2001). *La Sale Guerre* (Paris: La Découverte).

Splidsboel-Hansen, Flemming (1994). "The 1991 Chechen Revolution: The Response of Moscow," *Central Asia Survey,* vol. 13, no. 3.

Springborg, Robert (1989). *Mubarak's Egypt: Fragmentation of the Political Order* (Boulder, Colo.: Westview Press).

Sprinzak, Ehud (1998). "The Psychopolitical Formation of Extreme Left Terrorism in a Democracy: The Case of the Weathermen" in Walter Reich, ed., *Origins of Terrorism: Psychologies, Ideologies, Theologies, States of Mind* (Washington, D.C.: Woodrow Wilson Center Press).

Stern, Jessica (2000). "Pakistan's Jihad Culture," *Foreign Affairs,* vol. 79, no. 6 (November–December): 115–126.

Stowasser, Barbara Freyer (1987). *The Islamic Impulse* (London: Croom Helm).

Sullivan, Denis J. (1994). *Private Voluntary Organizations in Egypt: Islamic Development, Private Initiative, and State Control* (Gainesville: University Press of Florida).

Sullivan, Denis J., and Sana Abed-Kotob (1999). *Islam in Contemporary Egypt: Civil Society Versus the State* (Boulder, Colo.: Lynne Rienner).

Swindler, Ann (1986). "Culture in Action: Symbols and Strategies," *American Sociological Review,* vol. 5, no. 2: 273–286.

al-Tahiri, Nur al-Din (1992). *al-Jazair: Bayna al-Khiyar al-Islami wal-Khiyar al-Askari* (Casablanca: Uyun al-Maqalat).

Taji-Farouki, Suha (1996). *A Fundamental Quest: Hizb al-Tahrir and the Search for the Islamic Caliphate* (London: Grey Seal).

Tarrow, Sidney (1989). *Democracy and Disorder. Social Conflict, Protest and Politics in Italy, 1965–1975* (New York: Oxford University Press).

——— (1994). *Power in Movement: Social Movements, Collective Action and Politics* (Cambridge: Cambridge University Press).

——— (1996). "States and Opportunities: The Political Structuring of Social Movements" in Doug McAdam, John D. McCarthy, and Mayer N. Zald, eds., *Comparative Perspectives on Social Movements* (Cambridge: Cambridge University Press).

al-Tawil, Camille (1998). *al-Haraka al-Islamiyya al-Musalaha fi al-Jazair: min al-Inqadh ila al-Jama'a* (Beirut: Dar al-Nahar).

al-Tawil, Muhammed (1992). *al-Ikhwan fi al-Barlaman* (Cairo: al-Maktab al-Misri al-Hadith).

Tessler, Mark (1997). "The Origins of Popular Support for Islamist Movements: A Political Economy Analysis" in John P. Entelis, ed., *Islam, Democracy and the State in North Africa* (Bloomington: Indiana University Press).

al-Thawra al-Islamiyya fi al-Jazair: al-Nus al-Kamel lil-Barnamij Asiyasi li-Jabhat al-Inqadh al-Islamiyya. (1991). (Cairo: Dar Yafa lil-Dirasat wal-Abhath).

Tilly, Charles (1978). *From Mobilization to Revolution* (Reading, Mass.: Addison-Wesley).

——— (1979). "Repertoires of Contention in America and Britain, 1975–1830" in Mayer Zald and John D. McCarthy, eds., *The Dynamics of Social Movements* (Cambridge, Mass.: Winthrop).

Tilly, Charles, Louise Tilly, and Richard Tilly (1975). *The Rebellious Century, 1830–1930* (Cambridge, Mass.: Harvard University Press).

Tlimsani, Omar (1985). *Zikrayat la Muzakarat* (Cairo: Dar al-Tawzi'a wal Nashr al-Islamiya).

Trotsky, Leon (1961). *The History of the Russian Revolution* (New York: Monad Press).

Turner, Mark (1995). "Terrorism and Secession in the Southern Philippines: The Rise of the Abu Sayyaf," *Contemporary Southeast Asia,* vol. 17, no. 1.

Vandewalle, Dirk (1987). "Political Aspects of State Building in Rentier Economics: Algeria and Libya Compared" in Hazem Beblawi and Giacomo Luciani, eds., *The Rentier State* (London: Croom Helm).

Vatin, Jean-Claude (1981). "Religious Resistance and State Power in Algeria" in Alexander S. Cudsi and Ali E. Hillal Dessouki, eds., *Islam and Power* (Baltimore, Md.: Johns Hopkins University Press).

——— (1983). "Popular Puritanism Versus State Reformism: Islam in Algeria" in James P. Piscatori, ed., *Islam in the Political Process* (Cambridge: Cambridge University Press).

Vergès, Meriem (1997). "Genesis of a Mobilization: The Young Activists of Algeria's Islamic Salvation Front" in Joel Beinin and Joe Stork, eds., *Political Islam* (Berkeley and Los Angeles: University of California Press).

Voll, John O. (1991). "Fundamentalism in the Sunni Arab World: Egypt and the Sudan" in Martin E. Marty and R. Scott Appleby, eds., *Fundamentalism Observed* (Chicago: University of Chicago Press).

Von der Mehden, Fred R. (1986). *Religion and Modernization in Southeast Asia* (Syracuse, N.Y.: Syracuse University Press).

Voss, Kim (1996). "The Collapse of a Social Movement: The Interplay of Mobilizing Structures, Framing and Political Opportunities in the Knights of Labor" in Doug McAdam, John D. McCarthy, and Mayer N. Zald, eds., *Comparative Perspectives on Social Movements* (Cambridge: Cambridge University Press).

Walker, Edward E. (1998). "Islam in Chechnya," *Contemporary Caucasus Newsletter,* no. 6 (Fall).

Waltz, Susan (1986). "Islamist Appeal in Tunisia," *The Middle East Journal,* vol. 40, no. 4 (Autumn).

Wanas, al-Munsaf (1996). "al-Dawla al-Wataniyya wal Mujtama al-Madani fil Jazair: Muhawala fi Qirait Intifadhit Tishreen al-Awal/October 1988" in *al-Azma al-Jazairiyya: al-Khalfiyyat Asiyasiyya wal Ijtimaiyya wal Iqtisadiyya wal Thaqafiyya* (Beirut: Markaz Dirasat al-Wihda al-Arabiyya).

Wasmund, Klaus (1986). "The Political Socialisation of West German Terrorists" in Peter H. Merkl, ed., *Political Violence and Terror: Motifs and Motivations* (Berkeley and Los Angeles: University of California Press).

White, Robert W. (1989). "From Peaceful Protest to Guerrilla War: Micromobilization of the Provisional Irish Republican Army," *American Journal of Sociology,* vol. 94, no. 6: 1277–1302.

Wickham, Carrie Rosefsky (1997). "Islamic Mobilization and Political Change: The Islamist Trend in Egypt's Professional Associations" in Joel Beinin and Joe Stork, eds., *Political Islam* (Berkeley and Los Angeles: University of California Press).

Wickham-Crowley, Timothy P. (1991). *Exploring Revolution: Essays on Latin American Insurgency and Revolutionary Theory* (Armonk, N.Y.: M. E. Sharpe).

——— (1992). *Guerrillas and Revolution in Latin America: A Comparative Study of Insurgents and Regimes Since 1956* (Princeton, N.J.: Princeton University Press).

Wieviorka, Michael (1997). "ETA and Basque Political Violence" in David E. Apter, ed., *The Legitimization of Violence* (New York: United Nations Research Institute for Social Development).

Wiktorowicz, Quintan (2001). *The Management of Islamic Activism: Salafis, the Muslim Brotherhood, and State Power in Jordan* (Albany: State University of New York Press).

Williams, Rhys H. (1994). "Movement Dynamics and Social Change: Transforming Fundamentalist Ideology and Organizations" in Martin E. Matry and R. Scott Appleby, eds., *Accounting for Fundamentalism* (Chicago: University of Chicago Press).

Willis, Michael (1996). *The Islamist Challenge in Algeria: A Political History* (Reading, UK: Ithaca Press).

Wintrobe, Ronald (1998). *The Political Economy of Dictatorship* (Cambridge: Cambridge University Press).

Yepsah, Abdelkader (1994). "L'armée et le pouvoir en Algérie de 1962 à 1992," *Revue du Monde Musluman de la Méditerranée,* vol. 65: 74–94.

Yous, Nesroulah (2000). *Qui a tué à Bentalha? Algérie, chronique d'un massacre annoncé* (Paris: La Découverte).

Yousef, al-Sayid (1997). *al-Ikhwan al-Muslimun: Hal hia Sahwa Islamiya,* Volumes 1–6 (Cairo: Markaz al-Mahrousa lil-Bihouth wal-Tadrib wal-Nashr).

Zaki, Moheb (1995). *Civil Society and Democratization in Egypt, 1981–1994* (Cairo: Konrad Adenauer Foundation and the Ibn Khaldoun Center).

Zald, Mayer N., and Roberta Ash Garner (1987/1966). "Social Movement Organization: Growth, Decay, and Change" in Mayer N. Zald and John D. McCarthy, eds., *Social Movements in an Organizational Society: Collected Essays* (New Brunswick, N.J.: Transaction Books).

Zartman, I. William (1987). "The Military in the Politics of Succession: Alge-
    ria" in John W. Harbeson, ed., *The Military in African Politics* (New York:
    Praeger).
——— (1997). "The International Politics of Democracy in North Africa" in
    John P. Entelis, ed., *Islam, Democracy and the State in North Africa*
    (Bloomington: Indiana University Press).
Zeghal, Malika (1999). "Religion and Politics in Egypt: The Ulema of al-Azhar,
    Radical Islam, and the State (1952–1994)," *International Journal of Mid-
    dle East Studies*, vol. 31, no. 3 (August): 371–399.
Zeid, Ala Abdel Aziz Abu (1996). "al-Itar al-Siyasi wal-Qanuni al-Hakem li-
    Amaliyet al-Tahawel al-Dimuqrati fi Misr fi al-Fatra min 1976/1992" in
    Mustapha Kamel al-Sayid and Kamal al-Manoufa, eds., *Haqiqet al-
    Tadudiya al-Siyasiya fi Misr: Dirasat fi al-Tahawul al-Raismali wal-
    Musharaka al-Siyasiya* (Cairo: Markaz al-Bihouth al-Arabiya, Maktibet al-
    Madbouli).
Zimmermann, Ekkart (1980). "Macro-Comparative Research on Political Protest"
    in Ted Gurr, ed., *Handbook of Political Conflict: Theory and Research* (New
    York: Free Press).
——— (1983). *Political Violence, Crises and Revolutions* (Rochester, Vt.:
    Schenkman Publishing).
Zitouni, Jamal (1995). *Hidayat Rab al-'Alamin fi Tabyeen Usul al-Salafiyeen
    wama Yajib min al-Ahd ala al-Mujahedeen* (a 62-page pamphlet carrying
    the name Abu Abdel Rahman Amin and dated 27 Rabi'a al-Thani 1416).
Zubaida, Sami (1993). *Islam: The People and the State: Political Ideas and
    Movements in the Middle East* (London: I. B. Tauris).
Zviagelskaya, Irina (1997). "The Tajik Conflict: Problems of Regulation" in
    Mohammad Reza Djalili, Frederic Grare, and Shirin Akiner, eds., *Tajik-
    istan: The Trials of Independence* (New York: St. Martin's Press).

Daily Papers, Weekly Magazines, Other Journals and Reports of Record, and Human Rights Organizations

African Contemporary Record
Agence France Presse International (AFPI) (Paris)
Amnesty International (AI)
BBC News
Country Watch Reports
Christian Science Monitor
The Economist
Egyptian Organization for Human Rights (EOHR) (Cairo)
al-Hala al-Diniya fi Misr (Cairo: Markaz al-Dirasat al-Siyasiya wal-
    Istratijiya)
al-Hayat (London)
Human Rights Watch
al-Huwar al-Dawli

The Independent (London)
International Crisis Group
International Herald Tribune (IHT)
La Croix
al-Liwa al-Islami (Cairo)
Le Monde (Paris)
Le Monde Diplomatique
Middle East Contemporary Survey (MECS)
Middle East International (MEI)
Middle East Journal (MEJ)
Newsweek
New York Times
New Yorker
The Observer (London)
al-Sharq al-Awsat (London)
al-Taqrir al-Istratiji al-Arabi (Cairo: Markaz al-Dirasat al-Istratijiya fi al-
    Ahram)
Taqrir Misr al-Mahrousa wal-Aalam (Cairo: Markaz al-Mahrousa lil-Nashr)
Wall Street Journal
al-Wasat (London)
Washington Post

Index

243

About the Book

Rejecting theories of economic deprivation and psychological alienation, Mohammed Hafez offers a provocative analysis of the factors that contribute to protracted violence in the Muslim world today.

Hafez combines a sophisticated theoretical approach and detailed case studies to show that the primary source of Islamist insurgencies lies in the repressive political environments within which the vast majority of Muslims find themselves. Highlighting when and how institutional exclusion and indiscriminate repression contribute to large-scale rebellion, he provides a crucial dimenion to our understanding of Islamic politics.

Mohammed M. Hafez is a visiting professor in the department of political science at the University of Missouri–Kansas City.